The Foundations
of Karl Rahner

THE FOUNDATIONS OF KARL RAHNER

A Paraphrase of the
Foundations of Christian Faith,
with Introduction and Indices

MARK F. FISCHER

A Herder & Herder Book
The Crossroad Publishing Company

This printing: July 2015

The Crossroad Publishing Company
www.crossroadpublishing.com

This book is set in 10/12 Sabon.

Printed in the United States of America

Library of Congress Cataloging-in-Publication Data is available

0-8245-2342-3

Contents

The Unique Place of the *Foundations* among the Writings of Karl Rahner

Every Master of Divinity student at St. John's Seminary in Camarillo—the seminary of the Roman Catholic Archdiocese of Los Angeles—purchases a copy of Karl Rahner's *Foundations of Christian Faith*. For several years it has been a required textbook for priesthood candidates. Its central role in the seminary curriculum testifies to the book's thoroughness and depth. At a time when fundamentalism pretends to speak for all of Christianity, and when the Catholic Church too often assumes a defensive posture, the book offers a powerful theological vision. It presents a Christianity deeply rooted in the Catholic tradition and confidently embracing the insights of world culture and the human sciences. It is nothing less than a "basic course in faith," the literal translation of the book's German title, *Grundkurs des Glaubens*.[1]

This basic course, however, is anything but simple. To be honest, the book is so challenging that few students read it in its entirety. Indeed, one professor in the seminary's systematic theology department even confessed to me that he had never finished the text. Seminarians wince at Rahner's specialized vocabulary. They weary of his complex syntax. They struggle with the subtlety of his thought. The *Foundations* is a basic course, but its topic, Christian faith, is as deep as divinity itself. It does not lend itself to speed reading.

When students complain about textbooks, professors usually shrug their shoulders and recommend more strenuous study. That is what I did when I first heard seminarians grumble about Rahner's *Foundations*. No other

---

1. Karl Rahner, *Grundkurs des Glaubens: Einführung in den Begriff des Christentums* (1976); 8th ed., 1984; paperback edition (Freiburg—Basel—Vienna: Herder, 1997). In 1976, the book received the "Imprimi potest" (or permission to be published after a critical review) from Rahner's Jesuit superior and then the "Imprimatur" (a definitive approval for publication) from the Diocese of Freiburg im Breisgau.

book can take its place, I told them, and the English translation by William V. Dych is excellent. I advised them to apply themselves more vigorously. But student complaints persisted. Eventually I began to sympathize with them. For all its profundity, *Foundations of Christian Faith* is a difficult book.

So some years ago I began to write a paraphrase of it. My goal was not to create a substitute for Rahner's text but to summarize it.[2] I wanted to give students an overview of the chapters and subsections. Students could then compare my overview with Rahner's own words. I put my paraphrase on the Internet, and before long, many people were visiting the web site.

The reader might well ask, however, why students should devote themselves to a book so notoriously difficult—or even to a paraphrase of such a book. The answer has to do with Karl Rahner himself. Twenty years after his death in 1984, he still remains the object of intense theological study. His ecclesiology enhanced the church's catholicity and openness to the world; his name is intimately linked with the legacy of Vatican II; and he was among the leading Catholic theologians of the twentieth century.[3] Within his scholarly publications, *Foundations of Christian Faith* holds a unique place. Rahner himself indicated this, and the following essay will explain what he meant.

Rahner's Claims about the *Foundations*

In the 1976 Preface, Rahner made two claims about the uniqueness of the *Foundations* within his body of work. Although not a summary of his ear-

2. Although the summaries of each section in the text reflect my own judgment regarding selection and abbreviation, nevertheless they accurately paraphrase Rahner's thought. In that way they differ from the admittedly "personal interpretation" of the *Foundations* contained in the various essays edited by Leo J. O'Donovan, *A World of Grace: An Introduction to the Themes and Foundations of Karl Rahner's Theology* (New York: A Crossroad Book [The Seabury Press], 1980). The essays provide what O'Donovan calls a "running introduction" to the *Foundations*, rather than a summary of it (p. xi).

3. On Rahner and the church's catholicity, see Richard Lennan, *The Ecclesiology of Karl Rahner* (Oxford: Clarendon, 1995). Lennan summarizes the "unequivocally Catholic" aspects of Rahner's ecclesiology, starting on p. 263; on p. 229 he traces the genesis of *Foundations* in Rahner's 1969 book *Zur Reform des Theologiestudiums*. On the legacy of Vatican II, see John R. Sachs, "'Do Not Stifle the Spirit': Karl Rahner, the Legacy of Vatican II, and Its Urgency for Theology Today," *Proceedings* of the Catholic Theological Society of America 51 (June 6–9, 1996): 15–38. On Rahner as a leading Catholic theologian, see Miguel H. Díaz, *On Being Human: U.S. Hispanic and Rahnerian Perspectives* (Maryknoll: Orbis Books, 2001), xiii. Díaz argues that U.S. Hispanic theologians have found in Rahner's thought an enrichment of their own themes, such as solidarity with the oppressed and the theology of the Kingdom of God (p. 135).

lier efforts, he wrote, the book "has a somewhat more comprehensive and more systematic character than one might be accustomed to in the other theological writings of the author."[4] More comprehensive—this phrase is surprising, given the tremendous scope of Rahner's writings. What could be more comprehensive, for example, than Rahner's *Encyclopedia of Theology* (for which he served as general editor) or the *Theological Dictionary* (which he co-authored with Herbert Vorgrimler)? To say that *Foundations of Christian Faith* is somewhat more comprehensive than these all-encompassing works raises a question: what does it comprise that they do not?

Moreover, Rahner says the *Foundations* has a "more systematic character" than one might be accustomed to find in his other works. What could be more systematic, however, than the early works with which Rahner established his formidable reputation? Consider, for example, Rahner's 1939 doctoral thesis. Published as *Spirit in the World*, it analyzed a single question in St. Thomas's *Summa Theologica*. From this single question, Rahner drew the insight that no human thought can proceed without an image or representation. Even the most profound human thought—the thought, for example, of God—depends on mental imagery, on representations that St. Thomas called phantasms. Through these phantasms, Rahner concluded, spirit is present to the world. Rahner's thesis laid a systematic basis for his eventual doctrine of sacrament and symbol, through which God's Spirit becomes tangible. Yet Rahner claims that *Foundations of Christian Faith* has a more systematic character than even *Spirit in the World*.[5] How can this be?

Rahner sheds light on the more comprehensive and systematic character of *Foundations* in the book's introduction. Sketching the content of an introductory course in theology, he states that such a course must treat philosophy and theology as a unity. The traditional seminary curriculum, however, regards philosophy as a handmaid or prelude to theology. Before beginning theology, seminarians study philosophy, especially metaphysics

---

4. Karl Rahner, *Foundations of Christian Faith: An Introduction to the Idea of Christianity*, trans. William V. Dych (New York: Seabury Press [A Crossroad Book], 1978), xv. "Wenn hier eine Einführung geboten wird, dann darf der Leser auch nicht erwarten, daß dieses Buch eine abschließende Zusammenfassung der bisherigen theologischen Arbeit des Verfassers sei. Das ist es nicht, und das will es nicht sein, wenngleich dieser Grundkurs von seinem Thema her einen etwas umfassenderen und systematischeren Charakter hat, als man es bei den sonstigen theologischen Veröffentlichungen des Autors gewohnt sein mag" (*Grundkurs des Glaubens*, 9). Harvey D. Egan's book review of the *Grundkurs* drew attention to Rahner's claim that the book has a more systematic and comprehensive character (*Theological Studies* 38:3 [1977]: 555–59, at p. 556).

5. Indeed, Geffrey B. Kelly wrote that the *Foundations* is Rahner's "only major systematic work" ("Introduction," in *Karl Rahner: Theologian of the Graced Search for Meaning*, ed. Geffrey B. Kelly, vol. 8, The Making of Modern Theology: Nineteenth- and Twentieth-Century Texts [Minneapolis: Fortress Press, 1992], 22).

and ontology. These disciplines help students to appreciate transcendent realities such as truth and justice. Rahner, however, does not want to presume that his readers have completed a course in philosophy as a preparation for theology. He does not regard philosophy as merely the prelude to or foundation for theology but as a reflection on the Christian's understanding of the whole of human life. Theology, for its part, is not exclusively the understanding that follows upon the acceptance of revelation but encompasses every intellectual effort to understand Christianity. *The Foundations of Christian Faith* is more comprehensive because it comprises both disciplines as a "question and answer."[6]

Rahner asserts that his foundational course in theology will show people that they can believe with intellectual honesty "from the very *content* of Christian dogma itself."[7] This, I believe, is the heart of Rahner's claim that *Foundations* is more systematic than his other works. The content to which he refers is the self-communication of God to human beings. They in turn can receive God's very life. This is the dogmatic mystery that inspires confidence in believers. Rahner states that it is more fundamental than any other dogmatic mystery. The other dogmas—the unity of God, the two natures of Christ, and even the Trinity—presuppose God's fundamental offer. The other dogmas contain the self-communication of God, to be sure, as well as an understanding of human beings as hearers of the divine Word. But they do so as presuppositions. Rahner aimed to make the presuppositions explicit. If *Foundations* is more comprehensive because it contains both philosophy and theology, it is more systematic because it draws out the consequences of God's decision to share the divine life with human beings.

These claims about the more comprehensive and systematic character of *Foundations of Christian Faith* are not argued at any length in the book's introduction. They are so fundamental to Rahner's intention, however, that they deserve closer scrutiny.

First Claim: The Comprehensiveness of Foundations

To see how *Foundations* comprises both philosophy and theology, Rahner invites us to regard the human being as a question—a question in the philosophical sense.[8] It is the question of the origin and destiny of human-

---

6. *Foundations*, 11. In the next paragraph, Rahner seems to equate the philosophic dimension of his basic course with fundamental theology. "By its very nature the foundational course must necessarily be a quite specific *unity of fundamental theology and dogmatic theology*."

7. *Foundations*, 12. "In unserem theologischen Grundkurs kommt es gerade darauf an, dem Menschen auch aus der *Inhaltlichkeit* des christlichen Dogmas selbst heraus das Vertrauen zu geben, daß er in intellektueller Redlichkeit glauben kann" (*Grundkurs*, 23).

8. This paragraph and the next three quotes are from *Foundations*, 10–12.

ity. Human beings are able to reflect on this question because of their history (i.e., the way the question has been framed in the past) and because of their capacity for transcendence. The answers to this philosophical question from previous generations do not suffice and leave us dissatisfied. In every age human beings raise the question anew, moved by a desire to transcend the answers of the past and plumb reality more deeply. In searching for an answer, Rahner's procedure is eminently philosophical, and seems (at first) distinct from theology.

What is his answer to this question about origin and destiny, the question that human beings "have" and "are"? Rahner claims that the answer is Christianity itself. Christianity teaches that the human being has a basic orientation to the mystery of God. God is not eternally distant, says Rahner, but wants "to be the innermost center of our existence." God gives the divine self to human beings as a share in divinity (grace) and in the person of Jesus Christ (history). So the answer to the philosophical question about the origin and destiny of human beings is not only philosophical but a Christian answer as well, and thus a theological one.

Rahner's procedure of uniting philosophy and theology challenges traditional assumptions. Indeed it challenges the very pedagogy of theological formation. Every Catholic seminary requires the aspirants to the priesthood to complete a number of philosophy courses before they embark on theology proper. The study of being, ethics, logic, and philosophical anthropology—these are typical courses from the pretheology curriculum. Although official documents about seminary formation emphasize that the relation between philosophy and theology is complementary, nevertheless, theology occupies the superior position. Philosophy is supposed to lead the seminarian from human to divine realities.[9]

---

9. Even Rahner concedes that there are "theological data which possibly cannot be reached by a secular philosophy as such" (*Foundations*, 11). For an understanding of philosophy and theology in the curriculum of today's Catholic seminary, see the National Conference of [United States] Catholic Bishops, *Norms for Priestly Formation: A Compendium of Official Documents on Training Candidates for the Priesthood*, Compiled for Publication by the Bishops' Committee on Priestly Formation (Washington, D.C.: United States Catholic Conference, 1982). This compendium of norms includes the Sacred Congregation for Catholic Education's 1970 document *The Basic Plan for Priestly Formation*, where we read that a chronological progression from philosophy to theology is not strictly required but is the first of three options, the third of which is the option of studying philosophy and theology together (par. 60, p. 39). The same compendium also includes the congregation's 1972 document *The Study of Philosophy in Seminaries*. Here we read that philosophy is a prelude to theological reflection, because "an exclusive recourse to the light of revelation"—though superior to philosophy—"is not even possible" (chap. II, par. 3, p. 103). In this same vein, the National Conference of Catholic Bishops' *Program of Priestly Formation*, 4th ed. (Washington, D.C.: United States Catholic

Rahner's method, however, compresses the two by "philosophizing . . . within theology itself." In fact, Rahner criticizes the traditional pedagogy. It unfortunately begins with a philosophical approach, he says, an approach that treats the revelation of God as if it had to be "proven" or at least demonstrated to be possible. For the person who already believes, this approach can be unfruitful. It almost requires him or her to suspend belief, as it were, and pretend to be an Enlightenment-style philosopher, investigating the conditions for the possibility of faith. By contrast, Rahner's approach is directly Christian. "We are reflecting," he writes, "upon the concrete whole of the person's self-realization in Christ." His approach is not that of a systematic doubter but of a Christian who wants to know more clearly humanity's origin and destiny in God.

CRITIQUE OF RAHNER

Critics of Rahner fault him, however, for uniting philosophy and theology. Philosophy, they say, is the realm of human reason. Theology, by contrast, must begin with divine revelation. Rahner's attempt to unite the two, say the critics, blurs the distinction between the human and the divine. Ultimately it blurs the distinction between human nature and divine grace, they argue, even making God dependent on creation. In short, the "more comprehensive" character that Rahner claims for his *Foundations*, that is, the book's unity of philosophy and theology, is the very thing that his critics condemn.

One of Rahner's most vociferous opponents is the American theologian Paul D. Molnar. In two lengthy articles, Molnar has attacked Rahner for his doctrines of experience and revelation. Rahner's theology reduces God to a reflection on human experience, Molnar charges, thus making divine revelation unnecessary.[10] Although Molnar is a hostile critic, his careful analyses of *Foundations* highlight many distinctive features of the work. Let us take a moment to review Molnar's critique in broad outline so as to see

---

Conference, 1993) teaches that philosophy promotes reflection on the relation "between the human spirit and truth, that truth which is revealed to us fully in Jesus Christ" (par. 167, p. 35). All of this is summed up well in the encyclical letter of Pope John Paul II *On the Relationship between Faith and Reason: Fides et Ratio*, Vatican City, Sept. 14, 1998 (Washington, D.C.: United States Catholic Conference, 1998; text and format from Libreria Editrice Vaticana). Although the Holy Father insists on the "profound unity" of faith and philosophy (par. 48), nevertheless he concludes that revelation endows philosophical truths "with their fullest meaning" (par. 67).

10. Paul D. Molnar, "Can We Know God Directly? Rahner's Solution from Experience," *Theological Studies* 46:2 (1985): 228–61; and Molnar, "Is God Essentially Different from His Creatures? Rahner's Explanation from Revelation," *The Thomist* 51:4 (October, 1987): 575–631.

more clearly why Rahner calls *Foundations* "more comprehensive" than his other works.

Molnar insists on clear distinctions. To understand God, he argues, the Christian must choose a theological method over a philosophical one. Rahner, he charges, conflates the two. The mysterious God revealed the divine self to the Israelites, Molnar reminds us, and not to the other nations. God is the first cause, radically different from all creatures, who only know their creator indirectly, from God's effects upon creation and from distinct acts of historical self-revelation.[11] Molnar accuses Rahner of forgetting this. His method of uniting philosophy and theology reduces God to a necessary part of human existence. Molnar puts it this way: "By assuming that knowledge of God is a universal experience of man as he is, Rahner has precluded any real transcendence or freedom for God *independent* of what human experience ascribes to him."[12] If God can be known from human experience, then God is not transcendent. If human experience is the measure of God, then God cannot reveal divinity in sovereign freedom.

Starting from this premise, Molnar levels further charges against Rahner. The first is that Rahner's theology has not consistently held "scriptural faith" as the norm of God's being. Another is that Rahner tried to "deduce" the meaning of grace and revelation from human experience. A third charge is that Rahner erased the difference between creator and creature. In short, Molnar argues that Rahner's unity of philosophy and theology has not preserved the transcendence of God. It has failed to see that God's specific self-revelations in history not only surpass but may contradict our "natural" knowledge of God.[13]

Molnar's critique casts the features of Rahner's "more comprehensive" approach into high relief. Rahner did indeed hold that we know God in our reflection on experience. "All knowledge of God," Rahner said,[14] "is an a posteriori knowledge which comes from and through encountering the world." Molnar is entirely correct to argue that knowledge of God, for Rahner, is inseparable from experience of the world. Nowhere, however, does Rahner claim that the world supplies "direct" knowledge of God. In fact, Rahner takes pains to insist that we cannot know God as if God were an object among other realities that are present to us. The fact that the human being is able to encounter the divine in reflecting on experience does not reduce God to a product of human reflection. It rather points to a fundamental aspect of human experience. Rahner calls this a "supernatural exis-

---

11. Molnar, "Can We Know God Directly," *passim*, esp. 236–37.

12. Molnar, "Is God Essentially Different," 596.

13. Ibid. For Molnar's treatment of scriptural faith, see pp. 577, 597. On deducing the meaning of grace, see p. 596. On the contradictions between natural and revealed knowledge, see p. 593 n. 67.

14. Rahner, *Foundations*, 52.

tential," an orientation or receptivity toward God as the ground of human being.[15]

The supernatural existential expresses a fundamental Rahnerian insight: "Really and radically *every* person must be understood as the event of a supernatural self-communication of God."[16] Because every person can receive this communication, the supernatural existential illustrates Rahner's unity of philosophy and theology. The doctrine of the supernatural existential is a philosophical statement about the capacity of every person, distinct from an explicitly theological revelation. At the same time, it is a theological affirmation. It affirms that God invites human beings to share in the divine life. Not all accept the invitation, and people can refuse it. But the capacity to hear God's Word and obey it belongs to everyone.

Molnar dislikes the supernatural existential. From his viewpoint, a capacity extended to everyone is not gracious and free but rather a constituent of human nature. If it belongs to everyone, then God apparently owes it to us. With the supernatural existential, Molnar argues, Rahner has muddied the clear distinction between God and humanity. He has left us "unable to distinguish God from ourselves"[17] by confusing the realms of nature and of the supernatural. These, like the realms of philosophy and theology, should be rigorously distinguished.

RAHNER'S METHOD AND GOD'S INTENTION

It is fair to say, however, that *Foundations* had anticipated these objections. Indeed, Rahner conceded that the human capacity for receiving God's Word cannot be readily distinguished from the basic openness of the human spirit. "God's self-communication in grace," Rahner confessed,[18] "cannot . . . be differentiated from those basic structures of human transcendence" described in chapter II of *Foundations*. Rahner admits that it is almost impossible to say where the human capacity to hear God's Word stops and where grace begins. But this concession does not obscure the difference between humanity and divinity, as Molnar charges. It is rather an admission that every human capacity or talent is ultimately a gift from God. Yes, the supernatural existential does claim that something supernatural—namely, the capacity to hear God's message—is given to everyone. But it obliges neither God to give the divine self nor humanity to receive it.

Molnar contends that the supernatural existential cancels the need for an explicit historical revelation. If the capacity to hear God's Word in daily

15. David Coffey, "The Whole Rahner on the Supernatural Existential," *Theological Studies* 65 (2004): 95–118.

16. *Foundations*, 127.

17. Molnar, "Can We Know God," 239.

18. Rahner, *Foundations*, 129. The quotation in the next paragraph is from p. 128.

experience were to belong to everyone, Molnar argues, then the revelation of God to Moses and of the incarnate Word in Jesus would be unnecessary. But Molnar's critique runs aground on Rahner's sharp distinction between these supreme examples of revelation and the human capacity to respond to them. The supernatural existential enables humanity to hear God's Word in specific events and people. "God's self-communication as offer," Rahner wrote, "is also the necessary condition which makes its acceptance possible." Without something like a supernatural existential, people would not be able to recognize God in history. Critics may object that the human capacity for reflecting on experience lacks the clearly supernatural character of biblical theophanies and miracles. Philosophers may even recognize this capacity by the light of reason. But were it not for this capacity, people might never understand theophanies and miracles for the divine realities they express.

THE "MORE COMPREHENSIVE" METHOD AND GOD'S INTENTION

Let us take a moment to review our progress up to this point. We have identified Rahner's claim that *Foundations* is more comprehensive with his intention to unite philosophy and theology. Rahner philosophizes within theology by defining a universal human capacity (a capacity upon which philosophic reason can reflect) for receiving God's Word (and theologizing about it). Without this capacity, no one could discover in scripture and tradition, or even in theophanies and miracles, expressions of the transcendent God.

Critics have attacked the Rahnerian union of philosophy and theology as an improper confusion of the human and the divine. The proposed union appears to drag theological revelation to the same level as philosophical thought. It seems to shrink the divine to a human reflection on experience. And by fusing supernatural gift with a natural capacity, it seems to reduce divine grace to human nature. Rahner's union of philosophy and theology strikes some critics not as "more comprehensive" but as an affront to Christian tradition.

Their critique is unpersuasive. It attributes to Rahner a claim that he never made, raises objections he had already anticipated, and misunderstands his intention. The critique appears to rigidly exclude philosophy from theology.[19] But it also enables us to see distinctive features of Rahner's "more comprehensive" approach. By focusing not just on the revelation

19 . Leo J. O'Donovan, "A Journey into Time: The Legacy of Karl Rahner's Last Years," *Theological Studies* 46 (1985): 621–46. O'Donovan devotes a lengthy footnote (p. 625 n. 24) to a critique of Molnar's "Can We Know God." Molnar replies to O'Donovan in his own lengthy footnote in "Is God Essentially Different," pp. 578–79 n. 3.

bequeathed in scripture and tradition, but additionally on the human capability to recognize and receive that revelation, Rahner helps us understand God's intention for humanity. It is nothing less than a desire for people to discern the divine Word in history and accept the invitation to obey it. Rahner's union of philosophy and theology enables people to receive, through human experience and a subsequent reflection on it, genuine knowledge of God. This knowledge, however a posteriori and indirect, comes to people in the divine invitation to transcend themselves by responding to God's appeal.

Second Claim: The Systematic Character of Foundations

Let us turn now to Rahner's second claim about *Foundations*, the claim that it has a more systematic character than his other books. He expounds this assertion indirectly (without explicitly arguing for the book's systematic character) in the introduction. There he distinguishes between the large number of propositional truths in dogmatic theology and the "really absolute mysteries" in the content of Christian faith. We find the absolute mysteries, he says, in

> the self-communication of God in the depths of existence, called grace, and in history, called Jesus Christ, and this [self-communication] already includes the mystery of the Trinity in the economy of salvation and of the immanent Trinity.[20]

Grace and Christ, the "absolute" mysteries of God's self-communication (Rahner says in the same place), "constitute the basic content of faith." The theme of God's self-communication contains even the Trinity. Here, in a single sentence, Rahner brings us to the heart of his theological system. The sentence suggests why *Foundations* has a more systematic character than we are accustomed to find in Rahner's other writings. The book elaborates the insight that Christian faith is about God's gift of self.

This fundamental insight simplifies Christian faith, now concentrated into the mysteries of God's self-communication in grace and Christ. Readers will have to judge whether this simplification achieves Rahner's hope, namely, to help people believe with intellectual honesty from the very content of dogma.

---

20. *Foundations*, 12. "Wirklich absolute Mysterien gibt es eigentlich nur in der Selbstmitteilung Gottes in der Tiefe der Existenz—Gnade genannt—und in der Geschichte—Jesus Christus genannt—, womit auch schon das Geheimnis der heilsökonomischen und immanenten Trinität gegeben ist" (*Grundkurs*, 24).

STEP ONE: SELF-COMMUNICATION IN GRACE

Rahner's treatment of grace emphasizes its presence throughout world history and religion. It occupies the initial five chapters of *Foundations* and marks the first step in Rahner's systematic account of God's self-communication. Corresponding to grace is the second step in the systematic account, the treatment of Jesus Christ. The historical specificity of Jesus Christ, who appeared at a single time and place, complements the universality of the human experience of grace throughout history. By presenting God's gift of self in two steps, Rahner poses a question: what is the relation between the two? As an answer, let us start with grace, and then move on to Jesus Christ, before we see Rahner's synthesis.

Rahner begins with the depths of existence, that is, with an analysis of human beings. God has created them with a capacity for self-reflection, for acknowledging their limitations, and for transcending those limits by achieving the possibilities that life presents (chapter I). Transcending limits and achieving possibilities are gifts, gifts of a personal God. God offers these gifts by granting to people a time on earth to exercise their freedom and accomplish their life's work. People encounter this God explicitly when they recognize that the mysterious ground of existence is present as a Holy Spirit who fills them and meets them in holy places, people, and things (chapter II). At the same time, people concede that they do not always obey God's Spirit. This is the experience of guilt. Guilt threatens those who close themselves off from God's gifts. They refuse God's invitation to follow their conscience and thereby to transcend their former selves (chapter III). When people ignore their consciences, they are not merely refusing to act as they should. They are refusing a relationship with the God who speaks through the conscience. This relation, however, can be repaired. God offers forgiveness by offering a renewed friendship, a share in the trinitarian life (chapter IV). The friendship between God and humanity has expressed itself throughout history, and especially in the history of Christianity. Christianity enables people to recognize God's initiative as Holy Spirit and as the grace of divinization. God's initiative also motivates a free response to that grace (chapter V). In each of the first five chapters, Rahner expounds the absolute mystery of grace as a constant inspiration to human beings. It inspires people to receive divinity as the center of their lives.

This self-communication, Rahner emphasizes, is not granted exclusively to Christians. God offers the divine self "in the depths of existence," that is, to all people at all times. By creating human beings with a supernatural existential, with openness to divinity, God has enabled a divine-human communication throughout history. The peoples of the world have expressed their encounter with God in a variety of religious traditions. These traditions attest to God's ongoing initiative in sharing the divine life with humanity.

GOD'S INITIATIVE AS REVELATION

God's initiative throughout history can even be called revelation. God reveals divinity to human beings, Rahner says, not just in the miraculous events of biblical history. The appeal to conscience, the recognition of guilt, and the experience of forgiveness are also revelations, manifesting the grace of God in the depths of existence. God's universal and transcendental revelation expresses itself in a variety of special and categorical ways. These ways are species of the universal, and concrete (i.e., "categorical") expressions of the transcendent. They are the many historical revelations to which human culture and the world's religions attest.

The religious experiences of non-Christians deserve to be called revelations in that they express the self-communication of God. Christians usually apply this term, *revelation,* to the scriptures and the gospel as handed on in tradition. But the application of it to non-Christian experiences accords with a definite aspect of Christian usage. The application of the term corresponds to God's universal salvific will, to the Vatican II teaching that all can be saved, and to Christianity's preservation of primeval history (in the Hebrew Scriptures) as a preparation for Christ. In these ways Christians understand the Holy Spirit as the revelation of God to all.

What is the relationship between the many historical revelations and the Christian revelation? Rahner answers that, of all the historical revelations, Christianity is the most successful, the absolute, and the unsurpassed. At the same time, however, it too is a historical revelation. Like the other revelations, it manifests God's universal will to save all. In that sense it is, as Rahner says, "only a species, a segment of the universal."[21] There are more revelations of God than are to be found in historical Christianity.

God's transcendental gift of self both precedes every historical revelation (including Christianity) and gives rise to it. The gift *precedes* historical revelation because God first addresses the human being personally, in the person's heart. The gift *gives rise to* historical revelation because human beings want to share their experiences. As they interpret their encounter with God, they express it in words and symbols. Without God's gift of self, and without the human capacity to receive the gift, people would not recognize in the words of categorical history the transcendent Word of God.

---

21. *Foundations,* 155. "Allerdings ist diese Art von Offenbarungsgeschichte nur eine Spezies, ein Sektor der allgemeinen kategorialen Offenbarungsgeschichte, der geglückteste Fall der notwendigen Selbstauslegung der transzendentalen Offenbarung oder—besser gesagt—der volle Wesensvollzug der beiden Offenbarungen und ihrer einen Geschichte—der transzendentalen und kategorialen—in Wesenseinheit und -reinheit" (*Grundkurs,* 159). At the same time, the English translation of *Foundations* speaks of Christianity as successful (p. 140), absolute (p. 162), and unsurpassed (p. 174).

Let us summarize the stages in our discussion so far. Rahner's *Foundations of Christian Faith* is more systematic than his other works in that it elaborates a fundamental insight. It is the insight that people can believe in Jesus Christ with intellectual honesty from the very content of Christian faith. The basic content of faith is God's communication of the divine self in grace and history. Chapters I–V sketch God's gift of self, God's grace, offered by the Holy Spirit in the depths of human existence. The many historical religions, including Christianity, attest to that grace. It is ubiquitous and represents the first step of Rahner's presentation of the divine self-communication. Rahner's second step is Jesus Christ and the distinctiveness of Christianity. We now turn our attention to Rahner's Christology in order to see how he justifies the claim that Jesus Christ is the self-communication of God in history.

STEP TWO: SELF-COMMUNICATION IN CHRIST

Chapter VI of *Foundations* is the longest chapter, comprising almost one-third of the book's pages. It presents the historical revelation of God in Jesus Christ as the highest manifestation of God's ongoing self-communication. Christianity is highest, Rahner says, because it enables us to recognize God's self-communication for what it is, namely, a share in divinity. To understand this claim, we will summarize the treatment of Jesus Christ in chapter VI under the headings of Transcendence, Word, and Tradition.

Chapter VI proclaims Jesus Christ as a Word of *transcendence*. By responding to this Word, humanity transcends what it was and participates in God's own life. Through the incarnation, says Rahner, human nature "becomes the nature of God himself."[22] The unity of Jesus with the divine Word invites human beings to recognize God's intention. God intends the unity of human nature with God's own self. The union of Jesus and the Word gives people courage to hope for their own communion with God— in short, for salvation. This hope is based on the perfect realization of that union already achieved by Jesus Christ. So the first fifty-two pages of chapter VI present transcendence as:

---

22. Humanity's "orientation towards the abiding mystery whom we call God" (p. 217) reaches its climax "when this nature of man as so understood so gives itself to the mystery of fullness and so empties itself that it becomes the nature of God himself" (*Foundations*, 218). "Dieses geschieht in einem unüberbietbaren Maß in radikalster Strenge, wenn diese so verstandene Natur des Menschen, so sich weggebend an das Geheimnis der Fülle, sich so enteignet, daß sie Gottes selbst wird" (*Grundkurs*, 216). The quotation about humanity as "the utterance in which God could empty himself" occurs in *Foundations*, 224. Rahner's description of the resurrection (quoted in the next paragraph) as "the permanent, redeemed, final and definitive validity of the single and unique life of Jesus" occurs in *Foundations*, 266.

- the evolution of the human being in response to God's Word (part 1)
- participation in Jesus' relationship with his heavenly Father (part 2)
- the continual surpassing of our "old self" prompted by the unsatisfied longing for the divine (part 3), and
- the attainment of the goal of human nature, that is, union with God (part 4).

In short, transcendence is God's very intention for human beings. God wants humanity to speak the divine Word as Jesus did, to be "the utterance in which God could empty himself." Emptied into human nature, God enables that nature to transcend itself and become what God wants it to be.

After this focus on transcendence, chapter VI turns to the incarnate Word. The chapter argues that humanity encountered God's divine Word decisively and unsurpassably in Jesus of Nazareth. A historical analysis of the New Testament tradition, says Rahner, shows that Jesus understood himself as a prophet, indeed, as the final prophet or absolute savior. His function—to proclaim God's kingdom—was his very essence, his essence as divine Word. He accepted his death as the consequence of fidelity to the mission given him by his Father. Transcending every selfish motive, he made present in history the transcendent reality of God (part 5). Jesus' death was not his end. In the resurrection, the Father gave the Son's life a "permanent, redeemed, final, and definitive validity." From the time of the first disciples until today, people find in Jesus' resurrection the courage to hope for eternal life (part 6). In brief, Rahner's theology does not focus exclusively on the unique events of first-century Judea, in which Jesus Christ sacrificed himself for human salvation once and for all. Rahner adjusts this focus to avoid a mythological presentation of God as one who demands propitiation.[23] With this adjustment, Rahner emphasizes the hope of humanity. It is the transcendental hope for union with God's Word, a hope fully realized when the Word became flesh.

Finally, chapter VI reconciles traditional Christology with Rahner's transcendental Christology. According to classical Christology, the death of the divine Son made satisfaction for the sins of humanity. Rahner's transcendental Christology, on the other hand, emphasizes the human nature of Jesus. This second Christology complements the first by underlining the solidarity of Jesus with all humanity. We can hope to transcend death, in Rahner's Christology, because Jesus transcended it (part 7). Classical and transcendental Christology may seem incompatible because the one starts

---

23. "Rahner invokes the permissible aspect of demythologization and usually starts with an unrelenting attack on the common mythological idea of what belief in Christ entails" (Walter Kasper, *Jesus the Christ*, trans. V. Green [Kent, England: Burns & Oates Limited, and Mahwah, N.J.: Paulist Press, 1976], 48).

from the descent of the divine Logos and the other with the ascent in understanding of Jesus. But the Logos abided in Jesus, says Rahner, and led him to an ever-deeper understanding of the mission he had had from the beginning (part 8). This ascent reflects the personal relation of the Christian to Christ. Prompted by God's Word, we too ascend in understanding of and obedience to our vocation (part 9). What is true for those with an explicit Christian faith may also be true for those of different faiths. The Spirit of God and of Christ inspires them to heed God's Word as they understand it within their own traditions (part 10). Thus we can say that Christian dogma, which teaches that God's Word entered history only once in a hypostatic union with Jesus, does not exclude from salvation those of other faiths.[24] Rather, it reveals that God, through the Spirit, has communicated the divine self, even to those who do not know Christ in an explicit way. They too can hear God's Word and thus stand (however indirectly) in the Christian tradition.

Chapter VI, in short, marks the second step of Rahner's systematic argument. Recall that the two absolute mysteries—the self-communication of God in grace and in Jesus Christ—constitute the basic content of faith. Chapters I–V, with their focus on grace, took the first step. In the second step, Rahner explains how Jesus Christ is the self-communication of God in history. He defines this self-communication as nothing less than a relationship with God. In this relationship, God invites humanity to hear the divine Word and obey it, thereby transcending the merely human and participating in God's own life. Next, Rahner identifies God's Word with Jesus of Nazareth. Exploring the incarnation and Jesus' life, death, and resurrection, Rahner shows how the humanity of the Word genuinely expresses who God is. God "spoke" the Word of Jesus Christ, the sacrament and sign of God's will, thereby signifying and bringing about human salvation. Finally, Rahner shows how his transcendental Christology complements traditional Christology. The latter emphasizes the divinity of Son, the sender of the Spirit. The former emphasizes the humanity of Jesus, upon whom the Spirit descended. Both express the absolute mystery of Jesus Christ, through whom God communicates the divine self.

So the self-communication of God, expressed generally throughout human existence as grace, finds its unsurpassable historical expression in Jesus Christ. Rahner does not so much prove the claim that Jesus Christ is

---

24. Roger Haight questions Rahner's assertion (*Foundations*, 174) that the incarnation of the Logos is the "unsurpassable high point" of God's self-communication. "A consciousness of historicity," writes Haight, makes the thesis of a single incarnation of God "difficult to hold." Roger Haight, *Jesus Symbol of God* (Maryknoll: Orbis Books, 1999), 433. Haight (pp. 432–34) makes a number of other thought-provoking criticisms of Rahner, all within a general context of appreciation for and appropriation of Rahner's theology of the symbol and Christology from below.

the self-communication of God as he lends it precision. God communicates the divine self by inviting people into the union with the Word, Rahner says, the union that Jesus enjoyed. In him, people encounter both the gift of God and a free human response to it. Jesus Christ as both divine gift and human response reveals what it means to receive God's very life as a grace. Grace and Christ are the absolute mysteries of God's self-communication, said Rahner, which "already includes the mystery of the Trinity in the economy of salvation and of the immanent Trinity" (n. 20). But what is the relation between grace and Christ, and how is the Trinity included? To answer, let us turn to the trinitarian structure of Rahner's system.

THE BOOK'S TRINITARIAN STRUCTURE

Rahner already sketched his theology of the Trinity at the end of chapter IV, in the context of a discussion about the self-communication of God. In that chapter, Rahner emphasized the oneness of God. In particular, he called attention to the threat to God's unity posed by the traditional language of three divine persons. The traditional language leads to psychological spec- ulations about God's inner life. Rahner responded to the threat by asserting that the "immanent" Trinity (the inner life of the divine persons) is the "eco- nomic" Trinity (God acting in the history of salvation).[25] Human beings know God through the actions in history of the divine persons or, as Rah- ner would have it, as God's three modes of presence. The inner life of God is indeed the holy mystery of God's presence in history.

Rahner's treatment of the Trinity, we might say, subordinates it to the doctrines of grace and Jesus Christ. These are the absolute mysteries of the basic content of faith, namely, the self-communication of God. The subor- dination is clear from Rahner's comment about the Trinity as "included" in God's self-communication, as well as from the brief discussion of the Trin- ity in chapter IV and from other writings by Rahner.[26] In the systematic presentation of Rahner's theology, the primary focus is humanity's God- given orientation to God. Speculations about the inner life of the Trinity may distract Christians, Rahner implies, from this more fundamental topic.

25. *Foundations*, 136. Catherine Mowry LaCugna states that "There is wide agreement in Catholic and Protestant theology with Rahner's principle" of the equivalence of the immanent and economic Trinity. See *God for Us: The Trinity and Christian Life* (San Francisco: Harper- SanFrancisco, 1991), 211. She quibbles, however, with the phrase "economic Trinity," explaining that "There are not three but only two missions in the economy of salvation: the sending of the Son (Incarnation) and the sending of the Spirit (grace)" (p. 234 n. 7).

26. "The real doctrine of the Trinity is presented in Christology and pneumatology." These words are on the last page of Rahner's book *The Trinity* (which was originally vol. 2, chapter 5 of the 1967 series Mysterium Salutis), trans. Joseph Donceel (New York: Seabury Press, 1969), 120.

Yet it would be false to conclude that there is no substantial doctrine of the Trinity in *Foundations*. Implicit in its treatments of grace and Christ, *Foundations* presents the two "missions" of the Father, namely, the Spirit and the Word. The mission of the Word is treated so extensively, and the length and central place of Rahner's chapter on Jesus Christ are so striking, that the absence of a specific chapter on the Holy Spirit is conspicuous. However, I believe that chapters I–V, in which Rahner presents the mystery of grace, indirectly constitute a treatise on the Holy Spirit. Already in chapter II Rahner describes the human being as the finite spirit whom God fulfills with the gift of "his very own being." In other words, God is accomplishing the union of finite spirit and Holy Spirit as humanity's fulfillment. Then in chapter IV Rahner uses the language of 1 Corinthians to describe the human being as a temple in which God's Spirit dwells as a gift. This divine life is truly Holy Spirit, Rahner continues, "Insofar as he has come as the salvation which divinizes us." These passages[27] show that Rahner's treatment of grace in the first five chapters of *Foundations* is at the same time an indirect treatment of the Holy Spirit.

This indirect treatment, recapitulated in the book's epilogue, clarifies the trinitarian structure of *Foundations*. By systematically expounding grace and Jesus Christ, the book presents both the Holy Spirit and the incarnate Word, the two missions of the Father. Recognizing the existence of this trinitarian structure, however, does not explain the relation between grace and Christ. In fact, Rahner himself acknowledges that the relationship is problematic. To see how he solves the problem, let us turn to the final step in his systematic argument.

STEP THREE: THE COMPLEMENTARITY OF GRACE AND CHRIST

In chapter V, Rahner acknowledges that his emphasis on the ubiquity and constancy of grace throughout history poses a problem. He expresses it this way:

> If God as he is in himself has already communicated himself in his Holy Spirit always and everywhere and to every person as the innermost center of his [the individual person's] existence, whether he wants it or not, whether he reflects upon it or not, whether he accepts it or not, and if the whole history of creation is already borne by God's

27. The first of these passages occurs in *Foundations*, 83–84, where we read that God communicates "his very own being" in "the immediate vision of God as the fulfillment of the finite spirit in grace." The second passage occurs on p. 124. "God's self-communication to the human being, says Rahner, means "that in him as in a temple dwells the very spirit of God as a really divine gift." The third passage, about Holy Spirit as "the salvation that divinizes us," occurs on p. 136.

The Foundations of Karl Rahner

self-communication in this very creation, then there does not seem to be anything else which can take place on God's part.[28]

If God has already shared the divine life with humanity, what need is there for incarnation? Rahner's sentence touches on a number of characteristic themes. There is, first of all, the acknowledgement that God's self-communication in grace is what Christians call the Holy Spirit. The sentence also emphasizes that the Spirit communicates God to people as the center of human life, whether people know it or not. And finally, the sentence raises a fundamental question. If God extends the divine life as grace through the Spirit always and everywhere, then what more can an incarnation of the Word offer?

Rahner concedes that Christianity is only a part, a species, of the universal history of revelation. God has shared the Holy Spirit with people throughout history, and this universal history of revelation has manifested itself in the world's cultures and religions. To be sure, Jesus Christ is the criterion by which Christians distinguish the history of revelation in its fullness from misinterpretations of God's self-communication. But outside the circle of Christian faith, Jesus Christ cannot function as such a criterion. From the viewpoint of a historian of religion, Jesus Christ is merely one among other prophets.

Rahner moves from this impasse, first of all, by postulating a "caesura," a turning-point in history. It is the point, he says, at which "mankind becomes conscious of itself."[29] Before this caesura, humanity was situated in nature and threatened by it. In a few brief millennia, however, humanity changed, making itself the object of its own planning in an environment that it helped to create. The millennia-long "moment" of humanity's consciousness of itself marks this caesura.

Next, Rahner correlates the caesura and Jesus Christ. Just when humanity became conscious of itself, Christianity proclaimed the incarnation of

---

28. *Foundations*, p. 139. "Wenn Gott sich in seinem heiligen Pneuma als er selbst schon immer und überall jedem Menschen—ob er will oder nicht, ob er es reflektiert oder nicht, ob er es annimmt oder nicht—als die innerste Mitte seiner Existenz mitgeteilt hat, wenn alle Schöpfungsgeschichte schon getragen ist von einer Selbstmitteilung Gottes eben in der Schöpfung, dann scheint ja von Gott her gar nichts mehr geschehen zu können" (*Grundkurs*, p. 144).

29. *Foundations*, 169. This quotation, as well as the quotation in the next paragraph about the God-Man, are taken from the following passage: "In dieser Zäsur kommt die Menschheit nach einem fast unübersehbaren Verharren in einem fast naturalen Dasein zu sich selbst und nicht nur in introvertierter Reflexion, Kunst, Philosophie, sondern auch in einer in ihre Umwelt hinein extrovertierten Art und Reflexion, und in diese Periode hinein kommt gleichzeitig diese Menschheitsgeschichte zum Gottmenschen, zu der absoluten geschichtlichen Objektivation ihres transzendentalen Gottesverständnisses" (*Grundkurs*, 172).

the divine Word as the "God-Man." Rahner defines the term God-Man as "the absolute historical objectification of its [humanity's] transcendental understanding of God." In the God-Man, divinity and humanity unite. The holy mystery of the God who gives the divine self to humanity, and the man, Jesus, who accepts the divine gift, have become one. The God-Man corresponds to the turning-point of history, in which humanity became conscious of itself. Jesus Christ is a sacrament, objectifying absolutely the God that human beings understand, the God who invites them to transcend themselves by union with the divine.

Finally, Rahner links the question of human salvation with the two "moments" of salvation history. One moment is the event of God's self-communication. The second is the event of human freedom, the acceptance or rejection of God's offer.[30] This freedom, however, is not freedom from God but rather the God-given freedom to respond to God, the response of faith. Rahner calls it "the obedient acceptance of man's supernaturally elevated self-transcendence." In regard to God, obedience is freedom. The human being who obediently accepts God's self-gift "actualizes himself in freedom," says Rahner. The actualization of oneself in God fulfills and saves the human being. Salvation is not a state produced by God on a person but the free acceptance of God who wills to share divinity with all people.

Jesus Christ, the self-communication of God in history, accomplished salvation in a perfect way by uniting in himself God's offer and humanity's response. When people accept God's self-communication, grace elevates them. It enables them to transcend themselves by placing their trust in God. They obey God by taking responsibility for themselves, freely responding to God's Word. This is the Word, Jesus Christ, in whom "the God who communicates himself and the man who accepts God's self-communication become irrevocably one, and the history of revelation and salvation of the whole human race reaches its goal."[31] Whenever people follow in his footsteps by accepting God's offer, they "make" salvation history.

So after communicating the divine self in grace, what more can God do? Rahner's answer is that God can become incarnate. God can become the human nature that freely turns to God in love and loyalty. By becoming human, God makes human nature a dwelling place for divinity, allowing people to see in God their very own destiny and goal. Chapter V is the hinge

---

30. *Foundations*, 143–44, contains the passage about the "two moments" of acceptance or rejection of God's self-communication. Rahner discusses "the obedient acceptance of man's supernaturally elevated self-transcendence" on p. 152. Rahner's assertion about the person who "actualizes himself in freedom" occurs on p. 147.

31. *Foundations*, 169. "In dieser Objektivation werden der sich mitteilende Gott und der dies Selbstmitteilung Gottes annehmende Mensch (eben in Jesus Christus) unwiderruflich einer, und die Offenbarungs- und Heilsgeschichte der gesamten Menschheit—unbeschadet der individuellen Heilsfrage—kommt an ihr Ziel" (*Grundkurs*, 172).

xxvi

in *Foundations* between the chapters on grace and on Christ and illuminates their complementary relation. Grace is the constant offer of God, the offer that inspires all human beings. Jesus Christ is the sacrament of God in history, the sacrament which reveals divinity and embodies the full acceptance of God's offer on the part of human nature.

CONFIDENCE TO BELIEVE FROM DOGMA ITSELF

With this insight, the systematic character of Rahner's *Foundations* finally emerges. God's self-communication, we see, is the very foundation of Christian faith. God has communicated the divine self through the Holy Spirit, pouring the love of God into human hearts in all times and places. But at one time and place humanity encountered Jesus of Nazareth. Through him, people glimpsed in the flesh what God wants them to be— united in a kingdom of justice and peace, united with God unto death. And even the sting of death need not prove mortal. The resurrection of Jesus Christ, by which the Father gave the Son's human life an eternal validity, lends hope to all that death is not the end. In many and various ways God had spoken through the Holy Spirit, but in these last days God's Word became incarnate in Jesus Christ.

These "last days" constitute the millennia-long turning point of human history. They mark the caesura in which humanity has become conscious of itself as a creation dependent on a creator. This insight into human dependence did not dawn upon us on our own or as a product of reason. Rather, it is itself a gift of God, a gift that inspires us to respond in faith. Faith means taking responsibility for our lives in obedience to God. The sacrament of this faith is Jesus Christ. He united in himself the God who communicates and the human being who freely responds. Imitating him, we too can hope for communion with God.

The confidence and intellectual honesty of the believer features prominently in the last three chapters of *Foundations*. No one today can claim to have mastered all the theological disciplines, Rahner says, or can give an exhaustive and comprehensively scientific defense of Christianity. But Catholic Christians can confidently trust in their church. There, in a community of believers, they can have confidence that their faith is not a species of individualistic self-delusion but rather continues a mission that goes back to Jesus Christ (chapter VII). Christian faith is not an escape from reality. Rather, it embraces it as a gift from God, the God whom Catholics celebrate in the seven sacraments (chapter VIII). Projecting their understanding of reality into the future, Catholic Christians anticipate the destiny of creation as a whole. They express this destiny in eschatological statements. Far from being literal predictions of the end time, these statements express Christian hope, the hope that the future belongs to a providential God (chapter IX).

The last third of *Foundations* echoes Rahner's message that God invites people to accept reality as a divine gift for which they are responsible.

The central claim of *Foundations* is that the self-communication of God is not merely one aspect of the Christian message, but its very heart, its content, its central truth. To be sure, that basic content expresses itself in mysteries, the absolute mysteries of grace and Christ. They are the Father's missions of Spirit and Word. But human being can understand these mysteries because God has revealed them. Indeed, God has given people a "positive affinity" to the mysteries which constitute the basic content of faith.[32] God has created humanity with the capacity to hear and respond to the divine self-communication.

By focusing on God's gift of self, Rahner has undoubtedly simplified Christian faith. It does not consist, he says, "in a rather large number of individual propositions which are unfortunately unintelligible," but rather in the relationship between humanity and God. Many individual propositions support and explain this relationship, but they are subordinate to it. The very content of Christian dogma, Rahner implies, is this self-communication of God. This content, distinct from the various theological propositions, allows people to believe confidently and with intellectual honesty. And what do they believe? Rahner put it this way:

> Hence there is really only one question, whether this God wanted to be merely the eternally distant one, or whether beyond that he wanted to be the innermost center of our existence in free grace and in self-communication. But our whole existence, borne by this question, calls for the affirmation of this second possibility as actually realized.

God wants to be, and is, the center of human life. God stands not just at the center of Christian life, but as the basis, the origin, and the destiny of all creation. *Foundations of Christian Faith* dedicates itself to that thesis. That is why Rahner viewed it as somewhat more comprehensive and more systematic than his other writings, and why theological students view it as worthy of study.

---

32. *Foundations*, 12. The quotations in the next paragraph are also from p. 12.

Acknowledgments

In preparing *The Foundations of Karl Rahner,* I owe a debt of gratitude to my students at St. John's Seminary. Father Alexander H. Ha's Master of Arts thesis, "Rahner and Tillich in Dialogue with Christian Anthropology" (1995), first alerted me to the need for a synopsis of Rahner's Foundations. Then from 1998 to 2003 I had the opportunity to teach five seminars on Rahner, using my paraphrase as a text, and benefited from the give and take with students.

In the summer of 2000, Dr. Thomas Quinn of Frankfurt am Mein (who had taught me in the 1970s) presented me with a copy of *Grundkurs des Glaubens.* Later, he graciously proofread the index, giving special attention to the German language entries. Other proofreading help came from my youngest son, Paul Fischer.

My colleague at St. John's Seminary, Dr. Michael Downey, brought the paraphrase to the attention of the Crossroad Publishing Company, and his recommendation proved effective. Crossroad editor John Jones gave the paraphrase his careful attention, and entrusted the typesetting to Paul J. Kobelski of the HK Scriptorium. For all of these friends and colleagues I am grateful.

Rahner's Preface and Introduction

Preface

In his 1976 preface (pp. xi–xv), Karl Rahner said that he wrote *Foundations of Christian Faith*[1] for educated readers but not for specialists. He aims to present an idea of Christianity, a conceptual overview of Christian faith. The overview is intellectually honest but does not claim to be complete. It is a basic course, not the final word. Rahner says that it offers a kind of saving knowledge for everyone, not just for professional students of theology.

In the preface, Rahner makes two assertions. First, he says that an "idea" of Christianity exists. He calls it a formal concept. This concept can be induced from a study of the various expressions of Christianity. In other words, the many expressions of Christian faith reflect a single idea, a unity that we call Christian faith.

Rahner asserts, second, that his search for the idea of Christianity is somewhat "prescientific." It does not proceed in the ordinary scientific manner, with a comprehensive survey of theological literature and citations of all the relevant sources. A scientific survey, he says, may not yield an account of Christian faith. And that is Rahner's goal: to address Christian faith as a single whole that underlies the many theological specialty studies.

Introduction

The introduction (pp. 1–23) sketches the general aim of *Foundations*, its method, and the book's assumptions about spiritual knowledge. Part 1

---

1. The paraphrase is based on Karl Rahner, *Foundations of Christian Faith: An Introduction to the Idea of Christianity*, trans. William V. Dych (New York: Seabury Press [A Crossroad Book], 1978) and is correlated with the German original, *Grundkurs des Glaubens: Einführung in den Begriff des Christentums* (1976); 8th ed., 1984; paperback edition (Freiburg—Basel—Vienna: Herder, 1997).

shows how the book intends to help Christians (and those who want to be Christians) understand the relation between Christianity and the whole of existence.

Part 2 gives us an insight into the general method that Rahner pursues throughout *Foundations*. It is a method that unites philosophy and theology in faith. Against those who would subordinate philosophy to theology, Rahner wants to integrate the two. Philosophy presents the human being as a question, he writes, a question about the goal and meaning of life. Theology reflects on Christianity as an answer to that human question. It is the answer that God wants to share the divine life, and indeed offers it, to all humanity.

Part 3 identifies problems about how we can know ourselves and God. Some of these problems concern the relation between:

- the knower and Christian faith,
- our openness to reality and our limited knowledge of it, and
- what we know and how we conceptualize it.

In general, Rahner suggests that the bases of Christian faith are reliable. Although spiritual knowledge is limited and imperfect, it is nevertheless true knowledge, based on experience, rooted in history, leading to transcendence.

1. General Preliminary Reflections

(Intr. 1, p. 1). The goal of *Foundations*, says Rahner, is less religious edification than intellectual reflection. It asks about the idea of Christianity and about what makes faith possible. At the same time, however, it is no merely neutral history of religion, for it presupposes faith. What does it mean to ask about the possibility of faith? The following parts 2 and 3 provide an answer.

2. Preliminary Remarks on Methodology

(Intr. 2, p. 3). In this section on method, Rahner explains how his book is a response to the Second Vatican Council. The council recommended an introductory course for seminarians (A) that would summarize the major Christian teachings (B) in a way that recognizes the needs of the age (C). Such a course would acknowledge that theology today is pluralistic (D), and that Christians today can give an account of their faith even in a situation of pluralism (E). Finally, the course envisioned by Rahner would contain a fundamental theology that is also a philosophic reflection on human nature as God's creation (F). In short, *Foundations of Christian Faith* acknowledges the pluralism of modernity but insists that a single account of the faith is possible—not as an objective treatise but as an expression of faith in the God of Jesus Christ.

A. THE CALL OF VATICAN II FOR AN INTRODUCTORY COURSE

(Intr. 2.A, p. 3). The origin of *Foundations* is the Vatican II request, in *Optatam totius* 14, for an "introductory course" in Christianity. Such a course focuses on the mystery of Christ and integrates philosophy and theology. The goal is to make even the beginning student aware of (a) the meaning of theological studies, (b) the interrelation of the branches of theology, and (c) the pastoral intent of such study.

B. THE "THEOLOGICAL ENCYCLOPEDIA" IN THE NINETEENTH CENTURY

(Intr. 2.B, p. 4). This theological encyclopedia of the nineteenth century is a model for Rahner's enterprise. Although the actual encyclopedias of that period are not adequate today, their intent—namely, to present the major themes of Christianity in outline—continues to be a sound one.

C. THE ADDRESSEE OF CONTEMPORARY THEOLOGY

(Intr. 2.C, p. 5). In *Foundations*, Rahner presupposes that there is a contemporary crisis in which faith is challenged, and that this crisis can be overcome. How? By affirming our faith honestly and in an intellectual way. Although *Foundations* is aimed at the beginner, such a beginner today is not like the beginner of Rahner's youth, who could take Christianity for granted. The beginner whom Rahner addresses lives in a different situation, a situation in which the very possibility of belief is contested.

D. PLURALISM IN CONTEMPORARY THEOLOGY AND PHILOSOPHY

(Intr. 2.D, p. 7). There are so many subjects in contemporary theology and philosophy that no one can master them all. In this case, teamwork does not avail, for one must appropriate faith for oneself. Furthermore, there is no all-encompassing framework for understanding, and the theologian must be in dialogue with all the human sciences. Finally, one cannot treat philosophy and theology as a collection of facts, but rather must participate in (must affirm in faith) what one discovers and asserts. All of these observations suggest the pluralism of theology and philosophy.

E. THE JUSTIFICATION OF FAITH ON A "FIRST LEVEL OF REFLECTION"

(Intr. 2.E, p. 8). Theology's arguments for the credibility of faith (the traditional *analysis fidei*) do not establish faith. Rather, they are themselves a part of faith. Something like an "adequate" reflection on faith, a reflection that is scientifically thorough (i.e., a "second-level" reflection, one in which each theological discipline gives an account) is not possible. In Rahner's sense, all of us are *rudes* or beginners, for no one has an encyclopedic or all-comprehending faith. But it is possible for us to have a "first-level" reflection, a reflection in which we are able to give an account of our own faith. This is based on something like converging probabilities or the method of inference that J. H. Newman called the "illative" sense. *Foundations of Christian Faith* aims to supply it.

F. THE CONTENT OF THE INTRODUCTION

(Intr. 2.F, p. 10). The introductory course proposed by Rahner is a unity of philosophy and theology. The philosophy constitutes a "fundamental theology" in which we reflect on Christian existence and its foundations. The theology makes present what Catholics call dogma, namely, what has been revealed by God. The central and most important dogma is that God communicates the divine self to human beings, and that they are capable of receiving this communication. This is not only dogma but also the philosophic foundation of human existence.

By unifying philosophy and theology, Rahner intends (1) to identify the human being as the "universal question," (2) to show the transcendental and historical conditions that make revelation possible, and (3) to show Christianity as the "answer" to the question that the human being poses and in fact is.

Undoubtedly faith remains a mystery. But it is an intelligible mystery, says Rahner, a mystery that engages us at the heart of our being. Having said this, Rahner cautions us to be wary of a narrowly christological approach that prematurely leaps to Jesus Christ as the "answer" before adequately posing the question. Then he warns us to avoid an exclusively philosophical (and not also theological) approach to the problem. Finally, he warns us to be wary of a naive biblicism that might turn the foundational course into a course on exegesis.

3. Some Basic Epistemological Problems

(Intr. 3, p. 14). In his treatment of epistemology, Rahner anticipates the heart of his theology. That heart is the insight into transcendence, the insight that allows us to call his theology "transcendental." By that term, Rahner means that we, in the very act of reflecting on our limitations, overcome those limitations. This is especially true when we think about the meaning of our lives. As we reflect on how limited our understanding of that meaning is, we paradoxically experience a desire for, and the intuition of, greater meaning. In this experience and intuition, we have an indirect knowledge of God, who enables meaning and invites us to express it conceptually (A). Whenever human beings know anything at all, they know themselves along with it (B). Despite the fact that our knowledge is conditioned by history, that conditioning does not hinder our essential openness to experience (C). We know ourselves as capable of knowing more, of transcending what had limited us before (D). This experience of transcendence provides an indirect knowledge of God as the one who presents humanity with choices and who challenges it to grow (E).

A. THE RELATION BETWEEN REALITY AND CONCEPT, BETWEEN ORIGINAL SELF-POSSESSION AND REFLECTION

(Intr. 3.A, p. 14). Rahner distinguishes between an original experience—the experience, let us say, of an encounter with God as the one who calls us to a deeper understanding of ourselves—and the reflection on that experience. A rationalist might say that only the reflection, only the concept, of the experience is real. A modernist might say that reflection is a second-hand experience, an attempt to understand something which, in its original state, is much more fundamental. Rahner wants to say that the two form a unity. The experience of God strives to express itself in concepts. And the concepts one uses to express the experience may falsify it or be inadequate, and so must be purified.

B. THE SELF-PRESENCE OF THE SUBJECT IN KNOWLEDGE

(Intr. 3.B, p. 17). The traditional "correspondence theory" of truth (i.e., that truth is the concept that corresponds to the reality) assumes that the reality, the thing itself, is outside the mind. We have truth when the mind forms a concept adequate to the thing. But spiritual knowledge is such that one possesses the thing known and one's own self (the knower) together. We know ourselves in knowing any thing. That knowledge of ourselves, however, is often implicit and unreflected. Our reflection on what we experience is never the same as the experience itself. The reflection on God in our act of knowing is never the experience itself of God.

C. APRIORITY AND ESSENTIAL OPENNESS

(Intr. 3.C, p. 19). It is true to say that there are a priori conditions for knowing anything. For example, our own self-consciousness is a kind of law governing the way things are known to us. We know things in the way that our very human nature allows us to know them. Having said that, however, we must add: the human being is open by nature. That is why we call the human being a "knowing subject." Whenever we know anything—even when we know ourselves as conditioned by history and prejudiced by culture—we know that we are open to further experience. We are able to transcend ourselves.

D. TRANSCENDENTAL EXPERIENCE

(Intr. 3.D, p. 20). We know ourselves as capable of knowing more. That is the essence of transcendental experience. It is an "experience" in that we can know our capacity for transcendence in any and every experience whatsoever. And we call this experience "transcendental" because it points to a fundamental aspect of humanity. It is the human ability to know ourselves. Knowledge of ourselves is more than knowledge of this or that dimension of our lives. It is knowledge of ourselves as knowers—as those who, in the act of knowing anything, are simultaneously conscious of themselves and of what they are called to become.

E. UNTHEMATIC KNOWLEDGE OF GOD

(Intr. 3.E, p. 21). In transcendental experience, there is an intuition of God. Granted, this intuition is not always conscious of itself. The one who has it may not even know that it is an intuition of God. But that knowledge is still present. How? Because whenever we are aware of ourselves as knowers or seekers trying to understand the mystery of life, then God is present in that self-awareness: present as mystery, as the absolute and incomprehensible source of all that is. What we know, in knowing anything, is that our knowledge is a small vessel in a vast sea of mystery. Our own knowledge, small and incomplete, owes its existence to that vast sea as the mystery that bears it up.

·I·

The Hearer of the Message

This chapter's central theme is the human being, the one who is able to hear God's message. People do not hear this message as mere information about God, unrelated to their lives. No, they hear it, explicitly or inexplicitly, in every experience. In fact, Rahner says that this is what makes us human. We have been created with the ability to encounter the transcendent God in the experiences of daily life.

Chapter I sets out to explain this encounter and what makes it possible. The chapter has six sections. In part 1, Rahner shows that the philosophic analysis of human nature is interwoven with a theological reflection. In essence, he says, the human being is capable of a relationship with God. To ask about human nature, its capacity and its proper end, is ultimately a theological question.

In part 2, Rahner defines the hearer of the message as a person and as a subject. The word *person* means that the hearer cannot be reduced to a mere product of the forces that have shaped him or her. No, the hearer is capable not only of listening, but of freely responding. The word *subject* also has a technical meaning. Subjects are human beings capable of reflecting on themselves. They can ask themselves who they really are, and about what is their true self.

Part 3 states that the hearer of the message is a transcendent being. Hearers recognize that they are limited. But in that very recognition, they begin to imagine how they might surpass their limits. That is the first step to actually transcending them.

Part 4 describes the hearer of the message as responsible and free. Every person can ask whether one choice is better than another and make that choice. Whenever we do so, we take responsibility and act freely.

Part 5 links the hearer of the message to salvation. People who recognize their limits begin to imagine how they might transcend them. Transcendence presents them with choices. When they choose the better alternative, they are not only acting freely and responsibly. They become agents of salvation. They are realizing what God has called them to be.

In part 6, Rahner acknowledges that the hearer of the message is a dependent being. Even the free person is limited by time and place. We can envision only the possibilities that history has put at our disposal. Yet even in this limited and dependent way, the human person experiences spiritual freedom. We human beings are able to hear a message and freely respond to it. The message invites us to become what God means us to be.

1. The Interlocking of Philosophy and Theology

(I.1, p. 24). There is no philosophy that is absolutely free of theology, says Rahner. Whenever we say, "One person is capable of hearing another person," we mean that God has created us with the ability to hear. Persons are shaped by history. In history Christianity confronts them, Christianity not just as an institution, but as God's grace and message. So the philosophy that presumes that the human being is able to hear is not absolutely free of theology. In fact, it is an implicit theology.

And theology presupposes anthropology. Anthropology understands the human being as one created with the ability to hear God's Word. This anthropology enables us to understand how the Christian message can be heard and understood. When Christianity encounters people, it encounters them as hearers. People who encounter Christianity can be asked, "Do you recognize yourself in what Christianity says?"

2. Man as Person and Subject

(I.2, p. 26). In this section, Rahner defines what he means by "person" (A). This concept is essential, for Christianity is addressed to the human person. One needs to know what a person is, that is, to know the being with whom God speaks, in order to understand Christianity (B). The chief characteristic of human "persons" is that they can put their very being in question, and so can transcend it (C).

A. Personhood as Presupposition of the Christian Message

(I.2.A, p. 26). When we Christians speak of the human being as a "person," we mean something specific. We mean that the human being is capable of transcendence, responsibility, freedom, honesty in history, openness to mystery. The Christian message presupposes that its hearers are people with these capacities—in a word, are persons.

B. THE HIDDENNESS AND RISK OF PERSONAL EXPERIENCE

(I.2.B, p. 27). In the personal experience of hearing God's Word, the Word remains hidden. It is implicit in, for example, the Bible, dogmatics, ecclesiology, but not contained immediately in them. In them, God addresses the Christian believers. They hear God's Word in the media that we call the Word of God.

When we say that, we acknowledge that we are saying something general about the human being. We are creating a Christian anthropology. And like any anthropology, Rahner's is limited. In its general statements, anthropology attempts to view the human being as the effect of this or that cause. It may even tempt human beings to shift responsibility for their choices to something else—to history, let us say, or to nature. But the risk of shifting responsibility is worth taking. It is worth taking in order to say something about the human being as a whole, something true, however incomplete.

C. THE SPECIFIC CHARACTER OF PERSONAL EXPERIENCE

(I.2.C, p. 28). The character of personal experience is this: we "have" it in all that we do, but we do not always consciously reflect on it. In Rahner's anthropology, human beings experience themselves as "persons," as beings capable of transcendence. We are more than what a mechanistic anthropology says we are. And it is precisely that "more" that Rahner invites us to bring to conscious expression.

Once we recognize that we are products of history, psychology, etc., products of what is foreign to us, we then can put ourselves in question. We can ask about our true self. And that is what a "subject" is, namely, one who can put his or her very self in question.

The sciences tempt us to think that we can fully explain ourselves. But this is illusory. Transcendental experience suggests that I myself encompass every effort by science to explain me. The person transcends all attempts to reduce him or her to a system or to full comprehension.

3. Man as Transcendent Being

(I.3, p. 31). In this part, Rahner explains what he means by transcendence. This is the central concept in his "transcendental theology." God "calls" human beings to imagine those possibilities for the good that would realize their potential. In so doing, God enables them to transcend themselves (A). Although it is possible for persons to refuse to reflect on their experience (B), nevertheless the capacity for such a reflection is constitutive of being human. By reflecting on our limits, we begin to imagine new possibilities for ourselves (C) and to transcend our limits (D).

A. THE TRANSCENDENT STRUCTURE OF KNOWLEDGE

(I.3.A, p. 31). Whenever a person affirms the possibility that he or she can question things, even in a finite way, that person surpasses the finitude. Why? Because the horizon of finitude is always receding as one discovers more. And as the person experiences that horizon receding, the person experiences himself or herself as spirit. One is spirit whenever one acknowledges one's limits. In that acknowledgment, one has already surpassed the limits, at least as a possibility. Whenever we seek advice, guidance, or forgiveness, we are recognizing our limits and the possibility of surpassing them.

B. THE POSSIBILITY OF EVADING THE EXPERIENCE OF TRANSCENDENCE

(I.3.B, p. 32). One can evade the experience of transcendence in a variety of ways. One can naively say, "Self-reflection is a waste of time—why should I worry about it?" Or one can dully and unimaginatively "accept" one's existence without curiosity. This happens when we acknowledge that existence poses a question, but nevertheless refuse to pursue it. We may even despair. Despair arises when we stop pursuing the question because we disbelieve that there is any meaning to it.

C. THE PRE-APPREHENSION OF BEING

(I.3.C, p. 33). Being: Rahner says that we experience it in hope, in the movement toward freedom, in the assumption of responsibility. What does he mean? He means that, whenever we imagine a possibility for ourselves, we presuppose that there are such possibilities. They are the infinity of reality, the infinity of being. We grasp them as possibilities of the human spirit.

Yes, we are ourselves limited. But in our limits, we are connected to what is absolute. And that absolute (at this point Rahner calls it being, but he means God) can accomplish something—can accomplish in us what we hope for and desire. In short, we apprehend being because we are open to it. And whenever we ask about the mystery of our lives, we understand ourselves as persons who "receive" being. We receive it as a grace, the grace of freedom.

D. THE PRE-APPREHENSION AS CONSTITUTIVE OF PERSON

(I.3.D, p. 34). This openness to being makes us what we are, that is, persons. By being open, we experience ourselves as participating in the infinity of possibilities. This participation enables us to anticipate our own fulfillment. And that is a form of transcendence. We transcend what we are by being open to what being offers. This does not happen by deliberately trying to "think" transcendence. No, it happens indirectly. It may happen in a rare mystical experience, for example, or in the commonplace experience of loneliness.

4. Man as Responsible and Free

(I.4, p. 35). In this section Rahner defines freedom. For him, it is not a psychological phenomenon but a "transcendental experience" (A). We "know" it as the presupposition underlying our thinking and choices (B). Whenever we choose to act "responsibly," reflecting on our ability to make choices and deliberately choosing one course over another as more responsible, we experience freedom (C).

A. Freedom as Non-Particular Datum

(I.4.A, p. 35). One cannot discover freedom as a given. This was the attempt of scholastic psychology and contradicts the essence of freedom. Freedom is not one phenomenon among others in the realm of psychology. It is rather a transcendental experience. Such an experience grounds the concrete experience of freedom in, for example, jurisprudence and the philosophy of law. We do not discover freedom as a given but rather as a presupposition. It lies behind all our questioning about whether we are free and responsible. Our very questioning presupposes the freedom to question.

B. The Concrete Mediation of Freedom

(I.4.B, p. 36). Transcendental freedom is what classical philosophy called an idea. We reflect on it when it is objectified in the world in free choice and decisions but cannot be reduced to them. It lies behind every free act and thought, and so cannot remain unintelligible. We know originating freedom in the experience of objectified freedom. So one cannot point to a given act in history and say, "That is a pure product of freedom." Freedom is not a datum but an idea.

C. Responsibility and Freedom as Realities of Transcendental Experience

(I.4.C, p. 37). One's freedom is limited. But within those limits, one can act. And the recognition of that freedom is the recognition of transcendental experience. I experience myself as one who can assume responsibility and act freely, that is, as a "subject" within the horizon of being. To be sure, one can try to evade responsibility and pretend that one is merely a product of forces outside oneself. But that is a lie. Human beings are able to decide about themselves and to actualize themselves. The spiritual work of deciding and actualizing (rather than the concrete ability to do this or that) is the exercise of true freedom.

5. The Question of Personal Existence as a Question of Salvation

Is there such a thing as one's true self? Rahner says that there is, and whenever we choose to become what we are "called" to be, we become self-conscious agents in the history of salvation.

A. THE THEOLOGICAL AND ANTHROPOLOGICAL STARTING POINT FOR AN UNDERSTANDING OF "SALVATION"

(I.5.A, p. 39). Salvation is not a future that befalls someone from the outside. Nor is it something bestowed by moral judgment. Rather, salvation is the truth of ourselves before God. We are invited to understand ourselves truly and to realize our true selves. This is done "before God," that is, when we acknowledge who we are as God has created us. We are "saved" when we freely develop ourselves as God has allowed us to do. In that way we fulfill our destiny, we as persons destined to transcend ourselves. Such transcendence is invited by God and takes place in union with God.

B. SALVATION IN HISTORY

(I.5.B, p. 40). Our being, says Rahner, is not something we "have." Rather, it is experienced in all things, most of which are beyond our control: time, world, and history. Our experience of being is not at our disposal. But in the multitude of experiences, we encounter what is at our disposal. We encounter our own subjectivity and freedom.

Our experience of being in the world includes our feeling that we are alien and different. In that feeling, we discover ourselves and affirm ourselves. We attempt to become ourselves, to become what we are called to be. And the sum total of this human effort can be called the history of salvation. It is the effort of humanity to respond to the invitation to know itself as the being that can transcend itself. It does so in the fulfillment of the possibilities with which it was created, and in the attempt to realize its destiny. This history is the history of God, the God who calls human beings to recognize themselves for what they are and to become what they are meant to be.

6. Man as Dependent

(I.6, p. 42). Human beings are dependent on the world and on history, says Rahner in this brief section. But within that dependence, we exercise freedom and experience transcendence.

A. THE PRESENCE OF MYSTERY

(I.6.A, p. 42). We human beings experience ourselves as not being in control of our lives, but in being at the disposal of other things. In that experience, however, we imagine other possibilities, and so have a measure of freedom. That too is what we call transcendence. Hence we are both free and dependent on those things that limit our choices.

Even our transcendence is experienced as something we do not make for ourselves. It was established by another. Who is the other who enables us to transcend ourselves? We call that other the ineffable mystery.

B. MAN AS CONDITIONED BY WORLD AND BY HISTORY

(I.6.B, p. 42). It is true to say that, in the very experience of ourselves as conditioned, we have moved beyond that conditioning. Whenever we recognize ourselves as being at the disposal of others, as being conditioned and burdened, we take flight into the imagination, imagining ourselves as free. We experience spiritual freedom. But we cannot leave the limiting conditions behind. And that is our human situation: to be conditioned and limited, and yet to have transcended those conditions in freedom.

We experience freedom whenever we make choices. Yet that freedom is never wholly at our disposal. Rather, we make decisions as a synthesis: a synthesis of possibilities and choices. Only some things are possible to us. Every choice edges out other possible choices. And we come to the truth of reality by enduring and accepting the knowledge that reality is not in our hands. Yet we hope and persevere, knowing that we are, and are called to be, more than what we are.

·II·

Man in the Presence
of Absolute Mystery

The title of this chapter does not include the word "God." Strictly speaking, the title indicates that the chapter is about the human being. That human being, however, is in the presence of absolute mystery. The chapter focuses on this mystery. It asks what it is, why it is absolute, and how it is present.

Chapter II has five parts. Part 1 is a meditation on the word "God." The meditation distinguishes between the word and what it represents. Even if the word were to be stricken from the dictionary, says Rahner, the question implicit in the word—the question about the origin and destiny of life—would remain.

After part 1 has raised the question, part 2 discusses whether we can know God. It advances Rahner's central thesis, namely, that we encounter God in a transcendental experience of God's holy mystery. Whenever we experience our limits, imagining what lies beyond them, we begin to transcend them. In that experience, we recognize the mystery of our existence, whose origin and destiny are not yet clear. To know that mystery, says Rahner, is to know the source of transcendence.

The source of transcendence is not, however, a blind and impersonal force. Part 3 states that the source is a personal God. We speak of God as a person by way of analogy. God is not a person in the same sense that we human beings are. But God is indeed a person in that God cannot be reduced to a thing. God is the absolute ground of all things, "absolute" because irreducible to anything else.

The human being is related to God as a creature to the source of creation. Part 4 explains how human beings "know" God. We know God by knowing ourselves in relation to the mystery of our lives. This mystery is nothing other than what gives us our place in time and invites us to fulfill the possibilities allotted to us.

In part 5, Rahner states that the holy mystery is present "in" the world as its fundamental ground. It is "holy" because it enables us to be complete.

14

It helps us to be what we are meant to be. Doubtless we find God in historical religion and its holy places, people, and things. But God may not be confined to phenomena. Rather, the phenomena of this world, including the holy symbols, sanctuaries, and deeds of religion, mediate the presence of God and teach us how to discern it. But we already know this God immediately as our transcendent ground.

1. Meditation on the Word "God"

(II.1, p. 44). In the six sections of part 1, Rahner meditates on the reality of the word "God" (A), on its meaning (B), and on its very future as a word and concept (C). Then he reflects on what the human being would be like without the word "God" (D), on the function of the word (E), and on how human beings are presented with the word (F). Although the word is common to every language, it functions in an uncommon way by putting the meaning and destiny of life in question.

A. THE EXISTENCE OF THE WORD

(II.1.A, p. 44). Rahner begins by noting that, in many ways, the word "God" is a noun like any other. But unlike other nouns, "God" names something that does not appear in any place or time. Rahner's train of thought indirectly recalls to us the First Letter of John: "No one has ever seen God; if we love one another, God abides in us" (4:12). Yet this word is known and used by, and has an existence for, even those who claim to disbelieve in God.

B. WHAT DOES THE WORD "GOD" MEAN?

(II.1.B, p. 46). Although the word "God" functions like a proper name, it is not one. It differs from the proper names *Yahweh* and *Father*. Unlike them, "God" has a "blank face," since God is ineffable and does not enter the world. Because the word "God" is "silent," because it is not spoken by God, it can be overlooked and unheard. But the "blank face" of the word "God" is not only known in every culture, but takes on a variety of cultural contours.

C. DOES THIS WORD HAVE A FUTURE?

(II.1.C, p. 47). Karl Marx thought the very word, "God," as well as theism itself, would disappear. What does Rahner think? Either the word will disappear or it will survive as a question, he says, a question about the goal and meaning of human life.

D. REALITY WITHOUT THIS WORD

(II.1.D, p. 47). If the word "God" disappeared, then human beings would not be brought face to face with the whole of reality as the creation of this God. People would not be brought face to face with their own reality, with the individual's own existence as a whole. For Rahner, the ability to put reality into question is what constitutes the human being. Without a God who is the creator and sustainer of reality, there would be no one to question the meaning of reality, and the defining characteristic of the human would be absent. Humanity would henceforth no longer exist.

E. THE SURVIVAL OF THE WORD "GOD"

(II.1.E, p. 49). "God" is a word by which we refer to the one who brought into existence the whole of reality. With the word "God," all of language is placed in question. By asking about "God," we question whether it is possible in language to represent reality and find meaning in it.

F. THE ORIGINAL WORD SPOKEN TO US

(II.1.F, p. 50). Language presents us with the word "God." We do not create the word or what it represents. But the dictionary meaning of the word is not the whole of its reality. It only "represents the real word which becomes present for us from out of the wordless texture of all words" (p. 50). Rahner concludes this section with three references:

1. Tertullian. This second-century Latin father of the church taught that there is a soul (human and not divine) in every person. This soul, Christian from its origins, enables the person to hear the real Word of God.
2. Wittgenstein. This twentieth-century philosopher wrote that we should not speak about those things that we cannot understand, and this would seem to rule out all talk of God. But even Wittgenstein, as Rahner notes, disobeys his own dictum.
3. *Amor fati*. This Latin phrase, "love of fate," illumines the word "God": we human beings ought to love, to cherish, to revere, what is necessary in this life—whether we call it "fate" or "God."

2. The Knowledge of God

(II.2, p. 51). In this most challenging part of chapter II, Rahner begins with the fundamental idea that we know God in our reflection on experience, but not as some entity that we can "prove" independently of experience (A). Before any natural or revealed knowledge of God, we have an encounter with God (B). This encounter is given in the human experience of transcendence. This experience is mysterious, for it is both given to us (subjectively) and is something upon which we can (objectively) reflect (C). The mystery was recognized as early as Greek ontology. Ontology, the "science of being," showed that one both can express something as a concept and yet not capture everything in the concept (D). So instead of a concept, Rahner uses the phrase "holy mystery." He calls it the "term" of transcendence (E). Term is related to terminus, end, or goal. This term is both present in transcendence and as the way to transcendence. It enables us to know the reality of God, and is our experience of it (F). Finally, Rahner makes a comment on the proofs for the existence of God (G). They are signs that point to the reality, he says, and can enable the listener to reflect on the transcendental knowledge of God that he or she already has.

A. TRANSCENDENTAL AND A POSTERIORI KNOWLEDGE OF GOD

(II.2.A, p. 51). When Rahner speaks of "transcendental" knowledge of God, he means it is something "a posteriori." We know it, in other words, after the fact, for example, while reflecting on human experience. Our experience with others, Rahner says, enables us to know ourselves, whom we "see" as we reflect on our experience. So too we know the divine in reflecting on our experience of the world. The experience raises in our minds the question of who we are and what we ought to be.

But this knowledge is no mere reflection after the fact. It is what Rahner calls a "permanent existential," that is, a part of who we are. We encounter ourselves whenever we try to speak of our experience of God. It is we who are capable of an encounter with God. In this encounter, we find that we can transcend what we once thought to be our outermost horizon. The discovery of this experience itself is a mystery. The mystery is not reducible to what we can say about our transcendental knowledge.

To be sure, our knowledge of God remains a posteriori. We know God after the fact, after reflecting on our experience of meeting our limits, of imagining what lies beyond them, and of realizing the possibilities given us to respond to God's call. Our transcendental experience does not cancel the fact that we know it only afterwards, in the reflection on it. This cautions us to beware that God is not a thing we can "know" beforehand. We cannot indoctrinate another person about God, but only lead him or her to recognize the God whom they in an implicit way already know.

What can we know about God? Our knowledge of God is indirect, like the knowledge of "our subjective freedom, our transcendence, and the infinite openness of the spirit" (p. 53). We know the experience of God, even when we do not consciously reflect on the experience. Moreover, we know God, even when our conceptualization of God is unpersuasive to other people.

So we can finally say: the concept of God is not a concept we can grasp. It is, rather, what grasps us. We do not formulate a concept and ask if it is God. No, it is better to say that both the concept itself, as well as the reality, move us into the unknown.

B. The Different Ways of Knowing God and Their Intrinsic Unity

(II.2.B, p. 55). Traditionally, one speaks of "natural" knowledge of God, and of knowledge through "revelation" (in word and in deed). Rahner says, however, that there is a more "original experience," an experience on which both natural and revealed knowledge rely. The more original experience is a transcendental experience. It is not reducible to metaphysics, and it is fully compatible with the theological concept of grace. Transcendental experience is not purely "natural" because it takes place in freedom. We can choose to reflect on it or ignore it. This God-given freedom, the freedom to act responsibly and to make choices, is itself "supernatural."

C. Transcendental Knowledge of God as Experience of Mystery

(II.2.C, p. 57). Transcendental experience, says Rahner, is "the basic and original way of knowing God" (p. 58). More basic than "natural" and "revealed" knowledge? Yes, says Rahner. Natural and revealed knowledge is mediated. It comes to us through the media of categorical experiences. Transcendental experience, by contrast, is not a neutral power by which to know God. It does not enable us to "master" our experience. Instead, transcendental experience allows us to know ourselves as finite beings—finite beings who can transcend their finitude.

Are human beings united with their transcendence? Are we one with the gift and the impulse that moves us to realize our potential? This is an important and dangerous question. Since God "is" our transcendence, a "yes" might suggest that we are our own gods. But the unity we experience, says Rahner, is not that. It is rather the unity between the ground and the person who is grounded, between the Word and our response to it. There are two ways, says Rahner, to understand our knowledge of God in transcendence.

1. Subjective knowledge. This transcendental knowledge comes to light in conversation or even in something like Viktor E. Frankl's "logotherapy." Subjective knowledge enables us to see that our experiences (e.g., of love, of freedom, of joy, etc.) are experiences of transcendence. We bring our experience to light in discourse with another person.

2. Objective knowledge. This transcendental knowledge comes from a direct contemplation of the source of transcendence. We contemplate it and call it "God." But there is a danger in such objective knowledge. The danger is that, by speaking of God, we might lose sight of what we mean. What we mean is the source of the experience of transcendence, the holy mystery. It might be obscured by the concept we use to express it. If we try to describe the source as "absolute being," we might settle for an abstraction, not the source itself.

So Rahner proposes that we call the source of our original experience of transcendence the "holy mystery" (p. 60). He hopes that this phrase, this symbol of God, may not be easily confused with a stereotype, a myth, or a conventional image.

D. THE TERM OF TRANSCENDENCE AS THE INFINITE, THE INDEFINABLE, AND THE INEFFABLE

(II.2.D, p. 61). Rahner states that his goal is to express the source of our experience of transcendence without reducing it to a mere object, one topic among others, or a system. What gives him hope is that, whenever he tries to reflect on the meaning of transcendence, "an experience of transcendence takes place" (p. 62). The human being reaches out to or anticipates the "term" of transcendence. This technical word (German: *Woraufhin;* English: "where-to-there") means goal, end, or terminus. Every person implicitly anticipates an ultimate goal, and in the anticipation of it, grows toward it. The lure of God's future is the "term" of transcendence.

The transcendental experience (of God) and the categorical objects that mediate it (in the world) are united but different. If they were only united, their relationship would be pantheistic. God would then "be" our experience of the world. If the experience and the categorical objects were only different, their relation would be dualistic. God would be the unknowable "other." Rahner sees the relation between the two as unity in difference. "God establishes and is the difference" between the world and God (p. 63). Anyone searching for a God "contained in" reality seeks a false God. Those searching for a God wholly other and distant will never know God or themselves.

The earliest Greek philosophies touched upon the mysteries of first principles. Greek ontology saw that human beings cannot measure the first principles, but are themselves to be measured. True, we can have legitimately categorical knowledge of God—knowledge that we can categorize and classify. But we recognize that such categorical knowledge is not the whole. There is more to God than what we can say: that is why we acknowledge that God is infinite, indefinable, and ineffable.

E. The Term of Transcendence as the "Holy Mystery"

(II.2.E, p. 65). "Holy mystery" is Rahner's "term" of transcendence. Since "term" means "way of access to" as well as terminus or goal, "holy mystery" indicates the way to transcendence and remains the goal of transcendence. Rahner says that this holy mystery possesses absolute freedom. The holy mystery, the term of transcendence, *is* our freedom. In it we are free to be present, in whatever way we choose, to other "subjects of transcendence," other free persons.

Moreover, transcendence moves us toward holy mystery, its proper end. The experience of transcendence opens up to us the holy mystery. It is a "mystery" because we cannot fully fathom it. It is "holy" because it enables us to be complete. It allows us to be present to other persons in a communion of freedom and love. When we put ourselves "at the disposal of" transcendence, we move beyond ourselves and form relationships with others, above all, with God. Holy mystery includes the capacity to freely love.

Transcendence, Rahner concludes, does not depend on its "ground" or "term," that is, on holy mystery. Transcendence is not derived from or reducible to it. Rather, holy mystery is what we encounter in the experience of transcendence. Transcendence moves us in freedom and love toward its goal.

F. Transcendental Experience and Reality

(II.2.F, p. 66). Transcendence does not create God. Rather, transcendence is "borne by" God, who makes transcendence possible. Rahner calls the term or goal of transcendental experience a "holy mystery," namely, the unity of essence and existence. If it were existence alone, then we could experience it in the same way we experience anything else, like a sunset. If it were only an essence, without any concrete existence, then we could not experience it at all. But as the unity of essence and existence, holy mystery has a reality that is grounded for us in the experience of transcendence. That experience is a necessary part of the human being, the one who is created so as to hear God's Word.

G. Remarks on the Proofs for God's Existence

(II.2.G, p. 68). The proofs of God's existence are, in Rahner's view, "signs." They point to God but do not make God graspable or a mere concept. Just as we can only point to our experience of transcendence in words, but cannot reduce the experience to a concept, so we can point to God in "proofs." These proofs are not "ways" by which a previously unknown object can be known. By means of the proofs, however, one can show another person that they are already involved in the experience of transcendence and of holy mystery. The listener, presented with "proofs," is really being confronted with the light of his or her own spirit. He or she is faced with questions, anxiety, joy, moral obligation, and the anticipation of death—all of which recall the very experience of transcendence.

In the "proofs" of God, there is an element of causality. Causality in this case does not mean, for example, that one sees creation and is moved to belief in a first cause. Rather, causality is a way of indicating that being itself moves our judgment. Absolute being points to the relation between finite creation and its incomprehensible source.

3. God as Person

(II.3, p. 71). In this brief part, Rahner makes remarks about the word *person* as applied to God. He begins by noting that the word *Person* is analogous, and shows what analogical language about God can and cannot do (A). It can supply a concept, but the very inadequacy of the concept suggests that more lies beyond it. To give an example, Rahner analyzes the word *person* as applied to God, and shows that God is indeed a person (B). But God is not a person in the same sense that human beings are persons. By calling God a person our analogical language indicates the human desire to transcend the limits of understanding and know God more fully.

A. ANALOGOUS LANGUAGE ABOUT GOD

(II.3.A, p. 71). Language does not create, in and of itself, the direct experience of God. But it does allow us to express the reality of God in secondary and analogical concepts. Rahner's goal is to find words to express the experience of transcendence. God is disclosed, he says, by those things that are based and grounded in God. The ground itself (i.e., God) cannot be incorporated into a system alongside what is grounded. The ground is known only by analogy.

We human beings *are* the tension, says Rahner, between our categorical statements about God and the transcendent reality itself. We know God "by analogy." Analogy is not a hybrid between the univocity of God and the equivocation of categorical statements. Analogy is itself a category of tension. It is the tension between a categorical starting point (e.g., a statement "about" God) and the incomprehensible mystery that God is. Categorical language mediates God. Such language is a point of departure, for in it we glimpse what fundamentally lies beyond it.

B. On the Personal Being of God

(II.3.B, p. 73). Is God a "person"? Rahner offers two answers. First he says that, yes, God is a "person." Like human beings, God is irreducible to things, and is more than what anyone can say about God. Indeed, God is the ground of all things, and not grounded by anything else. This brings Rahner to his second answer. Insofar as God is not grounded by anything else, we can say no, God is not a person. God is not a person if by that we mean that God is in any way limited. The challenge for a transcendental theology such as Rahner's is to fill the traditional formula, "God is a person," with a personal experience of prayer—and not to reduce the formula to an impersonal principle. God would become an impersonal principle if we were to reduce God to a formula such as "the One who is not in Himself grounded." In an experience of prayer, however, the believer praises God as the mysterious source and sustainer of life.

4. Man's Relation to His Transcendent Ground: Creatureliness

(II.4, p. 75). In this section, Rahner uses the word *creatureliness* to characterize the relation to God of the human being. He says that only the whole of the Christian message enables us to understand the creator-creature relationship completely. It is not just that God "caused" human beings in a one-time event, but that creation is ongoing (A). Creation signals more than our difference from God. It also means that we depend on God as the ground of every action (B). This dependence, however, does not curtail human autonomy, because it is God who enables it (C). This autonomy leads to a reflection on how human beings, precisely as creatures, are able to make choices (D). The experience of choosing reveals the created world, not as a power independent of God, but as the raw material for humanity's own creative choices (E).

Two questions guide part 4. First, if we can know God by the light of reason, is God known precisely as the creator? And second, if God is known as creator, do we recognize that we are "creatures" by the light of reason? Vatican I did not define the role of natural reason, says Rahner, and he concludes that human beings experience their creatureliness immediately. They recognize that they are not their own ground.

A. Creatureliness: Not a Particular Instance
   of a Causal Relationship

(II.4.A, p. 76). In this section, Rahner is at pains to explain that we are not "creatures" simply because God has "caused" us. Rather, we know ourselves as creatures primarily in our transcendental experience. We are the only ones who can ask the question of "why" about ourselves. We are the only ones who can reply that we are "grounded" by God. Creatureliness is not a one-time experience that happens when we are created. No, it is the experience of all people who know themselves as being constantly in a relationship with a mystery. It is the mystery that gives everyone his or her own "time" or history.

B. Creatureliness as Radical Difference from and Radical Dependence on God

(II.4.B, p. 77). *Creatio ex nihilo* means that we are "from" God and "dependent on" God. God is absolutely different from human beings. How? Because God is the ground of all comprehension. Instead of being an object we know, God is what allows any knowledge whatsoever to take place. God's absolute being is thus the ground of every action. Absolute being, the answer to the question of why there is anything whatsoever and not nothing, is the horizon of every action and thought.

C. Radical Dependence on God and Genuine Autonomy

(II.4.C, p. 78). We are what we are precisely because we are created, not despite our creatureliness. We are not mere appearances behind which God and reality hide. No, we have a genuine autonomy. Creation means that God (1) retains us as God's own creation, and (2) sets us free in our own autonomy. We understand ourselves as creatures, not only in the experience of freedom but also in the experience of responsibility.

D. Transcendental Experience as the Origin of the Experience of Creatureliness

(II.4.D, p. 79). We experience creatureliness in transcendental experience. That is the experience of being "borne by an incomprehensible ground" (p. 80). We are living out of a mystery that can never be mastered. We recognize this mystery in prayer, a prayer that both acknowledges our own autonomy and responsibility, and also concedes that we are not our own ground. In this regard, we face two temptations. One is the temptation to experience ourselves as empty appearances that God controls. The second is to experience ourselves as something that is fundamentally independent of God.

E. The Experience of Creatureliness as Denuminizing the World

(II.4.E, p. 80). If the world is created, then the world is not a nature holy in itself. Nor is it a nature in which God shows forth as noumena or mere appearances. Rather, the world is material for the creative power of man. Rahner's words recall the passage from Genesis means in which God tells Adam to fill and subdue the earth. The message is to fulfill the possibilities that God presents to humanity.

5. Finding God in the World

(II.5, p. 81). God is both "in" the world and "outside" it as its fundamental ground. "In" the world, we know God in holy places, people, and things. Historical religions hold them sacred. But God is not a place, a human person, or a thing. Rather, we commonly say that God is "outside" the world. God is the world's foundation. In part 5, Rahner relates the inside and the outside. He does so by explaining his transcendental starting point (A). Then he goes on to say that our human immediacy to God is always mediated (B). Next, he affirms that God has truly revealed the divine self. We acknowledge this revelation as a mode of our transcendental relationship to God (C). Yes, God is "in" the world—primarily in a direct call to the human being. We recognize this call in the holy places, people, and things of Christianity (D).

A. THE TENSION BETWEEN A TRANSCENDENTAL STARTING POINT
AND HISTORICAL RELIGION

(II.5.A, p. 81). God is the "creative ground" of everything, but that does not mean that God has nothing in common with ordinary life. To be sure, no one has seen God. God is not a phenomenon, but is rather what underlies all phenomena. But if God were only an underlying ground, then God could not be found in historical religion. If God underlies everything, and is radically separate from those things, then God is "in" no religion at all, and it is meaningless to say that God is "here" but not "there." Historical religion, however, finds God in its sacred books, sacraments, and ordained leaders. It states that God is in sacred things. Some things are sacred, and there God dwells, according to historical religion. Other things are not sacred, and God is not in them.

The danger run by historical religion is that it does see God in phenomena, and indeed may reduce God to phenomena. This is a risk, but one worth running. Religions that refuse to see God in phenomena also run a risk. Their risk, says Rahner, is that they may "evaporate into a mist which perhaps does exist, but in practice it cannot be the source of religious life." In truth, God is neither a merely categorical object (such as reverence, holiness, the experience of awe) nor an abstract ground. Even the atheist can "reverence the ineffable in silence" (p. 82), and so is "religious" at a basic level. Even the simplest Christian senses that there is more to Christian faith than what is presented in the doctrine and celebrations of the church.

B. IMMEDIACY TO GOD AS MEDIATED IMMEDIACY

(II.5.B, p. 82). In order to grasp the "mediated immediacy" of God, we begin with what it does not mean. Real immediacy to God (i.e., what Christians mean when they speak of the beatific vision) does not imply that God is so immediate that the human being is "taken over" by God. Being "immediate" to God does not mean that freedom and independence, in short, everything creaturely, disappears. Rather, immediacy means that God, as the transcendental ground of all life, is present in and recognized through the finite person. In experiencing the infinite God, the finite person does not cease to exist.

The immediate vision of God, the beatific vision, is mediated by our experience both of God and of ourselves. When we speak of the beatific vision, we mean God fulfilling the human person. The vision is not an apprehension of God that cancels out my humanity, but an experience of myself as the spirit whom God fulfills. The beatific vision does not mean that the presence of God does away with the need for transcendental experience. Rather, when someone experiences the transcendent God, the encounter takes place in and through that finite human being. Our finite humanity glimpses the infinite God as the ground of our own transcendence.

C. THE ALTERNATIVE: "DEVOTION TO THE WORLD" OR TRUE SELF-COMMUNICATION OF GOD

(II.5.C, p. 84). Some might argue that God plays a minor role (if at all) in the rites and rituals of historical, categorical religions. God is rather, they would say, the transcendental ground of all structures in the world, including religion. A thoughtful person ought to be devoted, not to religion, but to the world. In this "natural religion" of devotion, and not in religious ritual, some might believe that they properly honor God as the world's transcendental ground.

Rahner contends, however, that God has really made a gift of the divine self to human beings, a self-communication which is revered and passed on in the form of a supernatural religion. How does he justify devotion to this supernatural religion?

To begin, Rahner concedes that God's holy mystery is truly experienced as the condition of the possibility for human activity in the world. Everyone may in fact experience God in this general, transcendental way. But the Christian would say more than that. In addition to a general experience of God present in a remote way as the world's transcendent ground, the Christian would also say that the holy mystery is present intimately.

God is present "in the mode of an absolute and forgiving closeness and of an absolute offer of himself" (p. 86). God's gift of self (which Rahner will articulate in later chapters) is the ground of historical religion. God is both an immediate transcendental ground and a mediated experience, mediated by historical events which actualize the divine gift of self and make it present.

D. GOD'S ACTIVITY IN AND THROUGH SECONDARY CAUSES

(II.5.D, p. 86). The question here is whether we can attribute to God the events we encounter in the world. Are any things "caused" by God? Rahner says that the chain of causality has its basis in God, but God cannot be understood as a link in the chain. If we believe that God is, in any way, "immediately present" to us, then we must say that the immediacy itself and its expression in things and events are embedded in the world. Immediacy is embedded. God is not.

Then what are those events and experiences that seem to be an intervention of God in the world? Rahner calls them a "concretion" of God's transcendental self-communication. Every "intervention," however concrete, is really an expression of something far more profound: God's presence as the transcendental ground of the world. This transcendental ground is like our own freedom and responsibility. They are always being objectified in free decisions and responsible actions, but the freedom and responsibility themselves are intangible.

When God "intervenes," such interventions should be understood as "divine" because of the fact that we have already experienced God as the transcendent ground of our lives. A "good idea," for example, can be called a "divine inspiration," and so it seems to the one who regards the idea as a moment in a living relation to God. The good idea is one of a multitude of concretions of my transcendental relation to God. But that "good idea" can also be explained by means of psychology. Good ideas are a "special providence." Bad ideas may concretize our relation to God as well. Our relationship to God's holy mystery finds its expression in the world, but transcends that expression.

· III ·

Man as a Being Threatened
Radically by Guilt

Christians can mistakenly believe that the world was evil before Christ and that, after his death, it essentially changed in a tangible way. Rahner avoids that misunderstanding. He defines guilt as the refusal, from the beginning of human history until now, to accept God's offer of self. Guilt is not merely a feeling of remorse about this or that sinful act. At its foundation, it is a rejection of God. It threatens the human being in a radical way, says Rahner, because the one who refuses God's self-communication refuses true freedom.

In part 1 of this chapter, Rahner shows just how difficult it is for people to extricate themselves from guilt. No one can escape the guilty situation—the situation of having refused God's gift of self—on one's own. Indeed, without God we cannot even recognize guilt for what it is. Once we admit that we have closed ourselves off from God, however, we can freely and responsibly choose the good that lies before us. With this choice we recognize God's offer of transcendence, the offer that we identify with divine mercy and forgiveness.

The freedom to act responsibly, Rahner says in part 2, is essential to God's communication with human beings. By following their consciences, people respond to God's invitation to hear the divine Word and obey it. In this way, they achieve their life's work and define themselves. But human freedom is never complete. We always act within a context imposed by history. We remain hearers of God's word, never the masters of it.

Hence we can never know how free we are or fully assess the moral quality of our actions. This is the argument of part 3. The self-righteous person is always capable of rejecting God. Such people delude themselves into thinking that they are acting freely and responsibly, but may in fact be doing the opposite. Conversely, a person may profess atheism in the name of human freedom, and thereby affirm God, albeit indirectly and inexplicitly. The mysterious God, who offers people freedom and invites them to act responsibly, remains the sole judge of the moral quality of their actions.

27

Human beings cannot escape the fact that their lives are determined by a history in which people refuse God's offer to them. That is the meaning, according to part 4, of original sin. It is not personal guilt, but the universal guilt of people in a history marked by repeated failures to respond to God's call. This guilt is radical because it threatens the root of human freedom.

1. The Topic and Its Difficulties

(III.1, p. 90). Rahner raises two questions: the nature of redemption and the manner in which it is achieved. First, he notes that our sinful acts are never wholly private. We can never reconcile ourselves by ourselves. So that is the first difficulty: how can we be reconciled to God, and to others, after we have done wrong. The second question is about how we are redeemed. Part of this is a temporal question. Rahner asks whether it is a "moment" or a "process." The answer is to come later.

In part 1, Rahner starts by showing that most people today regard the question of guilt as confusing or obscure. Next, he shows that we have to have a relationship with God in order to know guilt, and that the experience of guilt leads to an insight into God's love and forgiveness.

A. The Obscurity of the Question for People Today

(III.1.A, p. 91). The "normal" person does not fear God as the one before whom he or she shall be judged. Fear of God means respect, normally speaking, and not terror. Even Christians (whom we expect to fear God) do not have a particularly powerful impression of their own moral dispositions. Many people see death not as judgment, but as the resolution of the confusion of daily life or even as something absurd and meaningless.

But all people compare what they *should* be with what they *are*. Even though contemporary people not usually think of death as judgment, they do believe that the human being (rather than God) is the one who needs to be justified. They ought to be open at least to the Christian message, namely, that human beings are sinners in need of redemption.

B. The Circle between the Experience of Guilt and Forgiveness

(III.1.B, p. 93). More fundamental than the obscurity of guilt is the problem of the guilty person's relation to God. It seems paradoxical, but only when one has a "partnership" with God can one know guilt. Only with immediacy to God can we grasp it. Guilt means closing oneself off to God's self-communication.

Guilt and forgiveness, Rahner says, have a circular relationship. We experience guilt as closing oneself off to God. When one sees oneself doing this, one is moved to an insight. The insight is that the God to whom one is closed continues to extend an invitation. God is in fact not judgmental but loving and forgiving.

2. Man's Freedom and Responsibility

(III.2, p. 93). The freedom of the human being: that is the topic of part 2. Rahner asserts that this freedom is not something we have to rehabilitate by means of spiritual discipline, but is present in our every action and choice. Freedom is the essence of God's offer to humanity. But one act of freedom influences the next, Rahner says, and all contribute to the final achievement that is the human life. Every free act expresses our relation to God, the ground of human freedom. And so in every free act, we make a decision for or against God. But because every free act is conditioned by factors beyond the individual's control, the human being can never be certain of the moral quality of his or her decisions. There is no point at which one can say, "Now I finally understand God's communication, and I no longer have to listen."

A. FREEDOM IS RELATED TO THE SINGLE WHOLE OF HUMAN EXISTENCE

(III.2.A, p. 94). The concept of freedom can be understood falsely in terms of the Gnosticism we associate with Origen. He believed (according to Rahner) that life in the concrete is evil. Given this viewpoint, the Gnostic views freedom as something that existed before concrete life, even before history. As a counter concept, Rahner proposes that true freedom is "the capacity of the one subject to decide about himself in his single totality" (p. 94). It is not something which one has to "recover" by means of a rigorous spiritual discipline, but rather something one exercises constantly. Freedom did not exist before history (in some Gnostic aeon of perfection), but actualizes itself in a passage through time.

Freedom is not a "datum," a given, or a neutral faculty. It is not the mere ability to make choices. It is not a faculty whose morality one can only assess after it has been exercised. It is fundamentally the achievement of one's own person. By acting freely, one actualizes oneself.

B. FREEDOM AS THE FACULTY OF FINAL AND DEFINITIVE VALIDITY

(III.2.B, p. 95). It is a misunderstanding to assert that freedom is merely the capacity to do this or that, as if one decision has no bearing on the second decision. Rather, every decision conditions the next decision. Freedom is the capacity to do something definitive. Every act of freedom makes the achievement of one's life ever more final. Freedom is the capacity to achieve one's own self. It is the capacity to establish "the eternity which we ourselves are and are becoming" (p. 96). Every act contributes to the sum of who we are.

C. Transcendental Freedom and Its Categorical Objectifications

(III.2.C, p. 96). Freedom is an element of every human being, but it cannot be fully known or objectified. We can reflect upon it, and so make it a theme for thought. But even then it never becomes wholly an object. The very reflection on freedom is an exercise of it. We cannot define it without using the term as an implicit element of the definition.

Whenever the human being acts, he or she experiences freedom. But that freedom is never absolute. Freedom is subject to necessity. Whenever we act, we experience our freedom as limited. One consequence is that we can never be sure of the moral quality of our actions. Why not? Because our actions are "a synthesis of original freedom and imposed necessity" (p. 97). Our intentions alone do not determine the moral quality of our actions, and our intention to do good may nevertheless result in evil. That is why the attitude of "obedience," of listening to and of discerning God's self-communication, is so important.

3. The Possibility of a Decision against God

(III.3, p. 97). The human being can say "yes" to God, but that yes is directed to the invitation we *suppose* God is making. We never know God's will directly (A). This lack of knowledge complicates our understanding of sin and guilt. Even the person who rejects God usually does so in the name of freedom—irresponsible freedom (B). The "no" to God is possible in freedom because it is not usually an intellectual decision (C). Rather, it is a decision made manifest in one's actions (D). It is a no to the possibilities God offers, possibilities that we can refuse. And whether we refuse or accept God's offer, the decision is usually hidden, at least from others (E). Even an explicit no to God may be an implicit yes, an acknowledgement of the fundamental reality and goodness of God (F). Jesus' condemnations of his "evil generation" should not be interpreted as a prediction of that generation's fate, but rather an indication of the seriousness of our moral decisions (G). One can never know (in an ultimate sense) whether one's actions are sinful in God's eyes, but we know for certain that we cannot escape the possibility of evil (H). God grants the freedom to make a decision for or against

God, but the freedom God gives does not limit God's sovereignty and omnipotence (I).

A. UNTHEMATIC AFFIRMATION OR DENIAL OF GOD IN EVERY FREE ACT

(III.3.A, p. 98). Even when we say yes to God, we address God indirectly. Our yes to God "is not affirmed immediately to the God of original and transcendental experience, but only to the God of thematic, categorical reflection" (p. 98). In other words, we say yes to what we believe God asks. We can never be absolutely certain that we are saying yes to the absolute will of God.

Are we then to despair of ever really knowing and affirming God's will? No. For when we say yes to what we believe God is asking, we experience transcendence. It is the experience of ourselves reaching for what is forever beyond ourselves, namely the will of God. And in our decision to affirm God's will, we are making an "unthematic" yes to God. About the will of God that we affirm, we may well be mistaken. Our knowledge of that will is mediated. It is a synthesis of what we have been taught and our interpretation of that teaching. That interpretation may well be utterly unreflected.

B. THE HORIZON OF FREEDOM AS ITS "OBJECT"

(III.3.B, p. 99). In every decision, we choose what we think will make us more free. Even when we say no to God, we aim to affirm our freedom. And in that affirmation, we implicitly affirm the divine self. For it is God who created us in freedom. It is God who invites us to exercise that freedom responsibly.

C. THE POSSIBILITY OF ABSOLUTE CONTRADICTION

(III.3.C, p. 99). Some deny the possibility of saying both yes and no to God. They argue that we can only say yes. When we say no, these people contend, we are only refusing some finite reality, some imagined God. They argue that no one can really refuse the divine self. But Rahner disagrees. If we could not refuse God, he says, there would be no real freedom.

D. THE FREEDOM TO SAY YES OR NO TO GOD

(III.3.D, p. 100). Our freedom involves not just people, things, and actions, but God as well. Our freedom is freedom for our own final and definitive validity. We can choose to live our life in uprightness and truth, or in irresponsibility and falsehood. Every choice we make moves us toward the final and definitive achievement that arrives at the moment of death.

The concreteness of our transcendence consists not only in our choices, but also in God's offer to us. We can transcend who we are by realizing the potential given to us. Our freedom to do this is also the capacity to say yes or no to God. When we say no to God, this no is not primarily an intellectual act. The real no is actualized in our existence. We cannot equate it with the moral sum of our deeds. Nor can we define it in terms of the last act in our lives. It is rather who we are.

E. THE HIDDENNESS OF DECISION

(III.3.E, p. 101). Not just a one-time act of faith but our entire lives are an answer to God's question. God's question is about the human ability to transcend ourselves. Do we accept this transcendence and its divine source? The choice to hear God's invitation to transcendence, and to become what God invites us to be, may well be a "hidden" choice. It may not manifest itself in the usual mode of an upright life. Even a heinous crime may not manifest the totality of who a person is. It may only manifest what the person was before conversion. And what may seem upright—the bourgeois life of respectability—may conceal bitterness and despair.

F. YES AND NO TO GOD ARE NOT PARALLEL

(III.3.F, p. 102). One can say no to God, true, but that no is by no means parallel or equal to a yes to God. Why? Because when one says no to God, one is at least acknowledging that there is something true. The truth one acknowledges is the existence of God. And even when one says no, it comes in the midst of the more profound yes, the profound yes to God's existence. Hence the no is never absolute in itself. Rather, it takes place within the context of an implicit yes.

By contrast, an explicit yes to God may be a falsehood. It may be only a yes to a categorical and bourgeois ideal of God. And as such, it may conceal a no to the transcendental horizon of freedom—a no to the reality of God.

G. ON THE INTERPRETATION OF ESCHATOLOGICAL STATEMENTS

(III.3.G, p. 102). What does it mean to say no to God? One can only say this no when one is evil, when one understands the evil, and when one wants it. Is this what Jesus meant when the scriptures attribute to him statements about this "evil generation"? Do the "woes" and punishments that Jesus apparently called down on evildoers present us with an eyewitness account of how the world's wickedness will turn out? Rahner says no. Jesus' statements are possibilities. They are instructions about the seriousness of our moral decision making. Far from being relevant only to the end-times, they are statements about the human being of all times. As we human beings face the alternatives of death and eternal life, Jesus' eschatological statements demand that we take God, and the possibilities that face us, with the utmost seriousness.

H. The Possibility of Sin as a Permanent Existential

(III.3.H, p. 104). Every decision made by the human being is a synthesis of "original freedom" and "the necessities of freedom" (as discussed in section C). Every decision is "co-determined" by previous decisions. To these previous decisions we may be blind, and about them we may be incapable of reflection. Our actual situation is not completely accessible to reflection (as Rahner noted in section A). Even a thorough examination of conscience may not be a statement of absolute certainty.

One never knows perfectly whether objectively guilty actions manifest a no to God. They may well represent a manipulation of us which has the character of necessity. As Rahner says, "We never know with ultimate certainty whether we really are sinners" (p. 104). But we know with certainty that we really can be sinners. And we know that this possibility cannot be overcome.

I. The Abiding Sovereignty of God

(III.3.I, p. 105). Saying yes to God is not an alternative to freedom. Making a difficult moral choice may give us greater freedom than the easier, immoral choice. Yet it is true to say that "an evil will does indeed contradict God." The evil will that "freely" chooses wrongdoing makes a choice against God, and the good will that chooses righteousness under painful moral duress makes a choice for God that feels anything but free. But when the righteous person chooses to do good, even if "constrained by God," nevertheless that person still acts in freedom. God does not take over the human will.

God creates human beings as different from God. Even human freedom is God's creation. It does not limit God's sovereignty. So although we act freely, we never know the mind of God directly. Thus we can never know ("except in obedience," says Rahner) that our free choices will reach a good decision. Still we must make that decision. It is not a hypothetical decision that may or may not arise. It arises at every moment, and it has absolute consequences.

4. Original Sin

(III.4, p. 106). In this section, Rahner proposes a re-interpretation of the doctrine of original sin. It is reinterpreted in light of the experience of freedom and transcendence. He begins by showing how the free choices of those who have gone before us in history limit our freedom (A). He then goes on to say that, although we cannot judge the objective moral nature of another person's act, it is a fair guess that the evildoing of another can lead me to do evil (B). The guilt of another person shapes me and taints all my choices, even my good choices (C). This leads to the basic definition of original sin as the universal and ineradicable guilt of human beings whose evil has shaped all human generations (D). This original sin must be distinguished from personal guilt, defined as the person's refusal to heed God's call to freedom and transcendence (E). Original sin is more than the refusal to obey this or that commandment, but the refusal to accept God's offer of the divine self (F). In relation to that offer of transcendence, the biblical story of Adam's sin is an "inference," a story that explains the more basic idea of heeding or ignoring God (G). Original sin hinders our freedom to respond to God's call, and it is in that sense that the traditional "consequences" of original sin (i.e., toil, ignorance, and sickness) should be understood (H).

A. THE WORLD OF PERSONS AS THE REALM OF FREEDOM'S ACTUALIZATION

(III.4.A, p. 106). Our freedom is limited by the freedom of others. Indeed, all our choices are shaped by the choices of those who have gone before us. To be sure, we exercise freedom. But that freedom takes place within a world and within a history shaped by the decisions of others. So the "history of freedom" puts its stamp on us. Our freedom is not absolute, but rather a participation in freedom. Our decisions are thus never a pure manifestation of good or evil, but choices within a situation given to us. We do not know if they really objectify the good itself, or only look as if they do, given the situation we find ourselves in. Indeed, the goodness or evil of a decision can change its character as it becomes a part of another's free decision.

B. THE OBJECTIFICATION OF ANOTHER'S GUILT

(III.4.B, p. 108). When we suffer wrong from another, is that an actual manifestation of an evil intention? It can be, says Rahner, but there is no certainty. One can only be certain of one's own subjective evildoing. Although the personal guilt of another remains obscure, and equally obscure my own participation in an evil situation (which, as original sin, can shape me), nevertheless it seems true that "the situation" in which I find myself can lead me to evildoing. That is Rahner's sense of original sin.

C. ORIGINAL AND PERMANENT CO-DETERMINATION BY OTHERS' GUILT

(III.4.C, p. 109). Everyone is touched by the guilt of others. And when touched by another's guilt, I am "co-determined" by that guilt. It shapes my choices. Even my good acts are tainted by the guilt of others, and so can appear to be anything else but good. Example: I benefit from the wealth of my parents, and so am able to give charitably, but my parents' wealth was ill gotten, and so taints my charity. This is a form of Christian pessimism, says Rahner, but it has a truth to it. It dispels the myth of utopia.

D. The Christian Teaching about Original Sin

(III.4.D, p. 110). Our guilt is "original" in the sense that human beings have established this guilt throughout history. There is no point in history at which human beings have not been guilty of wrongdoing. The history of wrongdoing co-determines us, as we saw in the previous section. That is the meaning of original sin. To say that some original act of Adam and Eve has been transmitted in its moral quality, or transmitted biologically, is a form of mythology. Rather, original sin is the "situation" in which we find ourselves, a situation in which we exercise our freedom co-determined by the guilt of those who precede us. Example: every time we purchase a banana, our act is co-determined by the situation of those who picked the bananas and by those who profit from them. Original sin is "original" in the sense that it is universal and ineradicable.

E. "Original Sin" and Personal Guilt

(III.4.E, p. 111). Original sin is not personal guilt. Personal guilt lies in our refusal to accept the transcendence that God offers, that is, when we refuse to do the good to which we are called and which would realize our potential. Indeed, the word *sin* is used analogically; we know "sin" by looking at acts of wrongdoing, but we are unable to judge the moral intention of the sinner. The challenge to preachers is to find a way to express this idea, the idea of original sin and of personal guilt, to those who have only a rudimentary concept of God.

F. "Original Sin" in the Light of God's Self-Communication

(III.4.F, p. 112). In summary, original sin teaches that our human situation, in which choices are shaped by history, is "determined by guilt." History and guilt impair our freedom. How much is it impaired? That depends on the sin that lies at the foundation of original sin. If that foundational sin is a rejection of God's offer of the divine self, then it is weightier than a rejection of one or another divine commandment. A rejection of God's self-communication is the rejection of the condition for true freedom. This kind of original sin is as radical an existential as God's offer to humanity of the divine self. It has shaken the very foundations of human nature.

G. On the Hermeneutics of Scriptural Statements

(III.4.G, p. 114). One can gain an insight into original sin from the Christian experience of the history of salvation. That history culminates in the God-Man, Jesus Christ, who (unlike human guilt) is not just a product of human history. The encounter with Christ teaches us that we are called to transcendence, and that sin is a rejection of God's offer of transcendence. By contrast, the story of Adam's "original" sin is an "inference." We "infer" the existence of a primeval sin from our experience of the offer of transcendence and of our acceptance or rejection of it.

H. THE "CONSEQUENCES OF ORIGINAL SIN"

(III.4.H, p. 115). The church proclaims that toil, ignorance, sickness, pain, and death are the "consequences" of original sin. Experience teaches, however, that these would exist without original sin. So how are we to interpret the church's proclamation? Rahner's approach is to say that we interpret these consequences differently in our concrete situation of guilt, the situation that co-determines and limits our freedom. We cannot imagine life as it is—life with toil, ignorance, sickness, pain and death—as if we were not touched by the guilt of those who preceded us. In that sense, the loss of these gifts is the consequence of original sin.

Original sin must be understood as a limitation upon human freedom, Rahner says, not in the mythological terms inferred from a more basic, transcendental experience. The teaching about the preternatural gifts (Edenic life without pain, ignorance, etc.) expresses our longing for existence without guilt. We trace the loss of these gifts to the myth of Adam and Eve's loss of Eden. The myth, however, symbolizes something deeper. It symbolizes the no to God that human beings have uttered from the beginning.

·IV·

Man as the Event of God's Free
and Forgiving Self-Communication

The self-communication of God is transcendent. It transcends all of the tangible means in history by which we have known God, such as holy people, places, and things. God cannot be contained by them. If not, then how do we know God? Rahner answers that we know God when God communicates, that is, gives to us the divine self. The gift takes place in the human being, the person who is the "event" of God's call. When God gives people a share in the divine self, God not only frees them to respond. God also offers forgiveness. God forgives in the ever-renewed offer of a relationship with God.

Chapter IV elaborates this argument in four parts. In the brief part 1, Rahner clears up two misconceptions. One is that God's gift to human beings is a thing, that is, a message or revelation about God. No, says Rahner, God offers human beings a share in the divine life. The second misconception is that God's gift of self is either a historical event or a transcendental experience. Rahner states that God's communication with human beings is both. The historical gospel invites us to respond, and our response enables us to transcend who we were before.

How does the transcendent God communicate the divine life to human beings? This is the topic of part 2. God communicates by becoming "immediate" to us. In our own experience—our experience of self-reflection, self-knowledge, and self-transcendence—we recognize God as the one who has called and supported us. Recognizing our incompleteness, we long for something to fill our emptiness. God's love, says Rahner (p. 124), "creates the emptiness which it wants freely to fill." God fills the emptiness by inviting and enabling human beings to make free and responsible choices. In this way, God forms a relationship with humanity.

In the part 3, Rahner states that God's gift of self takes the form of a "supernatural existential." It is an existential because it is an offer to everyone. Every person is ordained to communion with God. Yet God's self-gift is supernatural. It is supernatural because communion with God would be impossible had God not given us the capacity for it. We who open ourselves to God's gift experience it as forgiveness. The acceptance of God's constant offer of a relationship overcomes the guilt of the past. God's own life is the source of our new life.

In part 4 of the chapter, Rahner shows the relationship between the human being and the trinitarian God. The language of "one God in three persons" is difficult to grasp because it suggests three individuals with their own inner life. This "immanent Trinity" is not the completely hidden inner life of God, but is identical to the Trinity of the economy of salvation. We view God "economically," that is, as active in history. The history of God, who reveals divinity in three persons and unites it with humanity, is the history of salvation.

1. Preliminary Remarks

(IV.1, p. 116). Rahner's preliminary remarks have to do first with the nature of self-communication as the giving of God's own self. Second, they have to do with the unity between the historical and the transcendental in this communication. God communicates not only in mighty deeds, prophetical individuals, the words of scripture and the traditions of the church. God also communicates in the intimate call of the conscience and of freedom.

A. On the Notion of "Self-Communication"

(IV.1.A, p. 116). When we say that God communicates with us, we do not mean that God says something "about" the divine self. We mean rather that God gives the divine self to human beings. "God in his own most proper reality," says Rahner, "makes himself the innermost constitutive element of man" (p. 116). God gives the divine to us and makes it essential to our very identity. This does not mean, however, that God is an element or a thing. The communication is a spiritual one, known to us through, for example, the call of conscience.

B. Starting Point in the Christian Message

(IV.1.B, p. 117). When we speak of God's self-communication, are we speaking of an historical event? Do we mean, for example, God's revelation to Abraham, and prophetic oracles, and the incarnation? Or are we speaking of a "transcendental" communication, that is, the experience of God's call and our desire to respond and hence to transcend ourselves (as Rahner described in I.4 and in II.2)?

Rahner says that he means both. God's self-communication takes place historically and transcendentally. On the one hand, we have a specifically Christian interpretation of God's communication to us. It is a communication that has been given in history and handed down in Christian tradition. On the other hand, God's communication is just a starting point. Having received it in history, we respond to it. Christians are invited to accept or reject the offer of transcendence in the tradition we have received. God's self-communication always has this twofold structure—a historical medium and a transcendent invitation to respond.

2. What Does the "Self-Communication of God" Mean?

(IV.2, p. 117). In this section, Rahner explains the ways in which God communicates. In the first place, he insists that God communicates not by sending a message, but by forming a relationship (A). The relationship consists of God's invitation and our response (B). We know God as the one who created us and who invites us to transcend our present situation, thereby realizing the possibilities that existence offers (C). God not only gives us these possibilities, but enables us to receive them and so becomes a gift which we can receive (D). Like parents who give their life to their child, God gives the divine life to us (E). This life is more than the simple capacity to hear God's call; it is also a transformation and a capacity to love as God loves (F). No doubt, this capacity is part of our human nature; but it is created freely by God, not "owed" or deducible by means of a system of logic (G). The offer of the divine self is not something added to human nature, but is the satisfaction of the very hunger God has created (H). The scriptures speak of this as the ability to be a child of God and a dwelling place of the Spirit (I). Our response is to accept the offer in gratitude and to surrender to the one who makes the offer (J).

A. GRACE OF JUSTIFICATION AND THE "BEATIFIC VISION"

(IV.2.A, p. 117). The human being, says Rahner, is "the event of God's absolute and forgiving self-communication" (p. 117). For Christians, the person is not primarily an animate body, or even an eternal soul, but rather an event. The event is a relationship with God. God gives us the divine self. Why? For the sake of our ability to know God and to possess God. How does this happen? It happens in the immediacy of experience, that is, our experience of transcendence, freedom, responsibility, and love.

In this event, the person experiences what Christian tradition calls the "grace of justification" and the "beatific vision." What is the beatific vision? In Christian tradition, it is the immediate encounter with God after death. But Rahner gives it a this-worldly interpretation. He calls it the fulfillment of our divinization. Divinization is a term from Greek patrology. It traditionally refers to the fullness of the Christian experience, the fullness of being alive, not in myself, but Christ living in me. For Rahner, divinization is the experience of grace par excellence. Grace divinizes the human being for the sake of the final goal of the beatific vision. It raises the person to the possibility of transcendence.

B. THE TWOFOLD MODALITY OF GOD'S SELF-COMMUNICATION

(IV.2.B, p. 118). There are two ways or modes by which God communicates the divine self. One is the offer and call of God to human freedom. It is God's invitation to transcendence. The other is our human response. Our ability to respond is a "permanent existential," a constituent part of who we are as human creatures of God.

From this twofold self-communication, three consequences flow. *One* is our acceptance of God's offer, based on what God grants in the offer itself (namely, the ability to hear the divine call and respond to it). The *second* consequence or proviso is that we do not misinterpret the divine self-communication. We must not interpret it as something created, such as a set of conditions we must meet on our own initiative. Even our acceptance of God's offer must be enabled and borne by God. The *third* consequence is that God empowers our very freedom. Although we can speak of "our" freedom, nevertheless that freedom comes from God as a gift.

C. GOD'S SELF-COMMUNICATION AND ABIDING PRESENCE AS MYSTERY

(IV.2.C, p. 119). "Man is the event of God's absolute self-communication," says Rahner. The meaning of "event" was treated in 2.A above. But how can God give us the divine self without turning that self into an object like any other? How can God be "present" without becoming a thing? The answer is that God is present as the "term" of transcendence. This means that we know God as we know ourselves, in the intimate experience of freedom to choose and in the call to act responsibly. Hence God, present as the "term of transcendence," is both the incalculably remote creator and ground of being and the intimately close conscience and call of freedom. The "term" (our transcendence) and the "object" (the divine being) coincide. So God communicates the divine self without ceasing to be divine. The original horizon of being is also our object of worship.

D. THE GIVER HIMSELF IS THE GIFT

(IV.2.D, p. 120). This paragraph explains how God can be both the giver and the gift itself. God is the cause of all things. And when God communicates with us, we are changed. God's gift of self becomes a part of our very being. The divine cause becomes a principle of the human effect. We become what God gives.

E. THE MODEL OF FORMAL CAUSALITY

(IV.2.E, p. 120). The language of Thomistic metaphysics proves helpful here. God's relation to us is an example, Rahner says, of "formal" causality. The very principle of God's being becomes constitutive of who we are. Example: the generation of children by their parents is formal causality. In causing children, the "principle" of the parents becomes a part of the children. This must be distinguished from "efficient" causality. In efficient causality (e.g., a bat striking a baseball), the effect differs from the cause (the bat does not become a part of the ball).

God "causes" us in that God communicates the divine self to us. But when we receive the gift of God, God does not thereby lose the divine self. God does not cause or produce something different from the divine self. Rather, God becomes a constitutive element in the fulfillment of the creature. Our "justification" by God is not something God does apart from us. It is rather the orientation of human beings, an orientation accomplished by God, to the absolute and divine mystery.

F. GOD'S SELF-COMMUNICATION FOR THE SAKE OF IMMEDIATE KNOWLEDGE AND LOVE

(IV.2.F, p. 122). What do we mean when we speak of God's self-communication? We mean that God becomes "immediate" to us. We know God through our own experience, through our own knowledge of ourselves. We know ourselves as the recipients and beneficiaries of God's call and as persons who desire to respond to it. Then God becomes immediate as the spiritual unity, the fundamental unity, of knowledge and love: knowledge of God who calls to us, love of God who asks us to respond.

The fact that we are created means that God is our efficient cause. But efficient causality is a deficient mode of God's self-communication. There is more to God's self-communication than the fact of creation. God is also, in Jesus Christ, selfless love incarnate. In other words, God is our formal cause as well. God's love for us, expressed in the life and death of Jesus, spills over from us to other persons. God communicates, not just by making us able to hear and respond to God's call, but by giving the divine self to us.

G. THE ABSOLUTE GRATUITY OF GOD'S SELF-COMMUNICATION

(IV.2.G, p. 123). Because God acts in freedom, we cannot claim that we merit the gift of the divine self. Some may argue that, because God created all human beings with the capacity to hear and respond to God, this potential is part of our human nature, and is not grace. But no, says Rahner, it is freely given. And it is "supernatural," not merely natural. Why not? Because God's gift of the divine self to human beings is added to nature, and cannot be deduced by means of logic.

H. Gratuitous Does Not Mean Extrinsic

(IV.2.H, p. 123). Although God communicates freely, the self-communication is not "extrinsic" or "accidental." God does not choose to communicate to some and not to others. The divine gift of self is more than a "super-nature" added to the merely human "nature" of a select few. And God is not indifferent to us. The divine self-communication cannot be reduced to a mere capacity for decision-making casually bestowed on all. Why? Because God creates in us an emptiness, a hunger for God, in order to fill it. God is love and does not want to remain alone with the divine self. Instead, says Rahner, God creates an emptiness that God wants to fill.

I. Remarks on the Church's Teaching

(IV.2.I, p. 124). There are numerous scriptures that foreshadow the doctrine of transcendental self-communication. The New Testament speaks of human beings becoming children of God, of the Spirit of God dwelling in us as in a temple, of our participation in God's own nature, of the hope of seeing God face to face, and of the seed of justification we now possess and which will bear much fruit. All of these suggest that God has become "immediate" (see II.5.B) through the mediation of our own self. In contrast, there are other mediations that do not make God present. The New Testament refers to these when it speaks of "principalities and powers," that is, the many mediations which are not God.

J. Christianity as the Religion of Immediacy to God
in His Self-Communication

(IV.2.J, p. 125). Christianity surpasses every other religion, Rahner says, because in Christianity God is immediate. God does not give some "numinous, mysterious gift which is different from himself, but . . . gives himself." This suggests that we are to surrender to God's "holy and ineffable mystery," to "accept it in freedom," and to allow it to become for us "in faith, hope, and love."

3. The Offer of Self-Communication
as "Supernatural Existential"

(IV.3, p. 126). What is the supernatural existential? It is the very being of the human person as ordained to communion with God (A). It is supernatural because communion with God would be impossible if God did not give us the capacity for it (B). The capacity is what Rahner means when he talks about our choice to transcend ourselves by responding to the offer God makes (C). The offer of God, and the capacity God gives to respond to it, are "grace." One cannot reduce grace to an object of reflection for it is hidden from us, but God can give us the ability to reflect on it (D). We are able to reflect on it both as the experience of our own lives and as the tradition of the church, an objective tradition in which we recognize our own subjective experience.

A. THE STATEMENT ABOUT GOD'S SELF-COMMUNICATION AS AN ONTOLOGICAL STATEMENT

(IV.3.A, p. 126). To say that "Man is the event of God's absolute self-communication" is not to make a statement about neutral or impersonal things. Nor is it a categorical statement in the philosophical sense (a statement indicating a fact, known by experience, which conforms to rules like any other fact). Rather, the statement is ontological. It has to do with the very being of human persons. It is not valid just for Christians, but for all people. But that does not make it any less supernatural. To be sure, not everyone will accept God's self-communication. People can protest against their essential being and against the divine self-communication that has formed them. But the communication always takes place.

B. THE SELF-COMMUNICATION AS THE CONDITION OF POSSIBILITY FOR ITS ACCEPTANCE

(IV.3.B, p. 128). God's self-communication is not only a free gift and a grace. It is also the "necessary condition that makes possible an acceptance of the gift" (p. 128). So when we receive God's gift of self, we receive not only the gift, but also the very possibility of receiving it. We are not in the position of accepting God's gift as if we were sovereign. Without God, we could not even grasp what is being offered.

C. MAN'S SUPERNATURALLY ELEVATED TRANSCENDENTALITY

(IV.3.C, p. 129). God's offer of the divine self is not experienced merely alongside other objects of our transcendental experience. It is not, for example, identical to our capacity for free decision, our capacity to act responsibly, our capacity to reach out to another in love. Rather, it is the condition for the possibility of each. Because it is so intimate, it can be overlooked, suppressed, denied, and falsely interpreted. But it can also be recognized and made a theme for reflection. We know it in closeness and immediacy as the basis for transcendence.

D. THE EXPERIENCE OF GRACE AND ITS HIDDENNESS

(IV.3.D, p. 129). What is the difference between grace and the other basic structures of transcendence? For example, what distinguishes grace from the experience of mystery, freedom, openness and creatureliness? Grace cannot be distinguished by simple acts of reflection and psychological introspection. It remains free, and cannot be predicted or manipulated. In short, it is hidden. But it does not fall outside the infinite possibility of our transcendence.

The experience of transcendence and our reflection on it are not the same. The experience of grace cannot be reduced to a reflection, any more than, say, the experience of the human spirit. And God's communication to us cannot be reduced to a matter of reflection because it is still unfinished. It is not yet the beatific vision.

What we can say is this: in grace, the human spirit moves both *within* its goal (i.e., the God who communicates) and *toward* its goal (the beatific vision). True, we cannot be certain that our reflection on transcendental experience is in fact an experience of God. God must "vouchsafe" it, for it is not an ever-present natural feature. Grace is rather a "modality" of transcendence. It is the power given by God of our movement toward the beatific vision. Although we may not express it with unambiguous certainty, nevertheless we can recognize our transcendental experience in the history of revelation and of Christianity.

The person who is open to transcendence experiences mystery, not just as a distant horizon, but as forgiveness and intimacy. God's gift of the divine self is forgiveness. Indeed, we can say that the experience of God's self-communication is "so universal, so unthematic and so 'unreligious' that it takes place, unnamed but really, wherever we are living out our existence" (p. 132). When we confront the abyss of existence and realize that the abyss accepts us and is our true and forgiving security, then we experience the divine mystery communicating itself to us.

4. Toward an Understanding of the Doctrine of the Trinity

(IV.4, p. 134). The language of "one God in three persons" is difficult to grasp because it suggests individual persons (A). These persons, Augustine said, have their own inner life as the "immanent Trinity" (B). But Rahner insists that this immanent Trinity is the Trinity of the economy of salvation, and that we need to view God as active in history (C).

A. The Problem of Conceptualization

(IV.4.A, p. 134). In ordinary language, we understand the word *person* as an individual. The person is a "free center of conscious and free activity which disposes of itself and differentiates itself from others" (p. 134). But that is not what we mean when we speak of the Trinity of persons in God. God is single and unique, and so the "persons" of God do not dispose of themselves as separate individuals. There is in God a single consciousness and a single freedom, not three of each. So a concept of "three persons in one God" is hard to grasp.

B. The Problem with a "Psychological Theory of the Trinity"

(IV.4.B, p. 135). The psychological theory was associated with St. Augustine. Augustine's theory presupposed the idea that the Father expresses the godhead in a Word that breathes Spirit. This is "the inner life of God." But Augustine did not explain this inner life. Rahner criticizes him and his psychological theory because they do not give enough weight to history. It does not treat our historical experience of being saved by Son and by Spirit. It is rather an "almost gnostic speculation about what goes on in the inner life of God."

C. The Trinity in the History and Economy of Salvation Is the Immanent Trinity

(IV.4.C, p. 136). The Trinity is not an assembly of "numinous powers." It is rather the true God, "given in the history of God's self-revelation" (p. 136). We call God "Holy Spirit" insofar as God divinizes us. We call God "Logos" insofar as God is present in history as Jesus Christ. We call God "Father" insofar as God is the ineffable and holy mystery who has come in the Son and the Spirit. The three are "modes of presence." They are different "for us," but they remain the one God. Although the psychological theory postulates differences in the three as the inner life of God, that postulate leaves us unsatisfied. The Trinity then becomes the mysterious God of infinite distance from us, instead of the "holy mystery" of God's presence in history. The immanent Trinity, with its own inner life, is simultaneously the economic tradition of salvation history.

·V·

The History of Salvation
and Revelation

This chapter lays out the relationship between the offer of grace and the revelation of grace in history. In part 1, Rahner explains how Christianity is both a "historical" religion, made concrete in history, and the "absolute" religion. It is historical in that it was founded upon the life, death, and resurrection of Jesus of Nazareth. It is absolute because, in the history of Jesus Christ, Christianity proclaims the transcendental experience of humanity with God. Part 2 presents the relation between transcendence and history. It shows that our experience of transcendence always takes place in history, that transcendental acts of freedom and conscience make history possible, and that the supernatural existential enables human beings to "make" salvation history with God. In part 3, Rahner describes the relation between world history and salvation history. When human beings respond to God's call, world history becomes salvific. It is the history of revelation, Rahner explains, because every individual expression of the encounter with God is a kind of revelation. Part 4 explains the relationship between the transcendental revelation of God (available to all people at least as an offer) and the special revelation of God in history (for example, the history of Israel). In part 5, Rahner describes the structure of the actual history of revelation. The Adam and Eve story, says Rahner, represents the transcendental encounter of humanity with God. Part 6 summarizes the notion of revelation. It notes that categorical or historical revelation mediates transcendental revelation.

1. Preliminary Reflections on the Problem

(V.1, p. 138). The transcendental experience of human beings has a history. It does not just exist in a static manner, but takes place in a constant dynamism. Christianity proclaims this transcendental experience as the encounter with God in Jesus Christ. This encounter is not a reality that is always the same. It is an ongoing history, a history borne by the freedom of God and of us.

How can Christianity claim to be both the absolute religion and a historical religion? In other words, how can it be both unsurpassable and still in process? Further, what can it mean to say that revelation has a history? It cannot simply mean that, in history, some events have revealed God and others have not. Salvation history cannot be just another aspect of history, given the Christian claim that God has communicated the divine self as the "center of everything which can be history at all" (p. 139). Nor can it be merely the expression in words and deeds of a revelatory experience which is ultimately transcendental, interior, and ineffable. It has to be more than "the process of limiting and mythologizing and reducing to a human level something which was already present . . . from the outset" (p. 139).

2. The Historical Mediation of Transcendentality and Transcendence

(V.2, p. 140). In this brief section, Rahner wants to show (1) that our experience of transcendence always takes place in the arena of human belief and action, (2) that our transcendental acts of freedom and conscience are what makes history possible as an interpretation of reality, and (3) that the supernatural existential is a gift of God, given over time, which enables human beings to "make" salvation history with God.

A. HISTORY AS THE EVENT OF TRANSCENDENCE

(V.2.A, p. 140). The foundational principle is that the human being is "historical" as a "transcendental subject." We experience transcendence as God's call to us, a summons to freedom and responsibility, a summons that takes place in history. It takes place in our day-to-day struggle for self-knowledge and self-realization. But it remains transcendent. We cannot reduce transcendental experience to any one historical moment. It is not, for example, the moment when we first realized the call of conscience, first celebrated Holy Communion, or first fell in love. But each of those historical moments can be said to have "mediated" transcendental experience.

The problem is that we no longer understand that our transcendental experience makes history possible. Without our concrete choices, choices to act and not act, choices responsible and irresponsible, choices that express our yearnings for or refusal of transcendence—there would be no history. We human beings are the only creatures who acknowledge such a thing as history. We postulate it. And we are able to do so because we recall and interpret human events from a certain standpoint. It is the hypothetical standpoint of the completion of history (p. 140). Although history is still underway, we hazard a belief about how things will all turn out. And from this hypothetical viewpoint, we interpret past and current events that are still in process.

The supernatural existential (see IV.3 above) itself has a history. This existential, defined as that which orients the human being toward God's self-communication, is a divine gift. It was given over time. It began in the obscurity of prehistory and has developed along with the development of human self-understanding and conscience. Thanks to that supernatural existential, human beings are able to hear and respond to God's call. That listening and response is the history of revelation. When we speak of the supernatural existential as a divine gift, we mean that God is free to give or not to give the divine self. We mean also that human beings are free to receive the divine self-communication or to mourn the absence of God's holy mystery. The salvific acts of God are mediated by history, and so are also the salvific acts of humanity (p. 142).

3. The History of Salvation and Revelation as Coextensive with the Whole of World History

(V.3, p. 142). What is the difference between world history and salvation history? That is the question with which we begin. Rahner says that the two histories are "co-existent." When the human being responds to God's call, he or she "makes" salvation history (A). Indeed, we can say that the history of salvation is the history of revelation. Every individual expression in word and deed of the encounter with God is a kind of revelation (B). Although it is commonly said that revelation "ended" with the death of the last disciple and the close of the New Testament, nevertheless it is fair to say (given a slightly different meaning of revelation) that revelation continues as it comes to self-awareness (C). Revelation is not just the expression, in scripture and tradition, of the "facts" of salvation, but the appropriation of them by the person in whom God enables the "facts" to become the word of God (D). And we experience the call of God, not just in the explicitly religious realm of worship and belief, but everywhere that God calls us to respond in freedom and responsibility (E).

A. HISTORY OF SALVATION AND WORLD HISTORY

(V.3.A, p. 142). Human history is co-existent, but not identical, with salvation history. Why not identical? Because human history is not only the history of our salvation. It is also the history of our guilt and rejection of

God. But God did not intend salvation merely for the few. Everyone finds salvation, says Rahner, "who does not close himself to God in an ultimate act of his life and his freedom" (p. 143). God wills to save all.

All history is the history of salvation insofar as all history is "the concrete, historical actualization of the acceptance or rejection of God's self-communication" (p. 143). Everything else is merely the "history of nature." There are two "moments" in salvation history. First, it is the event of God's self-communication. God communicates the divine self to us transcendentally, in the summons to transcend who we are and to become what we are in potential. The second moment in salvation history is the moment of human response. When we respond to God's invitation, we "make" history. When the human being accepts or rejects God's offer, the offer can be seen in history. Thus the self-communication of God, originally transcendental, is historical as well. And it does not have to be explicitly religious. Every response of the human being to God's call belongs to the history of the divine-human communication and relationship.

B. THE UNIVERSAL HISTORY OF SALVATION IS ALSO THE HISTORY OF REVELATION

(V.3.B, p. 144). No matter how popular, it is "careless" to identify the biblical history of revelation with the history of revelation in its entirety. There is more to the history of revelation, Rahner says, than what is in the Bible. Salvation history did not just begin with Abraham. The history of revelation takes place wherever human history takes place. Every individual's history of faith is part of the history of revelation. This is not the "natural" revelation of God that St. Paul describes in the first chapter of Romans, but a transcendental encounter with God. One cannot even approach God in the church or in the Bible without being already led by God's grace—without an invitation from God which may be called a revelation. Whatever is due to grace is an aspect of revelation.

The history of religion includes the history of true and false religions. And even the false ones can be said to exist in the order of grace, to be made possible by God, and to be practiced by people who accept or reject God. Why? Because one cannot even begin to have anything to do with God without first being "borne" or led by God's grace. Revelation is doubtless "beyond" merely natural knowledge, even the knowledge of the learned. But it cannot be reduced to the scripture and tradition of Catholicism. It is accessible, Rahner says, in every human experience. To be sure, that experience must be "gratuitously elevated"; that is, it must be the inner experience of God's own call. The experience is not merely God speaking "from without."

C. THE FOUNDATION OF THE THESIS IN THE DATA OF CATHOLIC DOGMATICS

(V.3.C, p. 146). Some would say that Rahner's thesis—the thesis that revelation cannot be limited to the explicit and official revelation of the church—is not "Catholic." But that is an inadequate understanding of Christianity. Christianity really does understand itself as an ongoing process, not a once-and-for-all deposit of faith. It is "the process by which the history of revelation reaches a quite definite and successful level of historical reflection" (p. 146). Christian faith has always understood itself as a process by which the history of revelation comes to self-awareness.

Contrary to the arguments of St. Augustine and Jean Calvin, Christians believe that salvation is promised to all. No one is "kept" from being lost. To be sure, one can forfeit salvation through personal guilt. But it is wrong to understand God as "producing" salvation in a person.

The history of salvation, the church's official history, must be accepted in freedom. And it cannot be accepted unless it is known as a history of salvation. To be sure, the person's acceptance of salvation history need not be an acceptance of dogmatic propositions. Salvation may occur outside the Christian context when an encounter with God is accepted freely and as known, even if not known explicitly. But it must be an acceptance in faith, a faith in God's own Word, a word that reveals God.

D. SUPPLEMENTARY THEOLOGICAL AND SPECULATIVE FOUNDATION

(V.3.D, p. 148). How does Rahner's thesis harmonize with official revelation? How does his idea of a "universal but still supernatural revelation" harmonize with the New and Old Testaments? Rahner's answer is that our ability to hear God's invitation and respond to it is given by God. "Man's transcendence is 'elevated' by God's self-communication as an offer to man's freedom" (pp. 148-49). This is not just an "ontic" or theoretical possibility, not just a statement of facts beyond our personhood and conscience. Nor is it the thematic and worked-out expression of a philosopher of religion. It is rather an essential and living reality, an "ontological" reality. One can even say that explicitly Christian teaching, produced by God, may be reduced to a merely human word if it is not carried and led by God's own self-communication.

Thomism would say that whenever our intentional acts are elevated by supernatural grace, then their object or goal is itself supernatural. So the intentionally pious acts of the Buddhist or Hindu are themselves supernatural. To be sure, they cannot reach their explicitly religious goal by a merely natural act. But the Buddhist or Hindu, moved by God, experiences "revelation."

E. On the Categorical Mediation of Supernaturally Elevated Transcendentality

(V.3.E, p. 151). Can we only experience transcendence in an encounter with specifically religious themes? At first sight, one might say yes. People experience the supernatural horizon, one might say, only if they use the word "God," only if they speak of God's law, only if they want to do God's will.

But no, that is false. "It is not the case," says Rahner, "that we have nothing to do with God until we make God conceptual and thematic to some extent" (p. 151). On the contrary, there is an original experience of God that is not explicitly religious. It is not thematic, not even an object of reflection. We experience it whenever we become for ourselves a free subject, free to respond to the possibilities which God offers. This happens when we experience ourselves before the holy mystery that transcends us. This experience is our "supernatural transcendentality." As a consequence of it, we can be said to experience God not just in religion, but everywhere.

There is for Christians no sacred realm where alone God is found. Even when we act morally for purely natural reasons, that moral action is supernaturally elevated. The observance of the natural moral law is "supernaturally elevated and salvific in itself" (p. 152).

The possibility of encountering God everywhere, not just in the traditionally sacred spaces, is implicit in the Vatican II teaching that all can be saved. To be sure, faith is necessary for salvation. But this faith cannot be defined narrowly as the explicit content of a tradition of revelation in the Old Testament and the New Testament. The faith necessary for salvation is nothing other than "the obedient acceptance of man's supernaturally elevated self-transcendence" (p. 152). Whenever one accepts one's own basic orientation toward God, one experiences a revelation of God.

4. On the Relationship between the History of Universal Transcendental Revelation and the Special, Categorical Revelation

(V.4, p. 153). If we can experience God anywhere, even in those realms that are not explicitly religious, then what does it mean to articulate that experience in an explicitly religious way? The answer has to do with history. History is the essential and necessary expression of the human encounter with God, the expression of revelation (A). The revelation spoken of here is primarily the transcendental revelation of God, the gift of God in call and in the empowerment of our response. Rahner calls it a "universal" and "transcendental" revelation to all people. This revelation expresses itself in "special" and "categorical" ways, for example, ways that we can categorize as visions and prophecies. The highest and most successful of these is the revelation of Jesus Christ (B). That means, however, that there are other "revelations of God" apart from what Christians know as revelation. These other revelations are the expression of a transcendental experience, expressions willed by God (C). Jesus Christ is the criterion for distinguishing between true and false interpretations of transcendental experience, a criterion available only in faith (D). The "bearers of revelation," such as prophets and disciples, bring to expression the experience of God's self-communication and can be said to "constitute" us. They constitute us because, through them, we actually enter into the history of revelation and salvation (E). The universal history of revelation expresses itself in the particular; the particular enables us to know and recognize the voice of God (F).

A. THE ESSENTIAL AND NECESSARY HISTORICAL SELF-INTERPRETATION OF SUPERNATURAL, TRANSCENDENTAL EXPERIENCE

(V.4.A, p. 153). Rahner starts from the premise that transcendental experience has a history. It is not just a subjective encounter that some have and others do not. Nor is it merely a recurring phenomenon that never develops. On the contrary, transcendental experience has the objectivity of something that is universally known. Moreover, it develops, and reached an unsurpassable peak in Jesus Christ. Christian history is the history of the shared transcendental experience of Christians. It is their interpretation of their own transcendental experience. In comparison to the history of transcendental experience, historical revelation (e.g., the historical "events" of the patriarchy, exodus, and even of Jesus of Nazareth) is a "secondary moment" in the total history of humanity. For historical revelation to be revelation, faith-filled people must recognize in it the expression of their transcendental encounter with God.

Does that mean that Christianity, the "absolute religion," is also a secondary moment? In Rahner's view, the early church experienced Jesus Christ as Lord. Theirs was a historical interpretation, an interpretation that took place in freedom and hope. There was a risk that the interpretation was wrong. But early Christians took the risk. They were confident that they, in Jesus, had met God's own Word. Historical interpretations of people and events may be mistaken interpretations. This one was not. But it was an interpretation, a "secondary moment." The early Christians recognized Jesus as the Word because of the transcendental encounter with God that they had already had.

It seems as if Rahner relativizes the history of revelation. Objective history is subordinate to the primary encounter in transcendental experience. But Rahner is saying something more profound. He is saying that the history of the church (the entire history, and not just the history of Jesus or of the saints) is the history of revelation. The history of the church does not stand outside history. It is revelation precisely because it stands within history.

B. On the Notion of a Categorical and Special History
    of Revelation

(V.4.B, p. 154). The history of Christianity is not merely one way among others of expressing the possibility of human self-transcendence. Christian history moves "in an irreversible direction towards a highest and comprehensive self-interpretation" (p. 154). Christians know revelation as culminating in the incarnation. That is the special sense in which the word *revelation* is normally used.

At the same time, however, there is a broader sense of revelation than the explicitly Christian. Rahner calls it the "universal, categorical history of revelation." It is not just "universal," that is, available (at least as an offer) to all people at all times. It is also "categorical," that is, a statement indicating a fact, known by experience, which conforms to rules like any other fact (see II.3.A; II.5.A; III.3.A; IV.3.A). In other words, the universal revelation of God as a supernatural existential expresses itself throughout human history. Compared to it, revelation in the usual Christian sense is only a species of a wider genus.

Hence there is a history of revelation that does not coincide with the Old Testament and the New Testament. This history of revelation is altogether real. It has taken place wherever God has addressed humanity through its conscience. But this revelation is "provisional and not yet completely successful," Rahner says. Moreover, it is "permeated and made obscure . . . by man's guilt" (p. 155). By contrast, the usual and full sense of Christian revelation is found where faithful people know it as guided and directed by God. There revelation "discovers its true self" (p. 155).

C. The Possibility of a Genuine History of Revelation
    outside the Old and New Testaments

(V.4.C, p. 156). Revelation in its purity is found in the New and Old Testaments. But it is not found only there. How is this possible? Rahner says no more than he said in the previous section, but he speculates that it is possible. It is possible, even if these other "histories of revelation" are brief and partial. He asserts that they are truly self-interpretations of a revelatory and transcendental experience of God. Such revelations are "positively willed and directed by God" because God wills to save all. They are "directed" by God in the sense that they stem from "the immanent powers of this [i.e., God's own] divine self-communication" (p. 156). Like the Christian history of revelation, other histories may not be deduced from an abstract principle or reduced to the consequences of a merely human logic. Like the Christian history, they are "experienced, suffered, and accepted in history."

The Christian historian of religion can acknowledge these other histories of revelation. Inevitably the Christian will interpret them with regard to their ultimate intentions. He or she may well see in these other histories the presence of the God of the Old Testament and the New Testament. The history of revelation can only be complete in Jesus Christ, says Rahner. But what, he asks, are the criteria by which one distinguishes between true and false revelations?

D. Jesus Christ as the Criterion

(V.4.D, p. 157). Jesus Christ alone is the "criterion" for distinguishing between true and false revelations. In Jesus Christ we distinguish between merely human and mistaken interpretations of the transcendental experience of God and legitimate interpretations. In Jesus we also distinguish true interpretations of Christianity's revelation from false interpretations of Christianity. To be sure, the criterion of Jesus Christ is not a merely neutral and impersonally scientific rule. It is not available, for example, to unbelieving historians of religion. It is available only in faith, and it is preeminent.

E. The Function of the Bearers of Revelation

(V.4.E, p. 158). What is the function of "bearers of revelation," such as the prophets? They bring to expression something that is present at a fundamental level everywhere and in everyone, namely, the ability to hear the call of God and respond to it. They express in an undoubtedly valid way the transcendental self-communication of God. When they do so, however, their expression is not merely human and natural. Truly prophetic speech differs from our own efforts to express the self-communication of God. How does it differ?

- It expresses a reality constituted by God.
- The expression can be said to be God's own.
- It is not an afterthought, but a part of God's self-communication, governed by God's will.
- The expression can be said to "constitute" us, for in hearing truly prophetic speech, we enter into the very history of salvation and revelation.

The light of faith and the light by which the prophets grasp God's message are the same. That "light" is the "divinized subjectivity" of the person (p. 159). The prophet is the believer who expresses correctly the experience of God. In the prophet's word, we recognize our own experience. This does not relativize the prophet. It is rather a corollary of our human experience. In that experience, others—namely, the "bearers of revelation"—become models for us. They are the norm by which we are empowered.

F. THE ORIENTATION TOWARD UNIVERSALITY IN THE PARTICULAR
AND SUCCESSFUL HISTORY OF REVELATION

(V.4.F, p. 161). The universal history of revelation and the particular history of revelation "condition" each other. The universal reaches its "essence" and "its full historical objectification" in the particular. Without the particular revelation of prophet and evangelist, we would not know or recognize the voice of God. The revelation we meet in the prophets and in the evangelists is not only official but also authoritative. Although they are "particular" expressions of revelation, they have a fundamental meaning for all. And in that sense, they can be said to be "universal." By them we recognize the experience of God's call to transcendence and can respond to it.

5. On the Structure of the Actual History of Revelation

(V.5, p. 162). How are we to interpret the history of revelation as presented in the Old Testament? Rahner offers two answers. First, he says that the Old Testament stories about Adam and Eve are inferences. The authors of Genesis inferred the existence of a transcendental encounter with God that must have happened to the very first human beings, and expressed it in the form of a story.

Second, Rahner offers an interpretation of the Old Testament history of revelation. Israelite history is but a brief moment in the millennia of transcendental encounters between God and humanity. But it is a more complete expression of the history of revelation than that contained in other religions. This history looks toward Christ as its fulfillment. In Christ, humanity and divinity reach a point of perfect union.

A. "PRIMEVAL REVELATION"

(V.5.A, p. 162). Did Adam and Eve exist? One cannot use the Bible, of course, to answer questions about natural science. But one can say that the first human beings, whenever and wherever they were, experienced God's

transcendental and categorical revelation. Humanity has always been oriented toward God through God's self-communication. And in that sense,
the biblical story of the first sin is a true one: it describes humanity's first
refusal of God's self-communication. But even at that moment, God's
absolute will to communicate with us encompassed Adam's guilt.

The revelation of God to Adam and Eve was kept alive, even in a situation conditioned by guilt. And we can say that God's universal revelation in
transcendental experience (however depraved and expressed in polytheistic
forms) is present in pre-Christian societies. The Genesis accounts of Adam
and Eve make an inference. They infer from our present transcendental
experience what must have been its historical ground. We know our origins
by means of aetiological myths, such as that of Adam and Eve, stories that
explain our origins. These are recognized as valid expressions of transcendental experience, hence as revelation.

Why do we resort to stories? Rahner explains this by means of the
Thomistic doctrine of the "conversion to the phantasm," which was the
subject of his first doctoral dissertation, published as *Spirit in the World*.
Not only the Bible but even the most abstract metaphysical language works
with "phantasms." This is St. Thomas's term for images, analogies, and
representations—the expression of transcendental realities.

B. IS IT POSSIBLE TO STRUCTURE THE WHOLE HISTORY OF REVELATION?

(V.5.B, p. 164). The history of religion shows a variety of supernatural
revelations. But this diversity has its own unity. All religions have a common
direction, seen from God's vantage point. From our vantage point, however,
the common direction is "hardly discernible" (p. 164). Scripture, for example, sheds little light on the structure of the universal history of revelation.
Old Testament stories of the Canaanites, Amalekites, and Jebusites tell us
little about the transcendental history of freedom.

Rahner's thesis is that, if we could see the broad picture, we would see
that the "biblical age" from Abraham to Christ is all part of the Christ
event. Religious struggles are attempts to clarify our experience of God's
communication with us. Only in recent millennia has the human race
"taken hold of its existence in the clarity and freedom of history" (p. 166).
Before this, there was no language to express the encounter with God. And
since there was no way of expressing the transcendental encounter, says
Rahner, humanity (in a philosophical or theological sense) did not exist
(p. 166). There was no precise or theological "history of revelation." Our
Christian history of revelation preserves, however, its connection with the
immense universal history of salvation.

The entire Christian history of revelation, from Abraham to the last of the writing prophets, is but a brief preparation for Christ. Apart from Christ, there is no unified interpretation of the Old Testament. Israelite history is the event of a dialogue with God. It offers a "prospective tendency towards an open future" (p. 167). True, in comparison to the transcendental encounters with God in the millennia of prehistory, the Old Testament history is but a brief moment. But that brief moment more completely expresses the transcendental relation we have with God than what we find in the history of other religions.

The history of Israel is also a history of guilt and alienation. It indicates that, even among those people who did not hear and respond to God correctly (e.g., the Canaanites, Amalekites, Jebusites, etc.), there was an experience of the transcendent. This experience pointed to Christ, the end-point of the fullness of salvation. So Old Testament history is a "decisive caesura" or turning point. It is the period in which human beings fundamentally changed. From being threatened by nature they were transformed, and began to create their own environment. They began to look toward the fulfillment of history. Unknown to them, they were looking toward Christ. The life of Christ is but one moment in history, but it is the decisive one. In that moment, God and the human being who accepts God's call became one.

6. A Summary of the Notion of Revelation

(V.6, p. 170). Transcendental revelation differs, first of all, from natural revelation. Natural revelation does not tell us about the human relation to God (A). Transcendental revelation, by contrast, transforms the recipient. It divinizes him or her, giving the person a participation in God's own reality (B). Categorical and historical revelation exists as a secondary moment in transcendental revelation. It "mediates" transcendental revelation (C). In the incarnation, revelation reaches its highest point. In it, God's own self is communicated (D).

A. "NATURAL" REVELATION AND GOD'S REAL SELF-REVELATION

(V.6.A, p. 170). "Natural" revelation "leaves God still unknown." Why? Because natural revelation suggests that we know God as an analogue to the mystery of nature. It asks the question of God, but leaves unanswered whether God wants us to be near or far. Real revelation is an event of dialogue. God speaks and we answer. Natural revelation does not tell us about the human relation to God. Only a transcendental encounter with God's real self-revelation can tell us that.

B. THE TRANSCENDENTAL ASPECT OF REVELATION

(V.6.B, p. 171). What do we mean when we say that God encounters the human being in revelation? We mean that God is "disclosed" to the person who "hears" God's voice. God "causes" that person to hear, and so transforms him or her. We call it "divinization." It means that the person is made capable of hearing God's summons and accepting the possibilities which God offers as the person's own possibilities.

This divinization is what tradition calls "sanctifying" or "justifying" grace. It is offered to all people at all times. It gives to humanity the very being of God as an object. In a word, it gives transcendence. That transcendence is a view to, and participation in, God's own reality.

The question of the human spirit is "answered" by God. God's answer is destined for all people in transcendental experience. It is not offered as something "alongside" everything else in a person's life. No, it is within and a part of the entirety of that life. It is the history of human transcendence.

C. THE CATEGORICAL, HISTORICAL ASPECT OF REVELATION

(V.6.C, p. 172). God's self-revelation is always mediated "categorically." That means that it is mediated absolutely or unqualifiedly in a particular and concrete sense (see II.3.A; II.5.A; III.3.A; IV.3.A; V.4.B). When something is "categorically true," we say that it corresponds to a form or idea that underlies all human experience. God's self-revelation conforms to what humans can experience, namely, historical existence. Thus we can say that God's self-revelation is always mediated in objective knowledge.

We humans try to interpret our experience of God's self-revelation by means of propositions. God thereby creates for us the possibility of salvation in and by means of those objects—for example, institutions and artifacts—which express the experience of grace. These objects exist within a human context. That means that they are intermixed with error and even sin. But given those limitations, categorical and historical revelation can be said to be true revelation. Indeed, the church's public, official, and ecclesially constituted revelation is the high point in the history of categorical revelation. Such revelation is accomplished:

- not for an individual but for a community;
- by those whom we call prophets; and
- by God in a way that is pure (however partial).

This pure revelation does not occur everywhere. It is but a moment in the universal history of salvation and revelation, where revelation can be misinterpreted and depraved. In the revelation of God in Jesus Christ, categorical revelation becomes absolute.

D. The Unsurpassable Climax of All Revelation

(V.6.D, p. 174). Why is the incarnation of the Logos unsurpassable? Rahner offers three answers. In the incarnation:

- what is communicated is God's own self;
- the mode of communication (namely, human reality) is made divine; and
- the recipient of the self-communication (i.e., Jesus' own self) has become one with God's self-communication.

The event of Christ is "the only really tangible caesura" or turning point in the history of salvation. In the light of Jesus Christ, the Old Testament is seen as an official history of revelation.

·VI·

Jesus Christ

This chapter (VI, p. 176), the longest in the book, shows the unity of Jesus of Nazareth with the eternal *Logos* or Word. In this Word, God intended from all eternity to reconcile us to the divine self. The chapter has ten parts. Part 1 presents Christology within an evolutionary view of the world. In this view, human beings evolve and transcend themselves in response to God's Word. Part 2 shows how transcendental Christology is based on an "absolute" relationship with God's offer of salvation. God does not save human beings from a distance. No, God saves humanity by offering a participation in the divine self.

Part 3 presents a transcendental Christology. It understands Jesus Christ as the one who enables human beings to transcend themselves. Jesus enjoyed a union with his heavenly Father, a union so complete that God finally and irrevocably affirmed Jesus' transcendence—and now offers transcendence to us as well. In part 4, Rahner explains the incarnation. He says that, by becoming incarnate, the Logos made the human reality God's own reality. When God took a human nature, human nature reached the goal toward which it had always tended. The thirty-five-page-long part 5 focuses on the theological understanding of the history of the life and death of Jesus of Nazareth. Rahner's main point is to show that Jesus knew himself to be the actual incarnation of God's offer of salvation. Part 6 focuses in twenty pages on the death and resurrection of Jesus. Rahner argues that the death of Jesus should not be understood as propitiation of divine anger, but rather as a sacrament of God's saving will for us. It is a sacrament that accomplished what it showed forth.

In part 7, Rahner reconciles his transcendental Christology with classical Christology. He wants to show that the death and resurrection of Jesus—in which God permanently validated the earthly life of Jesus—constitute an event in which all humanity may hope to participate. Part 8 aims to show the unity of Rahner's transcendental Christology with orthodox faith. God intended to reconcile all people through Jesus Christ by extending through him the offer to share God's very life. When people accept God's invitation to respond to life's possibilities, they express the hope that God will affirm them as God affirmed Jesus. Part 9 describes the personal relation of a Christian to Jesus Christ. Rahner says that the Christian's relation to Jesus Christ is identical with his or her life-work and destiny, that is, to the way one accepts God's offer of life and lives it freely and responsibly. Part 10 explores the topic of Jesus Christ in non-Christian religions. Christ is present in those religions, Rahner says, through the Holy Spirit. That Spirit can be said to have "caused" the incarnation, death, and resurrection of Christ. By analogy, Christ himself can be said to be the "final cause" of God's self-communication to humanity. Just as the two causes are united, so the explicit Christology of Christians is united with the implicit Christology of the non-Christian. It is implicit because the non-Christian (who may not know Jesus Christ) still may respond to God's transcendent Word.

Introduction

In the introduction to this chapter (p. 176), Rahner presents his doctrine of the "anonymous Christian." The Hindu, Buddhist, or Muslim may well accept what Christianity wants to convey, Rahner suggests, without that Hindu, Buddhist, or Muslim professing a Christian faith. Whenever a person accepts God's call to transcendence and responds to it, one becomes a Christian, even without knowing the name of Christ.

Still, one is only a Christian in the full sense of the word by means of Baptism and explicitly Christian faith. Rahner calls this "the historical and reflexive dimension of God's transcendental self-communication" (p. 176). It is "historical" because Christianity is not just an idea but has manifested itself in history. It is "reflexive" because that transcendental self-communication of God, offered to everyone in an interior way, is reflected in the life of Jesus. Without the history of Jesus, says Rahner, transcendental theology would not be recognized for what it is.

This chapter on Jesus Christ brings two elements together: transcendental and historical theology. The point of departure is the encounter with Jesus in history. The chapter then explicates what Rahner means by an "ascending Christology" or "Christology from below." This theology begins with the man Jesus of Nazareth, who showed himself to be the one whose life and words were affirmed and validated by God. The ascending Christology then connects this man with the eternal Word by whom God intended from all eternity to reconcile us to God's own self.

We recognize in the man Jesus the fullest expression of a transcendental encounter with God, an encounter in comparison to which our own experiences seem incomplete. The experience of the man Jesus enables us to ascend to a recognition in him of the divine Logos. To be sure, the classical "descending Christology," which begins with the idea of God entering human history, is also important. But the human, rather than the divine, is Rahner's starting point.

1. Christology within an Evolutionary View of the World

(VI.1, p. 178). The "evolutionary view" about which Rahner speaks does not refer mainly to an evolution on the part of Jesus Christ. Rather, it has to do with our own evolution and with the self-transcendence to which we are called (A). Transcending ourselves by responding to God's call is a kind of evolution. We evolve by opening ourselves to the God who unites all creation (B). Rahner calls this "active self-transcendence." He means that we transcend the merely material by knowing it for what it is, namely, the vehicle of spirit (C). Our proper end, the end of both matter and spirit, is to lead the material world into a consciousness of its spiritual vocation (D). Humanity is thus the shepherd of the cosmos, drawing it to God as its own innermost life and destiny (E). In this "evolutionary view," Christ is God's offer of self-communication. When we accept the offer, we enjoy membership in the very life of God (F). Christ is the "absolute savior," embodying God's offer and manifesting in himself the definitive acceptance of that offer by human beings (G). As divine Word, Christ established the world as the reality wherein the divine would show itself. As human being, he achieved a "hypostatic" union with God (H). This hypostatic union, accomplished definitively in Jesus alone, is part of a transcendence taking place in all human creatures (I).

A. EXPLANATION AND CLARIFICATION OF THE TOPIC

(VI.1.A, p. 178). Our question about Jesus proceeds from an evolutionary view of the world. Rahner intends to avoid the theories of Teilhard de Chardin, thereby presupposing (rather than presenting) the nature of evolution. An evolutionary starting point does not mean that we are trying to view the incarnation as a consequence of evolution (as in the heretical "consciousness Christology" of the early twentieth century). Nor are we trying to say that the incarnation is incompatible with evolution (and thus embracing a intellect-denying fideism). Rather, we seek a correlation of the two, namely, evolution and faith.

Evolution is the view of the contemporary person, the person in a pluralistic world. Such a person sees the diversity of religions and asks what is specific to the Christian religion. His or her question is not, "What is the message of Christ?" but rather, "How is it possible to take the question of a God-Man seriously?"

Rahner's method of procedure is straightforward. He poses questions about the unity of spirit and matter. He asks what is the nature of this unity from the standpoint of an evolutionary view. Further, he asks about the relation between the history of nature and that of the human being. His goal is to show that, in human beings, matter "discovers itself" in spirit. The human being is the one who transcends matter. The ultimate transcendence has already begun in the "hypostatic union" of two natures in Christ. In this incarnation is the beginning, Rahner says, of the divinization of the world.

B. THE UNITY OF ALL CREATED THINGS

(VI.1.B, p. 181). Matter and spirit do not exist "alongside" each other, unmixed and separate. Christianity presumes that they have much in common. It teaches the union of spirit and matter in the person. The Christian believes that the fulfillment of the human spirit is not an individual achievement. It must be understood as part of the fulfillment of the cosmos.

Natural science knows "about" matter, but "it cannot know *matter itself*" (p. 182). Why not? Because natural science abstracts from the person and seeks impersonal knowledge. Impersonal knowledge enables the scientist to calculate. But it does not enable the person to see the interrelationships between matter and the person. Rahner believes that we can only know matter in relation to the human being. Even the scientist cannot know the human being, not even in a "medical" and "physiological" way, as matter alone. To be sure, the person is not a "Platonic spirit" either. But knowledge of the person must be spiritual as well as material.

Rahner offers the following thesis: "*Spirit* is the single person insofar as he becomes conscious of himself in an absolute presence to himself" (p. 183). The human being is open to all of reality. He or she is oriented to the ground of reality, that is, God. This openness is not a possession but has the character of "being taken possession of." God draws us into mystery. We are "taken possession of" when we accept the mystery of God. So when we become conscious of ourselves as the presence of God's absolute call and mystery, we "become" spirit.

No doubt we experience ourselves and others as "matter." But we are deceived if we believe that matter is all that there is. Were we to view people as purely matter, then we might regard them as mere instruments at our disposal. But they are not, and matter is only a starting point. From matter we realize that there is a reality, an otherness, in which we live. We can communicate with others. In that communication, we realize that the "other" is more than matter. He or she is rather a finite spirit, like ourselves, reaching out in mutual knowledge and love. And in mutual knowledge and love all things are united, linked in freedom by the bonds of spirit.

C. The Notion of "Active Self-Transcendence"

(VI.1.C, p. 183). The fact that we are both matter and spirit can be mis-understood. We can misunderstand ourselves statically, as if the relation of matter and spirit in us never changes. And we can misunderstand ourselves as the mere containers of the two, matter and spirit, as if they were irrec-oncilable opposites.

A truer understanding of the relation between matter and spirit must realize, as Rahner says, "that it is of the intrinsic nature of matter to develop toward spirit" (p. 184). In time, the person changes. He or she develops. In this development, the person transcends his or her former self. Indeed, one surpasses oneself, and actually "increases" one's own being. This is "active self-transcendence." One transcends oneself, not just by passively accepting what God causes, but also by means of "the power of the absolute fullness of being" (p. 185).

For example, parents create their child, a new person, in an act that is (in the first instance) "merely" biological. Ultimately, however, that merely bio-logical act is of great spiritual consequence. And in the theory of natural selection, matter appears to develop, once again, toward more successful life, and even toward the evolution of the human being. All of these are examples of active self-transcendence, examples of matter developing toward spirit.

The highest dimensions of life and of spirit are variations of what existed previously. To be sure, new species evolve, and these are a development and a progression. But from Rahner's viewpoint, they are expressions of an underlying form or idea. The form or idea seeks to manifest itself. It has a *telos* or goal. And human beings not only possess themselves in that way, but also can be conscious of the form or idea that underlies them.

D. The Finality of the History of Nature and Spirit

(VI.1.D, p. 187). Human beings and nature have a single, common goal. The history of nature reaches its goal in the history of the human spirit. The goal of humanity is to continue the history of nature. It continues it by transforming the material world. Another way of expressing this idea is to say that nature culminates in spirit. Spirit, for its part, aims at the transfor-mation of nature.

The goal of humanity, says Rahner, "consists in the infinite fullness of God" (p. 188). The person, Rahner suggests, must simply accept God's hid-den and seemingly distant dynamism as providence. This seems to be an argument for fatalism or resignation. But it is not. Rahner states that there is reason for hope: that reason is the history of freedom, a history "encom-passed" by God's grace and will.

E. MAN'S PLACE IN THE COSMOS

(VI.1.E, p. 188). Under the influence of science, we commonly think of humanity as the product of chance whose destiny is extinction. That is the despair of our age. The Christian thinker, however, insists upon the dignity and abiding value of the person.

Is there any support for human dignity in a scientific worldview? Yes, says Rahner, it is the idea of the human person as the one who can now "direct" the very progression of culture and even of nature. This human person can hardly be a mere caprice or product of chance. He or she has the dignity of being a caretaker or shepherd of human destiny, and not just a mere product of chance. We must see, Rahner says, that a supposedly "brute nature" actually discovers its own goal in the human being. With that insight, we can avoid falling into the "Platonic dualism" which regards spirit as the enemy of matter.

If nature's goal is spirit, then the cosmos is related to its ground or source. The ground of being then becomes not a logical presupposition (e.g., an original "creative impulse") but rather a goal. The ground of being becomes the one toward whom the person strives. It is a magnet that draws us, enabling us to transcend what we were and to become what we are called to be. It is, in short, God's spirit. Persons are not just a product of the cosmos, but their union with God is the very goal of the cosmos. In the human being, the cosmos presses forward, reaching toward its own "self-presence in spirit" (p. 190).

Hence we human beings are able to anticipate our goal. It is nothing less than the goal of the cosmos. Our goal is the unity of a spirit that knows itself. Christianity calls it salvation, immortality of the soul, resurrection of the flesh. These terms "mean" the fulfillment of the cosmos. The cosmos "desires" to receive God, the God described by Rahner as "the immediate self-communication of its own ground" (p. 190). God desires this goal in and through the highest creatures, human beings.

What will it mean for the cosmos to achieve its goal? It will mean that the world will receive God in such a way that God becomes the world's innermost life. And this goal is already present, at least in anticipation. We see the world's goal in our own life-long struggle for existence and dignity, whereby we "act out of a formal anticipation of the whole" (p. 191). A person may claim to be uninterested in God. He or she may claim to rely, not on God, but on "science." But Rahner says that we are, by our nature, spiritual beings. We live in the midst of a mystery, a question about our goal and purpose. And this mystery or question remains, whether we choose to acknowledge it or not.

F. The Place of Christ in an Evolutionary View of the World

(VI.1.F, p. 192). The goal of the world, then, is to find itself in an encounter with God. We creatures of the world find ourselves in the manner or way that God has given to us. This is the way of self-transcendence. And since this is the way that God has given, then it is a fundamental clue to the nature of Christology.

God has created human beings in such a way that we can freely respond to God. We are spiritual beings, and when we respond to God, we are in communion with God. When God offered to humanity the divine self in Jesus Christ, we were invited to accept that offer. The acceptance of the offer "justified" us in St. Paul's sense of the word. It united us with Christ, made us members of his body, and so his justice before God became our own justice. To reject that offer is disbelief and sin.

G. On the Notion of Absolute Savior

(VI.1.G, p. 193). What do we mean by the term *savior*? In Rahner's view, savior is the historical person, Jesus Christ, whose life, death, and resurrection are a sacramental sign to us. They signify that God has communicated the divine self and has moved the cosmos towards its goal. To be sure, God has moved the cosmos closer to its goal in other ways than through Jesus Christ. God's self-communication began before the incarnation of the savior. But in Jesus Christ the self-communication becomes "irrevocable," "recognized," and "concrete" in a moment of history (p. 194).

Although God's self-communication is irrevocable and concrete, nevertheless it has not reached its conclusion. Christ, the "absolute savior," is only the beginning of the fullness of time. But in him the fullness has begun. It began in Old Testament times, for God's eternal Word was "at work" before the incarnation. And Jesus Christ, the future goal, is also the *causa finalis*, for he "caused" the cosmos to move toward its goal. Thus we say that the absolute savior is both God's "promise" (i.e., God's self-communication) and also the acceptance of God's self-communication (i.e., the acceptance which took place in the man Jesus himself).

H. Remarks on the Meaning of the Assertion
of a Hypostatic Union

(VI.1.H, p. 195). Christ, the absolute savior, must first of all be considered a human being. At the outset, we must consider him *not* as God acting in the world, but as a human person, that is, a part of the cosmos and of history. Jesus accepted God's grace through obedience, prayer, and willingness to accept death. Jesus had an immediacy to God, an immediacy to God in his very humanity.

Throughout Christian history, there has been a temptation of Gnosticism. It is the temptation to regard God as above and beyond the world. To be sure, this God draws close to the human spirit and offers a kind of knowledge. Such knowledge is akin to the human sciences such as psychotherapy in that the knowledge can free the human being from ignorance. But such knowledge is different from Gnosticism. Unlike the Gnostics, Christians believe that "God lays hold of matter when the Logos becomes flesh" (p. 196). We believe that, in the human being, matter is so ennobled that "matter becomes conscious of itself" (p. 196).

When the Logos became flesh, the corporeal or material part of the world was established as the Logos' own reality. Matter is different from the Logos, doubtless, yet it expresses the Logos. Matter allows the Logos to be present.

Matter and incarnation are thus two phases of God's self-communication. The divine Word established the world as the Word's very own material reality. The absolute savior and human matter have become one. Hence we can say that "God becomes world" (p. 197). The "self-transcendence" which we see in Jesus of Nazareth is the decisive moment toward which the cosmos is striving.

Does that mean that the self-transcendence of matter is "natural"? We witnessed this self-transcendence in a human being, Jesus of Nazareth. Was his self-transcendence purely a case of evolution? No, says Rahner, it is the goal of creation. It is related to earlier stages of human history, related not as a purely natural progression, but as a pure gift, a grace that built upon the earlier stages.

I. ON THE RELATIONSHIP BETWEEN HUMAN TRANSCENDENCE
AND HYPOSTATIC UNION

(VI.1.I, p. 198). In this section, Rahner speaks of the absolute transcendence of the human spirit of Jesus into God. It is a remarkable formulation: the human being, Jesus of Nazareth, has transcended his own human nature and achieved oneness with God. But then Rahner says something even more remarkable, namely, that this transcendence is not just a one-time event. Instead it is part of a transcendence taking place in all human creatures. All people potentially are in mutual intercommunication and have a common goal. To be sure, says Rahner, the transcendence was seen definitively only in the one person, Jesus of Nazareth. But all are invited to such transcendence. The only ones closed off to it are those who refuse it.

Was the hypostatic union of Jesus and the Logos a unique instance? No, says Rahner. The God-Man did not simply enter human existence once and for all, bring it to fulfillment, and leave it behind. There is a relation between the incarnation and our own self-transcendence. The entry of the Logos into human history is not just a once-and-for-all event, but also the means by which grace is bestowed on human beings. Thanks to Jesus Christ, all human beings know about the self-transcendence to which they are called. Undoubtedly the incarnation is a point of climax to which the whole world is directed. But it is a beginning, not an end. Through the incarnation, we receive God's very self, and are summoned into a new life with God.

Hence we can say that the hypostatic union of Jesus and Logos, man and God, is a union toward which all humanity strives. The incarnation is a concrete moment within the process by which the divinization of all creatures is realized. And the hypostatic union, fulfilled in one man, is also a promise to all people. It is the promise that God will bring about human transcendence by communicating the divine self (p. 201). Grace in us, and the hypostatic union in Jesus Christ, must be understood as aspects of the one decision and initiative of God.

"The hypostatic union takes place," says Rahner, "insofar as God wishes to communicate himself to all men in grace and glory" (p. 202). The difference between grace and hypostatic union is that Jesus is God's offer to us. We are not the offer but the recipients. What is offered in the two is the same, namely, self-transcendence and union with God.

2. On the Phenomenology of Our Relationship to Jesus Christ

(VI.2, p. 203). In this second part, Rahner wants to show that his transcendental Christology is based on a historical encounter with Jesus Christ. It begins in an actual relationship of faith (A). That relationship is not confined to the experience of professing Christians only, but is an "absolute" relationship. In other words, God offers a relationship through the divine Word to all people, including non-Christians (B). The relationship is self-validating. One knows it for oneself in one's own life. It expresses itself in conscience and intellectual honesty (C).

A. THE STARTING POINT IN AN ACTUAL FAITH RELATIONSHIP

(VI.2.A, p. 203). One does not produce a relationship with Jesus, Rahner admits, as the result of transcendental reflection. No, faith must precede theology. A relationship to Jesus Christ exists prior to theology. Once the relationship exists, then a person can ask what that relationship means and what it demands. But the relationship itself is common to Christians. It is lived out in churches throughout the world.

B. The Relationship to Jesus Christ as Absolute Savior

(VI.2.B, p. 204). A relationship—that is what we have in the experience of faith in Jesus Christ. A relationship with Jesus Christ means God's presence to us. It is the offer of salvation, forgiveness, and divine life.

This relationship is "absolute." It is not just a relationship with an individual, but between the human race and God's salvation. The relationship may be interpreted inadequately. It may be intermixed with an inadequate understanding of God and with false worship. Despite this, Christianity is present wherever the relationship exists. And when people interpret that relationship adequately in a profession of faith, that profession unites people, and there we find "ecclesial" Christianity.

C. The Relationship to Jesus Christ Is Self-Validating

(VI.2.C, p. 206). When a person grasps Jesus Christ as the mediator of God, then this relationship "validates itself." The relationship proves itself to be real, trustworthy, and salvific. And it does so "before the tribunal of man's existence, his conscience, and his intellectual honesty" (p. 206). No doubt a skeptic could cast doubt upon it from the outside. But the person who enjoys the relationship can be confident that he or she is not being deceived.

This relationship has to be understood from within. It cannot be imposed from without. When Christians preach about the relationship with Christ, they must show that this relationship is universal and freely embraced. All human beings "exist within the circle" of a relationship with Christ. Either they experience it concretely, hope for it, or reject it.

3. Transcendental Christology

(VI.3, p. 206). Transcendental Christology is the central concept of chapter VI. It refers to Jesus as the human being who first entered into a union with God so completely that God finally and irrevocably affirmed Jesus' transcendence. And it refers to Jesus as the one to whom we look for a sign that God's offer of transcendence is real. Rahner begins by overcoming the objection that his Christology substitutes a reflection on Jesus for a relationship with him (A). He then argues that such a transcendental Christology is important to our age because it enables us to distinguish the truth existing within the mythological expressions of Jesus' encounter with God (B). The presupposition is that all human beings are oriented toward this encounter and able to experience it in their concrete lives (C). Finally, Rahner traces the origin of transcendental Christology. It springs from our unsatisfied longing for an ever-deeper encounter with God (D).

A. SOME OBJECTIONS TO TRANSCENDENTAL CHRISTOLOGY

(VI.3.A, p. 206). Some will object that a transcendental Christology cannot supply the lack of a relationship with Jesus Christ. That is as true as to say that a theology cannot supply the lack of faith. One cannot deduce a relationship from a reflection. But there is more to the objection than that. By asking about the difference between Christology and faith, we raise a transcendental question. It is the question of how we can transcend a merely theoretical approach and enter into a more genuine relationship.

Transcendental Christology inquires about how a person can hear God's Word and obey its summons. To be sure, this question is logically prior to an actual relationship with Jesus Christ. There must be the possibility of a relationship before the relationship itself. That is a valid objection to transcendental Christology. But the question of logical priority is misleading. One cannot even understand such a thing as transcendental Christology until one has a concrete relationship with Jesus.

It is true to say that the incarnation is an event of grace. We cannot summon this event by an effort of intellectual speculation. The Christian, however, starts with an experience of a relationship with Christ. Then he or she can ask how the relationship developed. He or she can ask how human nature was "elevated" so as to enjoy the relationship.

B. THE IMPORTANCE OF TRANSCENDENTAL CHRISTOLOGY IN OUR AGE

(VI.3.B, p. 207). In this brief paragraph, Rahner states that traditional theology lacks a transcendental Christology. Traditional theology may seem to the modern person a merely "mythological" overlay to historical events. In other words, the modern may object that Jesus of Nazareth was "just a man" who was proclaimed Son of God after his death. Transcendental Christology enables us to distinguish between the genuine reality of faith and inadequate interpretations of it. It enables us to say what "Son of God" really means and to distinguish it from mythological images of Jesus, depicted (for example) with a halo.

C. THE PRESUPPOSITIONS OF TRANSCENDENTAL CHRISTOLOGY

(VI.3.C, p. 208). Transcendental Christology presupposes that all human beings are oriented toward and hope for an absolute savior. Further, it presupposes that the nature of human beings has been elevated by the grace of God's self-communication. The human being is also, as a spiritual being, open to a dialogue with God. The person can hope for God to offer God's own self. We cannot say whether this orientation of the human being is owing to an "elevated nature" or to his or her own "spiritual subjectivity."

But at any rate, a transcendental Christology presupposes both (1) what is necessary for human transcendence in general as well as (2) the concrete and historically contingent experience of individuals.

D. The Development of a Transcendental Christology

(VI.3.D, p. 208). Transcendental Christology can never be satisfied with merely conventional experiences of Jesus Christ and of the church. Why not? Because no finite experience can satisfy the human longing for absoluteness and absolute fulfillment. Rahner expands this thesis under five points:

1. *Unsatisfied Longing.* There is a transcendence for which we all long. We try to represent or mediate transcendence by means of an object, image, or person. In the gap between our longing for transcendence and the mediation of it, we experience God. Another way to express this is to point to the gap between the unity we seek and the plurality we experience.

2. *The Experience of Hope.* Human beings dare to hope that God cares for them. We see God's care in experiences which are themselves finite but which enable us to participate in "the infinite itself, in the unity of the fullness of meaning, in a Thou who is absolutely trustworthy" (p. 209). As we reflect on the hope for transcendence, we begin to see that hope itself is a manifestation of the hoped-for encounter with God. Yet we concede that hope is not enough. The hoped-for goal is not yet in our grasp. We may even refuse the goal of hope.

3. *Transcendent Promise.* Our hope takes place in history. Although we express this hope in words and actions that are finite and contingent, nevertheless the object of hope (the mystery of God) itself never becomes finite. God is revealed as a promise. The promise is not to be fulfilled in our merely human expressions of God. God is also revealed in the event of death. In the presence of death, we still can hope for eternal life—or we can resign ourselves in despair.

4. *Historical Promise.* Our hope searches in history for God's promises. These are promises of something final, irreversible, eschatological, promises such as the proclamation of the kingdom of God.

5. *Finality of God's Offer.* God's offer of the divine self can only be made complete to a person who "surrenders the future" in his or her death. By dying, the person reveals a final acceptance of God. God's offer can only be "final" when the human being accepts it in an irrevocable way.

In summary, Rahner's development of a transcendental Christology has a limited goal. It cannot create faith by showing that the absolute savior is found in Jesus of Nazareth. But such a Christology allows the Christian to understand what one has found in Jesus.

4. What Does It Mean to Say: "God Became Man"?

(VI.4, p. 212). This section asks how the notion of absolute savior can be identified with Jesus of Nazareth, whom Christians call the incarnate Logos and Son. Rahner begins with a sustained meditation on the meaning of "incarnation." He notes that the church's traditional teaching—the descending Christology according to which God descended to earth and became man—is a point of departure (A). He then foreshadows his own approach to the Trinity. His approach insists that the Logos is distinct. It is distinct not just because the Son proceeds from the Father, but because only the Logos became incarnate (B). By becoming incarnate, the Logos made the human reality God's own reality. When God took a human nature, human nature reached the goal toward which it had always tended (C). God "became" the human nature that God had prepared for the Logos, so that human nature might be divinized (D). The "lesser" (i.e., human nature) finds its foundation and goal in the "greater" (i.e., the Logos) (E). Hence we can say that humanity is a cipher or abbreviation for the Word of God. Divinized human nature expresses God's intention for us (F). For a true Christology, the affirmation of a dogmatic formula is less important than an existential decision. The important decision is to accept existence as an expression of God's love, and love extends beyond death (G).

A. The Question of the "Incarnation of God"

(VI.4.A, p. 212). The incarnation makes accessible the Trinity and our participation in the divine nature. That is its central importance. Because God became a human being, the gulf between divinity and humanity collapsed. We have been enabled to share God's own life. Rahner's goal is not to "prove" the teaching of the church. But in this section he starts with the church's traditional teaching of a descending Christology, the idea that God descended to earth and became man.

The official teaching is, for Rahner, a point of departure. His goal is to reinterpret the faith. Only in a reinterpretation does one know if one has rightly understood (made comprehensible for today) the ancient formulas of faith. The mystery of the incarnation is not something to be "solved." Rather, it is the very mystery that encompasses us. The desire to penetrate the mystery spurs our efforts to understand.

B. The "Word" of God

(VI.4.B, p. 214). God's "Word" or Logos is not the only person of the Godhead who could become flesh. The "Father" or the "Spirit" could have become incarnate, but did not. Rahner finds in the early patristic or pre-

Augustinian tradition an explanation. According to that tradition, only the Word has a relation to history. Only the Word made human history God's own. The Word is more than a part of the inner life of God (as in Augustine's "psychological" theory). We know the Logos most completely in history. We know it through its incarnation in a historical figure, Jesus of Nazareth.

C. Became "Man"

(VI.4.C, p. 215). People could simply assume that we know what "the human being" is. We could assume that "man" is a "human nature," the human nature that the Word took on. If we were to do that, we could approach human nature in a pragmatic and definable (and not metaphysical) way.

Rahner, however, rejects the idea of simply assuming what man is. The "rational animal" of Aristotle, the *zoon logikon*, is a concept without bounds. Why boundless? Because the human being is concerned about what is nameless and impossible to grasp, namely, the mystery of God. The human being is oriented toward the fullness of God. But in order to realize God's fullness, Rahner says, we must allow ourselves to be "grasped" by God.

He claims that we define ourselves by accepting or rejecting the mystery we are. This mystery is not a puzzle to be solved, but a "horizon." It is the horizon of all that is within our sight, the horizon that marks the limits of our knowledge. We are promised the vision of God, but that vision lies beyond our horizon. The promise is there, however, as something immediate. It is the immediacy of the incomprehensible God.

So when we think of God becoming human, we mean that God has assumed the human being's very orientation toward infinite mystery. God has taken that orientation as God's own reality. Thus our human nature, when the Word assumed it, had reached the very point to which it was always moving. "This nature of man . . . so gives itself to the mystery of fullness and so empties itself that it becomes the nature of God himself" (p. 218). The potential to obey God is thus identical with the human essence. The potential to obey God is the human nature that God becomes.

Is this, Rahner asks, a heretical "consciousness Christology," an understanding of Jesus as the one who "became Christ" by his consciousness of his closeness to God? No, he says, it is an ontological Christology. It has to do with the unique being of Jesus Christ. The potential to obey was fulfilled only once in human history, and the hypostatic union took place only once.

This Rahnerian kind of "ontological" Christology enables us to avoid a certain mistake. It avoids the mythological impression that God put on human trappings extrinsically, remaining God but "donning" human form.

God did not simply enter human history and "set things right" in the person of Jesus of Nazareth because God could not accomplish them from heaven. No, God entered history to unite human nature with divinity.

D. CAN THE IMMUTABLE "BECOME" SOMETHING?

(VI.4.D, p. 221). The incarnation forces a question upon us: how can the unchangeable God "become" something? The immutability of God is a well-established doctrine. So how can the Word become flesh?

Rahner's answer is this: the Logos assumes the reality of something that is capable of becoming. That "something" is the human reality of Jesus. The one who is not subject to change (i.e., the Logos) *can* be subject to change *in* something else (the man Jesus of Nazareth). The history of Jesus' life, death, and resurrection is "the event and history of God himself" (p. 221).

So God's immutability has to be understood dialectically. Immutability is not the only characteristic of God. It must be understood in relation to other qualities, such as God's willingness to become incarnate. We understand the tension between immutability and incarnation the way we understand the tension between the unity and plurality of God in the Trinity. God, who is immutable, can "become"; God can become "less" than what God remains.

In the incarnation, God "becomes" what has come from God. God becomes, but without changing the divine self. Rahner puts it this way: God "creates the human reality *by the very fact that* he assumes it as his own" (p. 222). God goes out of the divine self, becomes empty, and is *in* the emptying—in it as love. God does not just create in order for the creation to be separate. God creates in order to make creatures who are capable of being assumed by God. God creates human beings who can become part of God's own history.

E. THE "WORD" BECAME MAN

(VI.4.E, p. 223). Why was it only the Logos who could and did become man? First, we must affirm that the Word can and does express God's very self. That is why we call the divine person the "Word." Next, we must assert that, when God chooses to express the divine self, God does not do so by adopting a disguise. No, God is not putting on a human mask, but actually becoming a human being. Finally, we assert that this Logos, God's very own expression, is incarnate. Only the Logos (and not the Father or the Spirit) was incarnate.

Does the humanity of the Logos express who God is? Yes, Rahner says, it does so, both in the person of Jesus and as a providential plan for all people. Although the Word did not have to become flesh, nevertheless humanity *is* what it is because of the incarnation. The lesser (i.e., humanity) is grounded in the greater (i.e., God's self-expression in the Logos). The creator entered creation. Without Jesus Christ, we would not know what God intends for human beings.

F. MAN AS THE CIPHER OF GOD

(VI.4.F, p. 224). Humanity is the "cipher" of God, says Rahner, the "abbreviated Word of God." He means that the Word of God is not expressed in Jesus Christ alone. Rather, all human beings, all who exist "because there was to be a Son of Man," are a "shorthand" expression for God's Word. How can he say this? There are several steps in Rahner's logic. First, he says that human nature is the self-expression of the Word. This human nature says what we human beings are.

Next, he says that the self-expression of the Word in human nature redeems humanity. Our redemption is accomplished when the Word becomes incarnate among us. The Word shows us the human nature to which we are called. Doubtless the human nature spoken in Jesus Christ is not the same human nature that speaks in us. We are not the Word of God incarnate! Nevertheless, the human nature expressed in Jesus is the human nature to which God invites us.

After that, Rahner asserts that the human being "participates" in the mystery of God. This term, "participation," comes from Greek philosophy. It suggests our union with the mystery of God, and simultaneously the difference that exists between the mystery and us. Rahner puts it this way. He says that we participate in God's mystery in the same way that a question participates in the answer to that question. We human beings are a question. The question which we "are" is the why and wherefore of humanity. God answers that question in the Logos. The question (i.e., human being) participates in the answer (i.e., God's Logos).

Finally, Rahner expresses the close union of humanity and divinity. Thanks to Jesus Christ, he says, God "is" humanity and will remain so for eternity. Hence theology "is" anthropology, and Christology "is" the beginning and end of anthropology (p. 225). Anthropology is the theology that God speaks by uttering the Word as human flesh. Anthropology is our theology when we seek Christ and God via the human being. In Christ, the finite has received an infinite depth. The humanity of Christ receives its own validity, power, and reality—not just as a shadow of God's own, but precisely *as* God's own.

Modern humanity rejects the idea of God appearing in the trappings of a human being. In that rejection, modern humanity has the same instinct as the fathers of the church, who condemned docetism, apollinarism, monophysitism, and monothelitism. These heresies stated that Jesus Christ is God

appearing in human form. Many of us Christians know these to be heretical. But often our piety is mythological. We often underemphasize the
humanity of Jesus. By contrast, many critics of the church, who appear to
be enemies of Christianity, emphasize the humanity of Jesus. This emphasis
may express a profound but inexplicit believe in the incarnation.

G. ON THE IMPORTANCE AND THE LIMITS OF DOGMATIC FORMULAS

(VI.4.G, p. 227). Can someone who rejects the formula "Jesus Christ is
one divine person in two natures" still have a true and Christological faith?
Yes, says Rahner, it is possible. What then does it mean to have a true and
Christological faith? One must profess, says Rahner, that God has spoken
the ultimate word as the truth of human life. There are two parts of this
statement. First, God is real and has taken the initiative. God has spoken a
word. And second, this word (God's own Word) is the truth of human life.
By God's Word, the human being lives or dies. That for Rahner is true and
Christological faith. Anyone who, far from believing in explicit revelation,
accepts existence as the "mystery which lies hidden in the mystery of eternal love and bears life in the womb of death" (p. 228), does in fact say yes
to Christ. His or her yes, says Rahner, may be called "anonymous" Christianity.

5. On the Theological Understanding of the History of the Life and Death of Jesus of Nazareth

(VI.5, p. 228). This thirty-five-page part is divided into six subdivisions.
Subdivision (a) is a methodological reflection. Rahner describes the relationship between the transcendental experience of God and the historical
encounter with Jesus Christ. In subdivision (b), he treats the question about
the historical Jesus. One cannot arrive at faith in Christ from an historical
analysis of the New Testament, he concedes, but a historical analysis can
help us distinguish between objects of faith and the more amply docu-
mented grounds of faith. In subdivision (c), he summarizes the historical
results from exegesis upon which his analysis of Jesus rests. In subdivision
(d), Rahner argues that Jesus knew himself to be the actual incarnation of
God's offer of salvation. Subdivision (e) argues that Jesus had the confidence that, in his death, his claim to be the final proclamation of God would
be vindicated. In subdivision (f), Rahner states that the miracles of Jesus
should not be understood as suspensions of the laws of nature, but rather
as signs, addressed to an individual and meant to awaken faith, of which the
greatest is the resurrection.

(a) Preliminary Remarks

(VI.5.a, p. 228). In this subdivision, Rahner addresses a number of hermeneutical issues, issues about the interpretation of faith in Christ. First, he raises his question. He asks whether the divine self-communication, which he has described in transcendental terms, has actually taken place in the Jesus of history (A). He presupposes that the historical question about Jesus Christ is also a subjective one, for the meaning of Jesus can only be disclosed to faith (B). There is a circular structure of faith in which objective knowledge is combined with a subjective willingness to believe (C). To be sure, our knowledge of Jesus is "interpreted" knowledge. But it is not without objective grounds, for we have Jesus' own testimony to himself, recorded in the Gospels (D). Although history can be verified only in a relative sense, nevertheless it can have absolute significance (E). It has that significance because we human beings do make absolute commitments. True, we are never absolutely certain about the final wisdom and rightness of what we do. That does not prevent us from making absolute commitments based on contingent knowledge (F).

A. ON THE RELATIONSHIP OF THE PREVIOUS TRANSCENDENTAL INQUIRY
   TO HISTORICAL EVENTS

(VI.5.a.A, p. 228). Up to this point, Rahner has asked whether there can be a transcendental idea of God's self-communication. The transcendental issue differs, however, from the historical. Now he asks the historical question. It is whether this divine self-communication has in fact taken place— and whether it has taken place in Jesus of Nazareth.

B. THE ACCOUNTABILITY OF OUR FAITH IN JESUS AS THE CHRIST

(VI.5.a.B, p. 229). Rahner does not ask the objective question of Christian theology, "Is Jesus the Christ, and how does he show that he is?" His question is rather a subjective one. He asks, "How do I account for my faith in this Jesus as the Christ?" He asks the subjective question, he says, because he presupposes that his readers have a Western, Christian, and ecclesial faith. His thesis is an interesting one: he wants to show that what is "most objective" (i.e., the nature of Jesus Christ) is also "most subjective" (because it is disclosed to our act of faith).

C. THE CIRCULAR STRUCTURE OF FAITH KNOWLEDGE

(VI.5.a.C, p. 230). How does a person who does not believe in Jesus Christ come to faith? First, at a sociological level, says Rahner, that person has an experience. The nonbeliever experiences himself or herself within a "circle of knowledge," a circle he or she did not construct alone. So the first stage of faith is a form of socialization: one finds oneself in a society, a circle of knowledge about Jesus Christ that is plausible and shared.

Faith in the form of socialization does not mean that one has just accepted faith as a "given," a faith merely presupposed by those within the circle. For the individual must still give an account of the faith and make moral decisions. Although one's knowledge of the faith is incomplete, unreflected, and naive, nevertheless the one who accepts the faith from another is still involved in that faith.

The next stage of faith combines a subjective willingness to believe with the actual ground of the faith. It is the ground of faith, says Rahner, that justifies the willingness to believe. If someone believes my account of Jesus Christ, I have not therefore "produced" the other's faith. I have merely expressed it in a comprehensible way. I have put it in concepts. To those concepts, however, the other has responded. He or she recognizes in the Jesus I preach the one whose grace is already at work.

D. The Historical Dimension of Christian Faith

(VI.5.a.D, p. 232). In what sense, and with what right, does the believer assert that the events of Jesus' life are "historical" (p. 233)? Rahner asks this question because Christians in general (not to mention modern interpreters, such as Wolfhart Pannenberg) claim that faith has a quite definitive historical object. Still, our knowledge of the event of Jesus is not historical in a neutral sense. Rather, it is known through an authoritative interpretation, Jesus' own interpretation. And it is grasped within the circle of faith.

E. The Problem of the Universal Significance
of Particular Historical Events

(VI.5.a.E, p. 233). In the life, death, and resurrection of Jesus, something absolute has happened for the history of the world. That is the Christian claim. But such a claim runs into a problem, the problem of history. Modern humanity believes that we cannot know the past as well as we know the present. Modern humanity believes that the events of the past are less important than how we respond to them.

There is an incongruity between the merely relative verifiability of historical knowledge and the absolute significance of history. There is "verification" in the study of history, but it is "merely relative." The eighteenth-century Enlightenment asked whether something historical could be "existentielly" significant, that is, a matter of life or death. Rahner puts it this way: can salvation be dependent on a historical event, or must it depend on something more verifiable than history?

F. The Inevitable Incongruence between Relative Historical
Certainty and Absolute Commitment

(VI.5.a.F, p. 234). Why can we claim that historical events have an
"absolute" significance? Because they *do* have that significance in our real,
lived-out existence. We are asked to make absolute commitments throughout our lives. We make them in married life, in the heroism of the battle-
field, in religious communities. And we do so in the absence of theoretical
certainty. We are never absolutely certain about the final wisdom and rightness of what we do. No matter how thoroughly one tries to weigh a decision, the decision is ultimately made on the basis of a provisional
interpretation of reality. That interpretation is finite and historically contingent. Even a decision *not* to commit oneself can be an absolute decision.

(b) Observations from Hermeneutics and Fundamental Theology
on the Problem of Historical Knowledge
of the Preresurrection Jesus

(VI.5.b, p. 235). In this section, Rahner concedes that the New Testament
sources vary in their historical verifiability and reliability. But he insists that
an absolute historical verifiability is not only impossible to attain, but
unnecessary for faith. True, Jesus understood himself before his death and
resurrection in ways that differ from the understanding of the early church.
But these differences are not in contradiction (A). Indeed, one cannot "go
behind" the testimony of the first Christian generation to find, in a supposed "historical Jesus," something significant for theology that has nothing to do with faith (B). It is right and proper, however, to distinguish
between an "object" of faith (a truth in which we believe) and a "ground"
of faith (a truth for which there is more ample evidence) (C). Secular history
may be grasped without faith, yes, but not salvation history (D). Even the
earliest Christian witnesses interpreted what they saw with the eyes of faith,
just as Christians do today (E). Salvific knowledge is only possible within
the context of faith (F). And within faith, one is right to note that some
objects of faith are grounds of faith, and some are not (G). Rahner's goal is
to ground Christology in two ways: first, by showing how Jesus himself
understood his role: and second, by showing the central role of the resurrection (H).

A. Two Theses

(VI.5.b.A, p. 235). There are some (e.g., the followers of Rudolf Bultmann) who will say, "It doesn't really matter whether the stories of the New
Testament are true; what matters is that, in Jesus Christ, God calls me to
love and to obedience in faith." Rahner rejects this view. He says that Chris-

tians must have an abiding interest in the history and self-understanding of Jesus. His life and his death have theological relevance distinct from the relevance of his call to love and obedience. That is the first thesis: the thesis of the relevance of Jesus' history.

The second thesis is that the Jesus of history and the Jesus of faith are one and the same. To be sure, the accounts of the postresurrection Jesus are influenced by the faith of the early Christian community. But that does not mean that Jesus' self-understanding before the resurrection contradicts the understanding of him presented by the early Christian community. And our faith does not require that Jesus' self-understanding coincide precisely with the content of our faith today.

Rahner argues this in a clever way. He says that, if Jesus' life before the resurrection coincided unambiguously with the entire content of faith, then there would have been no need for the resurrection. The resurrection then would have been nothing other than God's seal of approval on a faith complete in itself.

B. Christian Faith Refers to the Concrete History of Jesus

(VI.5.b.B, p. 236). Research into the historical Jesus can lead to the erroneous conclusion that it is possible, by means of a neutral study of history, to get beyond the testimony of the first witnesses of Jesus. Some researchers believe that they can find something important for faith and for theology wholly apart from what the first Christians believed. But Rahner says that the effort to go beyond the Christ of faith to a Jesus of history is fruitless. Faith alone can decide what, of all that was transmitted in the New Testament record, is essential to faith. Faith has nothing distinguishable from itself that can be its ground.

Having said that, however, Rahner is at pains to emphasize that transcendentality and existentiality alone cannot ground faith. We cannot possess (manipulate or master) the transcendental and existential experience. We cannot transcend ourselves, nor can we make an existential decision for God, without a reference to real history. And for the Christians of the first century, the historical event of Jesus Christ was the ground of faith.

C. On the Relationship between the Object and the Ground of Faith

(VI.5.b.C, p. 238). Whoever says, "The historical event of Jesus Christ does not make Christian faith legitimate today," no longer has a traditional Christian faith. In such a person, the relation between faith and its historical ground have been severed. Every ground of faith, says Rahner, is an object of faith. Every miracle, every mighty deed, every selfless sacrifice—everything, in short, that we call a ground of faith—cannot by itself produce faith. These grounds of faith are also objects of faith, for in them we believe. We believe in them, and hence they undergird our faith.

Not every object of faith, however, is also a ground of faith. Jesus interpreted himself as the absolute savior, and his self-interpretation is an object of faith in which we believe. But this object of faith (Jesus' self-interpretation) is hard to transmit as a ground of faith. It is easier to proclaim the miracles of Jesus (and preeminently his resurrection) as objects of faith, because these objects also reveal their ground. Miracles ground faith but not from the outside. It is not as if, once having seen a miracle, we automatically believe. The grounds of faith are not extrinsic to faith. It takes faith to see something as a ground of faith.

Historical knowledge grounds faith but not from the outside. Rahner rejects the idea that the grounds of faith are extrinsic to faith itself. Why? Because faith is not possible without grace. Grace enables a real and effective grasp of the grounds of faith, such as miracles, mighty deeds, and resurrection.

D. On the Different Meanings of "History"

(VI.5.b.D, p. 240). The discussion of the necessity of faith for recognizing faith's ground and object enables us to distinguish between two "types" of history. Salvation history is real and objective, but it is grasped only within the assent of faith. The merely historical record of Jesus' life and death is accessible to knowledge, yes, but it may not be interested in faith.

E. The Faith of the First Witnesses and Our Faith

(VI.5.b.E, p. 241). Like us, the first witnesses could only grasp the events of salvation history from within faith. We enter into the structure of the faith of the first witnesses when we, having been given courage by their faith, and believing their testimony, say "I believe." Their faith, and that of subsequent generations from them to us, has become part of the grounds of our faith. But neither they nor we came to faith by means of experiences apart from faith. The grounds of faith are, from the very beginning, objects of faith

F. Salvific Knowledge Is Possible Only Within the Commitment of Faith

(VI.5.b.F, p. 242). Faith must necessarily be grounded by history. Why? Because salvation must take place in history. The historical object is an "object of faith"; and yet it "grounds" faith. So it must be recognized as what it is: namely, an object in which we believe. This recognition must take place if anything is to have significance.

An object remains insignificant without a faith. Faith recognizes an object in history as an object of faith, and without faith the object has no significance. The ability to recognize such an object for what it is (i.e., an object of faith) differs, however, from grace. We believers may be able to articulate the grounds of our faith. But when we do so, the articulation itself is an act of faith. No one will respond to it unless he or she first has had a transcendental experience of Jesus Christ. The transcendental experience allows one to see events of faith in the events of history.

G. On the Distinction between Articulations of the Object of Faith and the Ground of Faith

(VI.5.b.G, p. 243). We saw earlier (VI.5.b.C) that an object of faith (e.g., Jesus' self-interpretation as savior) is not always a ground of faith (like the miracles or the resurrection). Now Rahner goes further: some objects of faith, he says, like the virginal conception of Jesus, do not allow us to grasp the grounds of faith as much as do other objects of faith. Such objects, like Jesus' miracles, are not just objects but also grounds of faith.

Even for someone with faith it is not always possible to differentiate, by means of history, between object and ground. Some texts offer only an object of faith, not a ground of faith. Historically speaking, we want to establish with certainty what we can about those objects of faith that are also grounds of faith. Texts significant for dogmatic theology (e.g., texts about the virginal conception) are sometimes different texts from those significant for fundamental theology. Yet both are seen from within faith.

The believer is justified in distinguishing between the "minimum" of secure knowledge about the history of Jesus and other, less secure items of knowledge. These less secure objects of faith are true, but they go beyond the substance of the New Testament. The minimum items of knowledge, by contrast, are not only objects of faith but also grounds. In the past, says Rahner, we have judged the objects that go beyond the substance of the New Testament (e.g., those which are not also "grounds," such as the virginal conception) too generously.

H. The Minimal Historical Presuppositions of an Orthodox Christology to Be Established by Fundamental Theology

(VI.5.b.H, p. 245). Fundamental theology need only prove that two theses are credible in order to establish the grounds of faith for Christology. One thesis is that Jesus understood himself not merely as one in a line of prophets but as *the* eschatological prophet, that is, the absolute savior. The second thesis is that the resurrection of Jesus Christ is credible and mediates the savior in his total reality.

In fundamental theology, one does not have to prove that each and every detail of the New Testament record is reliable. Yes, it is "Catholic" to assert that the New Testament is inerrant. But the judgment about the historical value of the various New Testament sources is different from inerrancy. We need to make distinctions among the New Testament sources and their historically verifiable reliability.

(c) The Empirical Concrete Structure of the Life of Jesus

(VI.5.c, p. 246). In this subdivision, Rahner acknowledges that *Foundations* does not pretend to be a work of Scriptural exegesis (A). But *Foundations* is built upon the results of exegesis, and Rahner presents the essential elements in the historical knowledge of Jesus (B).

A. THE NATURE OF OUR PROCEDURE

(VI.5.c.A, p. 246). In *Foundations*, says Rahner, there is no attempt to do any detailed exegesis of scripture. Detailed exegesis belongs to a "second level" reflection which Rahner described on p. 8, that is, to a thoroughly scientific reflection. Although *Foundations* does presuppose the results of modern historical critical exegesis, its goal is a "first level" of reflection, an effort to present a general idea of Christianity.

B. A SUMMARY IN THESIS FORM

(VI.5.c.B, p. 247). Rahner lists and describes six essential elements in the historical knowledge of Jesus. The *first* is that Jesus intended to be a religious reformer, not a revolutionary. He was a member of his community's religious culture. The *second* is that Jesus was a radical reformer who broke the lordship of the law that had put itself in place of God. The *third* is that Jesus hoped at first for a victory in his religious mission. Gradually, however, he realized his mission was bringing him into mortal conflict with society. The *fourth* element is that Jesus accepted his death as the consequence of his fidelity to his mission and as imposed on him by God. The *fifth* element is that Jesus called for people to be converted because of the closeness of God's kingdom, a conversion that had political consequences. Such conversion did not require, however, that the only way to live discipleship was to be involved with the underprivileged and outcasts. The *sixth* element and the one above all others, says Rahner, is that we cannot decide a number of historical questions about Jesus. For example, we cannot speak definitively about his consciousness of his divine sonship, about the titles he used for himself, about the extent to which he believed that his death would have a saving consequence, and about whether he foresaw that his disciples would form a new community (even if we can say that he did found the church).

(d) On the Basic Self-Understanding
of the Preresurrection Jesus

(VI.5.d, p. 249). Rahner begins this subdivision by emphasizing the difference between the human and the divine natures in Jesus Christ (A). He notes that, although many say that Jesus was "mistaken" in expecting the immediate coming of the Kingdom of God, nevertheless a truly human Jesus could not have predicted the future. What Jesus was expressing, Rahner says, was his closeness to the Father (B). The function of Jesus was to proclaim the kingdom, Rahner says, and this function was also the essence of the divine Word (C). Jesus was not just the proclaimer of a message. He believed that, in his very person, the message of God had become incarnate (D).

A. The Truly Human Self-Consciousness of Jesus

(VI.5.d.A, p. 249). The human self-consciousness of Jesus was not "of one nature" with the consciousness of the divine Logos. The man Jesus was not a mere puppet or mouthpiece of the divine Word. On the contrary, Jesus (1) stood at a created distance from the divine in his freedom, obedience, and in worship; and he (2) had to learn, to grow in wisdom, and to suffer disappointment that God's kingdom did not arrive in the way he thought it would.

Rahner's way of explaining this is to say that Jesus' human self-consciousness had a history. Unlike the consciousness of the divine Word, Jesus' self-consciousness was not unchangeable. The two consciousnesses were different. That is why Christians were later to declare that Jesus Christ is one divine person with two natures.

B. The Problem of the "Imminent Expectation"

(VI.5.d.B, p. 249). Jesus spoke of his relation with God by means of apocalyptic language. His language implied "an imminent expectation and an eschatology of the present." In striking words and images, Jesus *denied* that there is a time between the arrival of God's kingdom and the present. But because Jesus spoke of the coming of the kingdom as "soon," and because he did not reconcile that "soon" with his affirmation that no one knows "the hour," many speak of an error in Jesus' expectation. They think that Jesus was mistaken.

But there is no reason to speak of an error, says Rahner, since a genuinely human consciousness must, by definition, have an unknown future. Jesus' imminent expectation was the truest way he could express his closeness to God. This closeness called for an unconditional decision. It was the decision to accept God's closeness and live by it, or not.

C. Jesus' Message about God's Kingdom as the Definitive Proclamation of Salvation

(VI.5.d.C, p. 250). Jesus proclaimed that God offers salvation here and now, says Rahner, and that God has decided for the freedom of human beings by means of the incarnation. In other words, God wants to "save" humanity and wants us to choose that salvation freely. God does not harmonize into a readily grasped system the *desire* for human freedom and the *will* to create a kingdom of grace for sinners. The two exist in tension.

Jesus proclaimed the kingdom of God, and not himself. His function (i.e., to proclaim the kingdom) is his *essence*, his essence as divine Word. His arrival is the arrival of the kingdom. Before Jesus, the offer of God's salvation was not irreversible. God had not made his offer in a definitive way. After the death and resurrection, a new situation for our decision making arose. Although all of history was directed to God's offer of salvation, nevertheless that offer was not, before Jesus Christ, final and irrevocable. After him, it was. Now every person is challenged to accept God's offer to humanity in a free decision.

D. The Connection between the Message and the Person of Jesus

(VI.5.d.D, p. 251). The Jesus of the Synoptic Gospels proclaimed that the last judgment of human beings by God is dependent on their decision regarding Jesus' own person. He implied that he "is" the closeness of God's kingdom. The coming of the kingdom, said Jesus, is identical to his own coming and person.

For some, it is impossible to ascribe to Jesus the status of one who achieved victory in death. Why impossible? Because the message of Jesus, they believe, is no different from the message of any other prophet. Such a message, they say, is independent of Jesus' own person (as were the messages of, say, Isaiah, Jeremiah, and Ezekiel). The message lives on despite the fate of the prophet and does not depend on the prophet's success or failure.

If Jesus' message were independent of his person, it would be impossible to ascribe to Jesus alone a "victory in death." But was his message really independent of his person? Rahner says no. "The preresurrection Jesus thought that this new closeness of the kingdom came to be *in and through* the totality of what he said and what he did" (p. 252). True, the focus of his preaching was the kingdom, not himself. But it is no less true that he identified the kingdom and himself *before* his death and resurrection.

Jesus believed and knew himself to be the final call of God. In Jesus, God promises the divine self (p. 253). Yes, Jesus' relation to God was unique in comparison to other human beings. But because it was unique, he was an example to us. We are to follow him. We are invited to have the same relation to God that Jesus had.

Did Jesus know himself, however, to be God's final call *before* his death and resurrection? Rahner said earlier (p. 235) that the resurrection added something unique to the content of faith, and he will explain the addition later (p. 279). But here he says that Jesus knew himself, even before the resurrection, to be the final call of God. He asserts that Jesus "could have" known and experienced himself as absolute savior before his crucifixion. How? Because Jesus knew himself to be "that radical and victorious offer of God." Further, he knew that God's offer to him "is significant, valid and irrevocable for *all* men" (p. 254).

(e) The Relationship of the Preresurrection Jesus to His Death

(VI.5.e, p. 254). In this brief section of part 5, Rahner asserts (1) that Jesus met his death freely and understood it "at least" as the fate of a prophet; (2) that the meaning of his fate was "hidden in the intention of God," an intention known to Jesus as "a forgiving closeness to the world"; and (3) that one can leave open the question of whether Jesus understood his death explicitly as an "expiatory sacrifice." To be sure, Jesus' death is atonement for sins. By sending Jesus, the Father expressed his salvific will for all human beings. In that sense, Jesus' life and death achieved an atonement or reconciliation willed by God. But Jesus understood this concept, Rahner argues, in terms of a unique claim. It was the claim of an identity between his message and his person. He understood that "in this death he will be vindicated by God with regard to his claim" (p. 255). The idea of an expiatory sacrifice should not be understood as changing the mind of an angry God, as if God did not intend human salvation before the death of Jesus.

(f) Miracles in the Life of Jesus and Their Weight in Fundamental Theology

(VI.5.f, p. 255). Jesus was a miracle worker, and Rahner poses a question about the significance of the miracles for our faith (A). The church presents the miracles of Jesus as a justification of Jesus' claims, but modern people often see the miracles as mere stories that reflect a prerational view of the world (B). A proper understanding of miracles, however, requires that they be seen as signs which disclose a particular truth and which are addressed to a particular person or group (C). While it may be true to say that miracles interrupt the so-called laws of nature, it would be better to say that we do not fully understand these "laws," and that the laws of biology and matter are integrated into the spiritual in ways we do not fully comprehend (D). A better understanding of miracles regards them as material signs of an experience that would be better described as spiritual. The experience of miracles depends on the spiritual receptivity of the participant (E). Miracles are a "call" from God, a call that may come through wonders or through the most ordinary means, a call that invites faith (F). The greatest miracle is the resurrection. It is well attested, a "ground" (and not just an object) of faith, and the validation of Jesus' life (G).

A. QUESTIONS ON THE IMPORTANCE OF THE MIRACLES OF JESUS FOR OUR RELATIONSHIP TO HIM IN FAITH

(VI.5.f.A, p. 255). Rahner starts with the assumption that Jesus was a miracle worker, and that Jesus perceived in his miracles a sign that a new closeness to God's kingdom was being brought about in his person. Given that assumption, Rahner asks what is the significance of miracles for our faith. He poses three questions:

1. If historical criticism rightly shows that the miracle stories have been embellished, then what is left of these miracles?
2. Once we have seen what is left of the miracle stories, then how are we to interpret them (knowing from modern science, for example, that sudden cures do not have to be seen as miracles worked directly by God)?
3. Do the miracles have a function that can be called indispensable in making the claims of Jesus legitimate?

B. OFFICIAL CHURCH TEACHING AND THE CONTEMPORARY HORIZON OF UNDERSTANDING

(VI.5.f.B, p. 256). The tradition of the church says that the claim of Jesus as the definitive arrival of God's kingdom is made legitimate by his miracles and resurrection. Vatican I's *Dei filius* obliges us to regard the miracles as a cogent justification of Jesus' claim, although not apart from the resurrection (which may be understood as one of the miracles). But this tradition of the church raises a stumbling block for some people. It is easier to acknowledge the resurrection as an *object* of faith than to see it as a *ground* of faith (see above, pp. 238 and 243). Many people simply do not understand what a miracle is supposed to be. They see it as a mythological expression that does not fit with a rational view of the world. Still other people do not understand the relation between the miracles in general and *the* miracle of resurrection. In the New Testament, the miracles are used to portray Jesus and his life. But the resurrection is the greatest of the miracles and had a unique place in the apostolic preaching.

C. On the General Notion of Miracle

(VI.5.f.C, p. 257). Miracles are not extrinsic to the reality they witness to. They confirm the reality. Indeed, says Rahner, a miracle is dependent on and conditioned by what it is supposed to disclose. Moreover, miracles vary according to what they are meant to show. Each discloses a distinctive aspect of God's salvific activity. Finally, miracles are addressed to a person. "They are not *facta bruta*," says Rahner, "but an address to a knowing subject in a quite definite historical situation" (p. 258). It is absurd to define all miracles as God's effort to correct the course of the world. God did not make a mistake that then had to be put right by a miracle.

D. Miracles and the Laws of Nature

(VI.5.f.D, p. 258). Rahner concedes that miracles are an interruption in the laws of nature, if by that we simply mean that God exists in sovereign freedom and omnipotence. No "laws" can bind God. But problems arise if we regard miracles as interruptions in the laws of nature. It is hard to show certainly and positively that the laws of nature have been suspended. So Rahner asks: can we do without the idea of suspending the laws of nature?

He thinks we can. First, he says, we must admit that the laws of nature are not fully comprehensible. We are accustomed to think that the laws of nature govern the "lower dimensions" of matter and biology. We assume that the "higher dimensions" of freedom and spirit are different. But Rahner states that there is a continuum between the lower and the higher. Matter and biology are one in being with freedom and spirit, and they are "open to" each other. The lower dimensions can be "subsumed into" freedom. And when that happens, their fundamental structures are not altered but expanded.

For this reason, the world of matter and biology can manifest the world of freedom, history, and spirit. The lower is integrated with the higher and does not thereby lose its own laws and structure. Moreover, the meaning of the human spirit cannot be derived from the material and the biological. Human spirit takes the material and biological into its service.

E. Miracles from the Perspective of the Relationship
   between God and World

(VI.5.f.E, p. 260). Rahner proposes what he calls an "alternative" and "better" concept of miracle. He says that a miracle takes place whenever the eyes of a person are so open to God's mystery that the person experiences in a concrete event a communication of God. This communication affirms what the person has already known in a transcendental experience of grace.

Such a concept is better, Rahner suggests, because it affirms the intrinsic relationship between God and the world. God did not create human beings so different from the divine self that they have nothing to do with God. No, God created human nature with God as its "ultimate and highest dynamism." So the world and history are not so "other" from God that God must occasionally intervene in order to communicate with them. The world and history are rather "moments" within God's own self-communication. They are presupposed by God as the condition for the possibility of God communicating the divine self.

Hence the "laws of nature" are themselves a part of God's intention. They are part of God's own gift of self. God does not need to intervene and break the laws of nature, for nature and its laws are the very means by which God is revealed.

F. MIRACLE AS CALL

(VI.5.f.F, p. 261). At the most basic level, a miracle functions as a "call." It is also a sign, a sign that a person is morally obliged to obey. Such a sign may be a miracle for one person but not for another.

An example is the answer to prayer. When we speak of something as an answer to prayer, we are not saying that God has intervened in such a way that the laws of nature are broken. A sudden cure may be experienced as a sign of God's love. Moreover, it may imply a moral obligation for the cured person to act in response to God's love. So the existence of a miracle presupposes a certain kind of person. It is the person who is open to God's call.

What is this openness? It is a willingness, first of all, to believe. It is a willingness, moreover, to affirm one's own finitude and to be humble. Rahner asks whether a natural scientist could have this openness and experience a miracle. Perhaps not, Rahner says, in his or her work as a scientist. In scientific work, one looks for quantifiable answers, not for signs of God's self-communication. In the scientific method, the scientist must deliberately limit his or her horizon to that of science. But the scientist, says Rahner, is more than a practitioner of a scientific method.

G. THE VARIOUS MIRACLES OF JESUS AND THE UNIQUE MIRACLE
   OF HIS RESURRECTION

(VI.5.f.G, p. 263). Jesus' resurrection unites itself with the sign value of his life as a whole. The resurrection has to be understood in the context of his whole life. But the resurrection is not merely one among other miracles in Jesus' life. It is the central miracle. The other miracles cannot be eliminated historically, but they are more remote from us than the resurrection. They are more removed from us in their importance and in their ability to be known. By contrast, the resurrection is a miracle, a call we are obliged to heed.

6. The Theology of the Death and Resurrection of Jesus

(VI.6, p. 264). This twenty-page part is divided into seven subdivisions. In subdivision (a), Rahner lays out his main aims: to recover the original experience of Jesus Christ and its intellectual presuppositions. Subdivision (b) defines the resurrection as a validation of the "cause" of Jesus' life and a sacrament of God's will. In subdivision (c), Rahner states that the resurrection must be interpreted within the context of humanity's hope for a new spiritual life (not the prolongation of earthly existence) after death. Subdivision (d) affirms that both the first Christian generation and we have experienced the death and resurrection of Jesus as a confirmation of our own transcendental hopes. In subdivision (e), Rahner suggests that the resurrection of Jesus moved history into a new stage. It is the stage after which humanity could really believe that God would offer a final confirmation and affirmation of human life. Subdivision (f) shows how the resurrection was not merely the confirmation of Jesus' life, but offers something new to our understanding of God's intention for human beings. In subdivision (g), Rahner argues that the death of Jesus should not be understood as propitiation of the Father, but rather as a sacrament of God's saving will for us, a sacrament that accomplished what it showed forth.

(a) Preliminary Remarks

(VI.6.a, p. 264). In his brief preliminary remarks, Rahner states what he will not do in part 6. He will not attempt to present either a New Testament theology or the "official" theology of the church as reflected in the authoritative documents of Christian tradition. Why not? Because the difference between the New Testament Christologies and the Christology of the church is no greater than the difference between the Christologies of the first witnesses and those of the New Testament authors. Rahner is primarily concerned with the experience of the disciples regarding Jesus. He wants to show the continuity between what the disciples believed and what the New Testament authors wrote.

In part 6, he proposes to accomplish two main aims. First, he wants to establish the intellectual presuppositions of the original experience of Jesus Christ. Second, he wants to establish the original experience itself, an experience that he believes can be found "behind the explicit New Testament Christology" (p. 265).

(b) Intellectual Presuppositions for Discussing the Resurrection

(VI.6.b, p. 266). This brief subdivision begins with a key thesis: namely, that the death and resurrection of Jesus belong together, for the resurrection is the validation of Jesus' life after his death on the cross (A). Resurrection does not mean the resuscitation of Jesus' body after death, but rather the affirmation by God of Jesus' "cause" and person. Moreover, it is the sacrament of God's will for all humanity, a sign of the kind of response to God's Word affirmed in Jesus that God invites from all people (B).

A. THE UNITY OF THE DEATH AND RESURRECTION OF JESUS

(VI.6.b.A, p. 266). There is a unity between Jesus' death and resurrection, Rahner says, even though the two are separated by three days. Although he does not deny a time interval between the two, he claims that the interval is not important. He puts it this way: Jesus' death is subsumed into his resurrection.

What, then, is resurrection? It is, Rahner says, the "permanent, redeemed, final, and definitive validity" of Jesus' life (p. 266). His life had that validity on account of his death. It was achieved through his death in freedom and obedience.

B. THE MEANING OF "RESURRECTION"

(VI.6.b.B, p. 266). In explaining the meaning of resurrection, Rahner begins by saying what resurrection is not. It is not, he says, the resuscitation of a physical body. Rather, it is the salvation of a person by God. By salvation he does not mean a rescue from physical death, but rather the full acceptance of the person by God. Rahner calls salvation and resurrection the "validation" of a person's "cause," that is, of what the person was dedicated to.

The validation of Jesus' cause does not mean that he was committed merely to an idea that lived on after his death. Jesus' cause was not an idea separate from his person. His cause and his person were one. Resurrection is the validity of Jesus' claim to be the absolute savior (see pp. 193 and 251–54).

It is undoubtedly right to say, "Jesus is risen into the faith of his disciples." But that does not mean that he lives on only in their memory, merely as an idea. Their faith, and our faith as well, is not just a concept but also a liberation. Rahner puts it this way: faith "knows itself to be a divinely effected liberation from all the powers of finiteness, of guilt and of death, and knows itself to be empowered for this by the fact that this liberation has taken place in Jesus himself and has become manifest for us" (p. 268). In short, faith represents a basic attitude of trust in God.

(c) Transcendental Hope in the Resurrection as the Horizon for Experiencing the Resurrection of Jesus

(VI.6.c, p. 268). Under five articles, this subdivision lays out a doctrine of the resurrection that harmonizes with Rahner's transcendental Christology. He begins by asserting that Jesus' resurrection is the hope for every human being, a hope that, in Jesus, has already been fulfilled (A). Every human being knows that he or she will die, and this knowledge characterizes the human situation (B). Death is the final end of one's material existence, but not the end of the love and fidelity, which belong to one's spiritual self (C). After death come eternity and afterlife, in which the free actions of one's life reach their fulfillment and become the final achievement of one's whole existence (D). Eternal life belongs not to the soul alone, separated from the body, but to the whole human being, who longs for permanent validation and who finds in Jesus' resurrection the hope for it (E).

A. Summary Thesis

(VI.6.c.A, p. 268). Resurrection is not an assertion about the "physical" part of a human being. Resurrection does not mean that the body was resuscitated apart from the spirit. Instead, resurrection is an assertion about the whole of a human being. It affirms that the human being's whole life—body, soul, and spirit—is "permanently valid and redeemable" (p. 268).

Thus we can say that Rahner's view of resurrection is not, at least at this point, a positive statement about how a person will live in his or her final state. Rahner's intention is rather to exclude any treatment of the body apart from the rest of the person.

Resurrection poses a question. It asks whether the hope that every person has (i.e., the hope for transcendence) is merely a hope still looking for fulfillment. Or is it a hope that, in the person of Jesus Christ, has already been fulfilled? Rahner affirms the second as his summary thesis.

B. Knowledge of One's Own Death

(VI.6.c.B, p. 269). Human beings, alone of all creatures, know that they will die. This knowledge is a "piece" of their dying. People are not only confronted with death, but with the finality brought about by death. Death is not just the cessation of life, says Rahner, but the culmination of it. Death presents us with the totality of human experience. It confronts us with the final meaning of our lives.

C. ANTHROPOLOGICAL REFLECTIONS ON DEATH AND THE FINALITY OF EXISTENCE

(VI.6.c.C, p. 270). Some may say that to be preoccupied with death is unhealthy. Rahner disagrees. He says that to ignore the question of one's own death is to make a decision, however indirectly. It is the decision to look away from the reality of one's life. It is a failure to engage the question of life's meaning.

When one dies, then one's metabolism returns to dust. But are the other things that existed (such as our love, fidelity, responsibility, and freedom), are these over as well? No, says Rahner, certainly not. We may fail to notice them any longer, but they endure.

It could well be, he says, that they continue to exist, not just for the living, but for the deceased person as well. Rahner poses a question: "When the deceased is gone, can his real self not continue to exist, transformed and transposed beyond physical time and space?" (p. 271). Rahner's implicit answer is yes; the real self can continue. Why? Because love and fidelity do not reach fulfillment in time and space.

D. WHAT DO "AFTERLIFE" AND "ETERNITY" MEAN?

(VI.6.c.D, p. 271). Rahner starts with an assertion: the existence that arises out of death is no mere "continuation." It lacks the undetermined openness of life before death. Death does indeed mark an end. But both the person who thinks that death is "the end of everything" and the person who thinks that life after death is a "continuation" are mistaken.

After death, there is a new kind of existence. It is a final and definitive existence. The time that came to be "temporarily" is over. Rahner puts it this way: "eternity subsumes time." What was temporary, open, and undetermined is now final and definitive.

How can we imagine eternity without thinking of it as endless continuation? Through death, says Rahner, "there comes to be the final and definitive validity of man's existence which has been achieved and has come to maturity in freedom" (p. 272). In comparison to eternal life, our brief existence is the mere flash of a momentary spark. When it is over, we cease the process of becoming. Our earthly lives are "a process in which there comes to be in freedom and responsibility something which is, and definitively is, because it is of value to be what it is" (p. 272). No longer "becoming," our lives achieve definitive existence.

Eternity, then, is no mere continuation. Eternity rather is the realm in which freedom and responsibility come to be. In time, the eternal and transcendent principles of freedom and responsibility are actualizing themselves toward fulfillment. What is the reward of the good life? Not its endless continuation in an afterlife. Eternal life is "the finality and definitiveness of . . . [the deceased person's] freedom." It is the achievement of the "free act of his whole existence" (p. 272).

What about those people who claim that they have never had the experience of eternity in time? For Rahner, consciousness of the experience is less important than the experience itself. Those who claim they have never experienced eternity may still have made real choices in freedom and responsibility, choices that indeed are the experience of eternity, without having acknowledged them as such. Such people had the experience of eternity but did not recognize it. This is regrettable in itself. But the denial by some people that they are in fact free and responsible is still more regrettable.

E. The Experience of Immortality: Nature or Grace?

(VI.6.c.E, p. 273). Rahner does not try to distinguish what, in the experience of "eternity in time," belongs to human nature and what belongs to grace. Instead, he assumes that the experience of eternity springs from grace. His concern is the relation between the experience of eternity in time and the resurrection of Jesus. We have the right and obligation, he says, to see whether this experience has become tangible in history. He calls this experience the "transcendental experience in grace of our eternal validity as moral persons" (p. 273). In short, we are able to recognize our own permanent validity, a recognition that has the character of eternity.

This brings Rahner to the person of Jesus. He asks whether our own experience of eternity is illusory or whether it has ever been confirmed. The example of Jesus' life, death, and resurrection, Rahner suggests, confirms our own individual experiences of eternity. In his resurrection, Jesus experienced a "final and definitive fulfillment" (p. 273). His fulfillment hints that our own fulfillment is also possible.

Rahner rejects the idea, which he attributes to the "Greek and Platonic tradition in church teaching" (p. 273), that the body and the soul are split, and that only the soul has eternal life. The question about eternal life is not about the body or the soul, Rahner says, but about the eternal life of the whole person—in a word, about resurrection. That is the "horizon" for any inquiry about Jesus' resurrection. The inquiry is shaped by our own expectation of death. What can happen to human beings, asks Rahner, who expect to find, at the moment of death, the summation of their final validity? The answer is shaped by the history of Jesus' resurrection.

(d) On Understanding the Resurrection of Jesus

(VI.6.d, p. 274). In the two articles of this subsection, Rahner notes *first* that the resurrection of Jesus is unique, and *second* that there exists between Christians and the apostolic witnesses to the resurrection a unity.

A. FAITH IN THE RESURRECTION OF JESUS AS A UNIQUE FACT

(VI.6.d.A, p. 274). There are many people who we wish were still alive. One thinks, for instance, of the great martyrs and prophets. Yet we do not believe in their resurrection. Only Jesus is believed to be resurrected. If the resurrection were untrue, asks Rahner, then why do we not encounter this so-called untruth more often? Why do we not tell resurrection stories about the martyrs and prophets? Why is it only Jesus whom we believe to be resurrected? The answer is that the resurrection of Jesus is unique.

B. THE UNITY OF THE APOSTOLIC EXPERIENCE OF THE RESURRECTION AND OUR OWN

(VI.6.d.B, p. 274). Our faith is tied to that of the resurrection witnesses. Christians do not accord to mystics, for instance, the character of being resurrection witnesses, despite the fact that the mystics claim to have seen the resurrected Jesus. They accord this character to the ordinary people about whom the New Testament speaks. But those who (in the period immediately after Jesus' death) saw him in his resurrected state are not "witnesses" in a secular sense. If we judged their testimony according to the standards of a secular "witness account," then their testimony would be judged incredible. But those standards do not apply, because we are not (as in the secular model) totally "outside" the experience of the apostolic witnesses.

Why not? Because "we hear this witness of the apostles with that transcendental hope in resurrection" (p. 275). We hear, says Rahner, with "grace" and with the "witness of the Holy Spirit." To hear the accounts of the resurrection with transcendental hope means that we have "the courage to stand beyond death . . . by gazing upon the risen Jesus" (p. 275). In courage we believe that there is a correspondence between our transcendental hope and the real presence of Jesus' resurrection.

We "experience" Jesus' resurrection because we experience Jesus' cause as living and victorious. We implicitly assume the existence of transcendental hope. We are able to express this hope only by means of the apostolic witness to Jesus as the risen one. As St. Paul said, the Holy Spirit is poured out into our hearts (Rom. 5:5) precisely as faith in resurrection.

(e) The Resurrection Experience of the First Disciples

(VI.6.e, p. 276). In this brief subsection, Rahner wants to clarify the extent of the credibility of the apostolic witness to the resurrection. He makes four points about the distinctiveness of the resurrection, based on an analysis of the Gospel texts:

1. The experience was not a "visionary" experience in the typical sense (i.e., a self-induced vision), but rather was given from without.
2. It was not an experience "in general," but was about a concrete individual, Jesus of Nazareth, whose life and teachings were known.
3. The experience was given in faith, yes, but it is not just an "object" of faith. It is one of the "grounds" of faith.
4. It was not awaited or predicted, and it has not happened since.

To be sure, the Gospel texts are secondary literature and not eyewitness accounts. They are dramatic embellishments, not scientific biography. But no one can pretend that he or she understands the experience of the apostolic witnesses better than they understood it themselves. The Gospel accounts are the most reliable accounts available.

The resurrection is not historical in the sense that it belongs to the ordinary, repeatable realm of historical experiences. It is unique and lies outside the normal realm of history. It is the event by which our ongoing history is assumed into its final and definitive state.

With a transcendental hope in the resurrection one may conceivably reject the apostolic accounts as unhistorical, says Rahner—at least in abstract, conceptual theory. But for the Christian in modern society, the rejection of the apostolic witness is more likely (and more regrettably) a rejection of transcendental hope in resurrection. Jesus' resurrection differs from the resurrection we hope for ourselves. In his resurrection, he was made "Lord" and "Messiah," exalted and enthroned. To be sure, only Jesus enjoyed what we call the hypostatic union. That was unique. Yet we too are graced, just as Jesus was, with God's self-communication.

The Pharisees taught the reality of the resurrection long before Jesus. Belief in the resurrection was not wholly new. But only after Jesus can we speak of our own transcendental hope in resurrection. Our own hope is linked to the historical experience of Jesus. We hope for the definitive validation that he experienced.

(f) The Original Theology of the Resurrection of Jesus
as the Starting Point of All Christology

(VI.6.f, 279). Rahner returns to the starting point of chapter VI, section 6. He asks, "What is really experienced, witnessed and believed with the resurrection of Jesus?" (p. 279). He does not want to start by assuming the metaphysical, divine sonship of Jesus. The resurrection is not merely a confirmation of the divine sonship that "we knew about all along." Why does Rahner not start with the customary assumption of divine sonship? Because the resurrection taught us something new about Jesus. It taught us the unsurpassability of his claim that God has expressed the divine self in a human being (A). And it taught that this unity of God and humanity has not been achieved merely in transcendental hope, but in a man (B).

A. THE VINDICATION AND ACCEPTANCE OF JESUS' CLAIM TO BE THE ABSOLUTE SAVIOR

(VI.6.f.A, p. 279). In the resurrection, Jesus' claim is seen to be of permanent validity. What was Jesus' claim? It is the claim that, with Jesus, "a new and unsurpassable closeness to God . . . will prevail victoriously and is inseparable from him" (p. 279). God's kingdom has come—and we must decide whether or not to accept the God who has come so close.

Then Rahner raises a question about the relation between Jesus and prophets of old. Jesus can be called a prophet, says Rahner, because he confronts us with a "word of God" which cannot be reduced to an eternal truth and which calls us to decision. But he is more than a prophet, says Rahner. A prophet allows God's Word to be greater than the prophet himself. In Jesus, however, the final Word is himself present. "There is nothing to say beyond it, because God has really . . . offered *himself* in Jesus" (p. 280).

Before Jesus, the religious categories about family, marriage, nation, law, temple, and Sabbath were seen to be the mediation and representation of God. After Jesus, they no longer have that same mediating function. There is "a new and real immediacy of God coming from God himself" (p. 280). That is the sense in which Jesus is not just a prophet, but also the absolute savior.

B. THE POINT OF DEPARTURE FOR "LATE" NEW TESTAMENT CHRISTOLOGY

(VI.6.f.B, p. 280). Late New Testament Christology and that of the church start with the assumption that Jesus is the Son and Word of God. By this, they mean something prior to the notion expressed in the Prologue of John's Gospel of a preexistent Logos. They mean that Jesus is Son and Word because Jesus' human reality has been assumed by God as God's own self-expression. Jesus was not "adopted" by God or made a mere "servant." If he were, then Jesus would be merely a provisional expression of God, an expression that can be superseded. But Jesus is not provisional; he is the final expression of God.

Although Jesus Christ is this final expression, nevertheless there is more than one way to talk about it. In the New Testament, one sees a variety of rudimentary Christologies. There are, for example, the Son of Man Christology, the Kyrios Christology, and the Servant Christology. Classical Christology, which describes Jesus as one in being with the Father and as one person with two natures, is not the only way of expressing the reality of Jesus Christ.

Rahner's point of departure is "the unity between the historically tangible claim of Jesus and the experience of his resurrection" (p. 281). Rahner calls it an "ascending" Christology. It begins with the humanity of Jesus, with the encounter between Jesus and other people as expressed in the New Testament and by the early witnesses in faith. Jesus is, first of all, a man. Ascending Christology regards him as a "redeemed man" who makes a claim on us. This type of Christology resolves the dilemma, Rahner says, between the so-called functional and essential Christologies. Functional Christologies describe how Jesus functions for human beings. They focus on his life as the confirmation of our transcendental hope. Essential Christologies describe the nature of Jesus. They define what he "really was" in history as the Word made flesh. Rahner says that functional and essential Christologies form a unity, just as there is a unity between our transcendental hope in resurrection and the historical experience of Jesus.

(g) On the Theology of the Death of Jesus
from the Perspective of the Resurrection

(VI.6.g, p. 282). This subdivision analyzes the death of Jesus in two brief articles. In the first, Rahner criticizes the notion of sacrifice as a propitiation of the Father by the Son. This doctrine does not do justice to God's own initiative. God did not wait to be propitiated, but sent the Word to reconcile human beings to the divine self. In the second article, he presents a "demythologized" view of the salvation accomplished by Jesus' death. He says that the life and death of Jesus are a sacrament of God's will, a sacrament through which God caused the salvation of humanity.

A. The Interpretation of the Death of Jesus as Cause of Salvation

(VI.6.g.A, p. 282). In this section, Rahner acknowledges that the death of Jesus was, for the New Testament writers, a "cause" of salvation. The death of Jesus in the New Testament "blots out our sinfulness before God and establishes a salvific relationship." It is a sacrifice of blood poured out for the many and offered to God. What did the New Testament writers mean by this?

First, Rahner calls the imagery of blood sacrifice a help toward understanding Jesus' death. In the first century, he says, "The idea of propitiating the divinity by means of a sacrifice was a current notion" (p. 282). But how is this imagery connected to Jesus, both before and after the resurrection?

In response, Rahner first raises a question about the salvific efficacy of Jesus' death. Earlier he had shown that the idea of God "changing his mind" (p. 255) as a result of Jesus' death was problematic.

Rahner's next step is to assert that Jesus' death is a free act of obedience. God, by sending the Son, made the Son's obedience possible. And God, who allowed the Word to "make satisfaction," gave us in Jesus the possibility of saving ourselves by believing and thus appropriating God's salvation freely.

Whoever asserts this, Rahner says, is "perhaps" correct. Believers do have a share in the sacrifice of Christ. But this assertion also implicitly criticizes and "desacralizes" the notion of sacrifice. Why? Because Jesus is no longer purely a sacrificial offering or an instrument of propitiation. He is rather the one sent by God to make peace with humanity. God has taken the initiative, not we human beings.

In Jesus, God is reconciling the world to God's own self. This does not happen, however, as if Jesus' actions changed God's mind. Such an assertion distorts the image of God. In order to avoid this distortion, we must answer several questions. First, how does the death of Christ as God's grace free us? And second, can we even say that the preresurrection Jesus interpreted his coming death as an expiatory sacrifice? These two questions, plus the question about whether resurrection clarifies the salvific significance of Jesus' death, remain to be answered.

B. THE FOUNDATION OF THE SOTERIOLOGICAL INTERPRETATION OF THE DEATH OF JESUS

(VI.6.g.B, p. 283). Rahner begins with the assumption that human history is one history and that one person's destiny can have significance for others. He then states his belief that the death of Jesus is God's own initiative, because in the event of Jesus Christ, the following conditions have been met:

- God has brought forth a human being who is God's final Word and offer;
- this Word is grasped in history and not merely in transcendental hope;
- this Word "prevails victoriously" in the person of Jesus of Nazareth, even in the history which ends with his death; and
- the human response of Jesus to the presence in him of God's Word is shown to be accepted by God by means of the resurrection.

Rahner says that, if these conditions are met, then we can say that the death of Jesus indeed reached its fulfillment in the resurrection. In it, God's desire to save human beings reached fulfillment.

This, then, is the salvific efficacy of Jesus' death. His life and death are the "cause" of God's salvific will in a sacramental sense. God's will has created the "sign" of Jesus' life and death, and through the sign God's will causes what it signifies. It causes human salvation.

Understood this way, the late soteriology of the New Testament and of the church—the soteriology of blood sacrifice—is "secondary and somewhat derivative." It derives from the original experience of the first Christian generation. Rahner expresses it this way: "We are saved because this man who is one of us has been saved by God" (p. 284). To be sure, the secondary and derivative late Christology remains legitimate. But it must be rightly understood. In Jesus, God gives the world the possibility of making satisfaction for the sins of the world.

7. The Content, Permanent Validity, and Limits of Classical Christology and Soteriology

(VI.7, p. 285). This brief part is divided into three subdivisions. In subdivision (a), Rahner lays out the theology according to which God descended from heaven and, in the form of Jesus, made satisfaction for our sins. In subdivision (b), he states that this classical theology, while permanently valid, must still be explained for people today. In subdivision (c), he argues that the greatest limit of the classical Christology and soteriology is that it may suggest that the death and resurrection of Jesus are singularities, accomplished once and for all. It is better to say that they form an event in which all humanity may participate.

(a) The Content of Classical Christology and Soteriology

(VI.7.a, p. 285). The classical Christology of the church is the topic of this subdivision. Rahner wants to show that his transcendental Christology is at least compatible with the classical Christology of the church's tradition (A). He then characterizes the classical Christology as a "descending" Christology. It starts from the premise that God "descended" from heaven and was born as a man. This Christology is of course legitimate, but it can be misunderstood as suggesting that God merely wore the disguise of humanity (B). With this descending Christology comes a soteriology of satisfaction. Jesus made "satisfaction" for our sins by dying for us (C).

A. Preliminary Remarks

(VI.7.a.A, p. 285). Rahner promises, under the next heading, to offer a brief summary of classical Christology, the Christology that he asserts is a straightforward development of the late Christology that can be found in the New Testament. He states that this classical Christology is to be measured against the original experience of the risen Jesus. Rahner assumes that the "functional" statements of New Testament Christology (e.g., Christ "gave himself for our sins," Gal. 1:4) imply "ontological" statements (e.g., Chalcedon's one person in two natures). So it is legitimate to link classical Christology and late New Testament Christology, despite their differences. "The Word became flesh" is a statement of late New Testament Christology, and it expresses the classical Christology of Nicaea, the Christology of the Father and Son as one in being.

B. The Official Christology of the Church

(VI.7.a.B, p. 286). The official Christology of the church is a "descending Christology," which Rahner described on p. 212. This descending Christology begins with the assertion that "God in his Logos became man." Implicit in this is the doctrine of the Trinity. The Logos is "born of" and "expressed by" the Father in an eternal "generation." The Logos assumed a complete human nature in a union called "hypostatic" (i.e., the natures are not mingled, but all human attributes are borne by this hypostasis or person). Although the human and divine natures exist in a single hypostasis, nevertheless the two natures differ. The subject, Jesus Christ, does not arise out of the natures and cannot be reduced to one or the other. Rather, he is the "subject" of the preexistent Logos.

Then Rahner explains some of the implications of this classical Christology. Because the natures are unmixed, he says, we have to affirm that the influence of the Logos on the human nature of Jesus is like the influence of God on other free creatures (p. 287). The human reality of Jesus is not merely an "instrument" of the Logos. Rahner cautions the reader to be wary of the heresy known as monothelitism, the heresy that there existed in Jesus Christ only one will, the will of God. The danger of this heresy is that it would make the man Jesus little more than an instrument of God. We must rather emphasize Jesus' own free will. "The created subjectivity [of Jesus] is distinct from the subjectivity of the Logos," says Rahner, "and faces God at a created distance in freedom, in obedience and in prayer, and it is not omniscient" (p. 287). Jesus had to grow in wisdom and knowledge.

How can we say that the eternal Son of God died, for example, or that Jesus of Nazareth is God? God cannot die, and a man cannot be God. We say that the Son of God died and that Jesus is God, Rahner states, by means of the doctrine of the *communicatio idiomatum*, that is, the interchange of predicates. The experience of faith requires such an exchange of predicates. The doctrine of hypostatic union defends the legitimacy of the titles of majesty applied to the New Testament Jesus. But we must reject the temptation to obscure his humanity.

C. CLASSICAL SOTERIOLOGY

(VI.7.a.C, p. 288). Since at least the time of Anselm of Canterbury, the church has taught that the obedience of the Son, confirmed in the sacrifice of the cross, "represents infinite satisfaction vis-à-vis the God who was offended by sin" (p. 288). God accepted the satisfaction of Christ on behalf of humanity. The Son's obedience satisfies God's justice and liberates us from the penalties imposed for sin. We are saved because Christ paid the price of our sins. This is the church's teaching. But it may wrongly suggest that Jesus' death was merely the propitiation of an angry God and not also a self-sacrifice in which every faithful person participates.

(b) The Legitimacy of the Classical Doctrine of Incarnation

(VI.7.b, p. 288). In this brief section, Rahner argues that the incarnation prevents Jesus from being seen as one in a line of prophets. It may blind us to Jesus' role in the context of Hebrew prophecy. To be sure, Rahner does not deny the uniqueness of the incarnation. He emphasizes that Jesus is God's own gift of self. He insists that God is not represented by someone other than and different from God. He even concedes that the classical theology of incarnation may be for some the only way of expressing the relation between Jesus and God. It has permanent validity.

But even those for whom the classical theology is the only way to express the relation between Jesus and God, even they have an obligation to explain that theology. They have to show that this classical theology is not just mythology (in the pejorative sense). They have to explain, in other words, how Jesus Christ stood in a line of prophets and must be interpreted in the context of the faith of Israel. This is, in a sense, one justification for Rahner's own theology. He is trying to widen the discourse so that it can be understood by modern humanity.

(c) The Limits of Classical Christology and Soteriology

(VI.7.c, p. 289). This subdivision criticizes classical theology for insufficiently acknowledging the solidarity that exists between human beings and the man Jesus, who leads humanity in an ascending movement to unity with God (A). Expressions that Christian usage sanctions, such as the statement that "Jesus 'is' God," must be seen as the expression of unity, a unity that is not an identity (B). The unity of God and the man Jesus should not confuse the two (C). The death and resurrection of Jesus was not a one-time anomaly in the history of the world, but an event in which we participate and thus are saved (D).

A. The Problem of Horizons of Understanding

(VI.7.c.A, p. 289). Why is the classical descending Christology inadequate? It overlooks, says Rahner, the point at which we have access to the mystery that Christology expresses. It overlooks the point that, from the outset, the incarnate Word of God takes our "cause" as God's own. The incarnate Word finds solidarity with human beings. Jesus leads us to back to God in an ascending motion, a motion initiated by God. Instead, the classical Christology concentrates one-sidedly on God's condescension.

B. The Problem of the "Is" Formulas

(VI.7.c.B, p. 290). When we say that Jesus "is" God, there is a danger that we might understand this monophysitically (and thus heretically). When we say, "Jesus is God," we exchange predicates according to the *communicatio idiomatum*. We are not identifying subject and predicate. Rather, we are asserting that there is a "unity between realities which are really different and which are at an infinite distance from each other" (p. 290). Chalcedon said that the two natures are unseparated (*adiairetos*) and unmixed (*asynchtos*). The phrase "Jesus is God" risks mixing the two. Those who have problems with the phrase "Jesus is God" are not, therefore, necessarily heterodox.

The Christological statements are legitimate and permanently valid, but they suggest a false identity, a monophysitism. The really Christian sense of the statement, "Jesus is God," is that the two realities are united but different and at an infinite distance from each other. We need to broaden, Rahner says, the ways we express this ancient doctrine.

C. The Indetermination of the Point of Unity in the Hypostatic Union

(VI.7.c.C, p. 292). Traditional Christology leaves "very formal and indetermined" the unity of the human and the divine, as well as the unity of the divine persons, in the hypostatic union. If we use the term *person*, we risk confusing people. The word *person* may falsely suggest that the Logos identifies the human nature with the divine nature. Someone might mistakenly infer that there is only one nature and only one will. It is important to realize, says Rahner, that the man Jesus is absolutely different from God. And whether we speak of "hypostatic union" or of "person," we overlook the salvific meaning of the incarnation if we think that Jesus was really God in the disguise of a human being. The salvific meaning, according to Rahner, is this: "We are saved because this man who is one of us has been saved by God" (p. 284).

D. Inadequate Expression of the Soteriological Significance
  of the Christ Event

(VI.7.c.D, p. 292). Classical Christology, with its assertion that all are saved in Christ, creates problems for individualistic Westerners. The idea that the whole of humanity is "assumed"—lifted up and recapitulated in the individual reality of Jesus—often strikes the Western mentality as foreign. Rahner wants to express the idea that Jesus Christ himself *is* a salvific event, not just one who performs redemptive activity. How can we convey the truth that, in Jesus, the salvific destiny of all humanity was achieved for the first time? If we could express this, then we could more easily avoid the impression that Jesus is one in *nature* with the Father.

8. On the Question of New Approaches to Orthodox Christology

(VI.8, p. 293). In this part, Rahner aims to expand what he said in chapter VI, part 3, on transcendental Christology. In subdivision (a), he begins by showing that the insight of fundamental theology—namely, that every person of good will is moving within God's grace—has consequences for dogmatic theology. The "grace of God" by which one responds to God's invitation is none other than the grace of Christ. Then, in subdivision (b), Rahner shows what his "Christology from below" or "ascending Christology" entails. It portrays the man Jesus as the one in whom God intended from all eternity to reconcile human beings. Their free and responsible acceptance of God's invitation to respond to life's possibilities is made in the hope that God will affirm them as God affirmed Jesus. And in subdivision (c), Rahner treats some of the difficulties of his ascending Christology, such as the consciousness of Jesus regarding his identity, the preexistence of the Word in Jesus, and the propriety of speaking of the death of God.

(a) The Need for Closer Unity between Fundamental Theology
and Dogmatic Theology in Christology

(VI.8.a, p. 294). The first rule of Rahner's "new approach" to orthodox Christology is to acknowledge that every person of "morally good will" is living by grace. Even if the faith of baptized Christians is not a refined faith, still it is a faith to which they are (at least implicitly) committed (A). Every person who seeks, in transcendental grace, to realize the possibilities that God has given, is living out a "searching" Christology (B). God is making an appeal: an appeal, first of all, through the experience of love of neighbor, a love that expresses an implicit of Christ (C). God also appeals to human beings when they are faced with death, and so confronted with the ground of existence (D). Finally, God makes an appeal through our hope, a hope for a future that transcends our present (E).

A. PRIORITY OF THE LIVED ACTUALIZATION OF EXISTENCE TO REFLECTION UPON IT

(VI.8.a.A, p. 294). As a first step in establishing closer relations between fundamental and dogmatic theology, Rahner acknowledges their basic assumptions. Both fundamental and dogmatic theology assume, whenever they try to give an account of the faith to non-Christians, that the non-Christian is a person of morally good will. Such a person of good will exists "in the interior grace of God and in Christ," says Rahner (p. 294). The grace of God expresses itself in the person's natural goodness, and the word of God that the morally good person hears is none other than the Word made flesh.

Christians may and must accept the Christology they are already living out, even if it is not a very refined faith, for it is the Christology to which they are implicitly committed. The Christian may understand faith as no more than "one abstract and conceivable possibility among others," but that is (in Rahner's view) enough. Even with that minimal understanding, the Christian is still grasped by the claim of Jesus. The Christian has been grasped in faith. Such a grasp is more important, says Rahner, than a merely scientific reflection.

B. APPEALS IN A "SEARCHING CHRISTOLOGY"

(VI.8.a.B, p. 295). Fundamental theology appeals to a global under-standing of existence that is "Christian" because of an "antecedent grace." Rahner asserts that every person is living out at least a "searching Christol-ogy" if that person accepts his or her existence "resolutely." This means that the person is seeking, in a transcendental hope, for the possibilities that God has offered. These are the possibilities that the Christian recognizes in Jesus of Nazareth. There are three "ways" or "appeals" which God makes to human beings. Rahner describes them under the next three headings.

C. THE APPEAL TO AN ABSOLUTE LOVE OF NEIGHBOR

(VI.8.a.C, p. 295). The statement of Jesus, "Whatsoever you do to the least of my brothers, so you do to me," must be rightly interpreted. "An absolute love that gives itself radically and unconditionally to another per-son," says Rahner, "affirms Christ implicitly in faith and love" (p. 296). Whenever we truly love another, we are in a situation of faith. But does this mean that any given human love can be called "absolute"? Of course not.

Love of neighbor, even the love of neighbor demanded by God's law, differs from love of God.

In the love of neighbor, God makes a transcendental appeal. God is inviting the human being to seek someone who can be loved with absoluteness, the absoluteness with which the Christian loves God. So fundamental theology tries to show that our love for another human being expresses an implicit love and faith in Christ. Human love expresses a response to God's invitation, the invitation to realize the possibilities that God has given. God invites us to enter into a relationship of love with God's own self. By doing so, we realize the possibility of becoming one with God.

D. The Appeal to Readiness for Death

(VI.8.a.D, p. 296). The way the average sermon treats Christ's death is inadequate, says Rahner. It usually regards the crucifixion "as an external and meritorious cause of redemption." By contrast, Rahner proposes a theology of death. This theology of death connects the death of Jesus to human existence. It acknowledges that, in death, we are radically powerless. By acknowledging this powerlessness, we also acknowledge the ground of all reality, namely, the holy mystery of God. God both gives the possibility of transcendence and invites us to surrender ourselves to the divine self. When we surrender ourselves to the divine self in death, we surrender ourselves to the ground of our being. In the fact of death, God appeals to us to acknowledge our source and our goal.

E. The Appeal to Hope in the Future

(VI.8.a.E, p. 297). Genuine hope is not the longing for an eternally distant and sought-after (but unrealizable) goal. It is not, Rahner seems to suggest, the longing for a mythical heaven that is merely the prolongation of our earthly life. Nor is it the longing for something that has not yet come. The goal of Christian life is not one that abolishes us and absorbs us into God's absoluteness.

Hope is rather the desire for an attainable goal. It is a longing for something that, while the goal itself is in progress, has already left its mark on history. The goal of human life can be seen in our history, says Rahner, a history already moving within its goal. So whenever we hope in the future, God is appealing to us. God invites us to see in our future a life that transcends our present life, a life to which there is already a reliable testimony.

(b) The Task of a "Christology from Below"

(VI.8.b, p. 298). Christology from below, Rahner's so-called ascending Christology, is the topic of this subdivision. Rahner starts with the concept of the supernatural existential. It expresses the capacity of every human to hear God's invitation, and so to hope for a future in God's Word, in the "absolute savior" (A). The event of the absolute savior becomes an "eschatological event" for us when we accept God's offer to respond freely and responsibly to life (B). A Christology from below must show how, in the incarnation, God has committed the divine self to a definite and historical Word; humanity finds in Jesus the one by whom God intended from all eternity to reconcile us to the divine self (C). This theology is perfectly compatible, Rahner says, with a theology of eternal, divine Sonship. Human beings find in the man Jesus the self-expression of God in its eternal possibility (D).

A. Man as a Being Oriented toward Immediacy to God

(VI.8.b.A, p. 298). The human being has a "natural" desire for the beatific vision. Rahner explains this by referring to his discussion of the supernatural existential (pp. 126ff.). The supernatural existential is a grace or gift of God, and so is supernatural. But it is also an existential, which means that it belongs to the basic ontological constitution of every person. The basic orientation toward God manifests itself in everyday life, in the realm of what Rahner calls history. It does so in our free choice to respond or not respond to God's Word. And so Rahner says that God "actualizes" the human being's basic orientation toward God.

B. The Unity between the Eschatological Event of Salvation and the Absolute Savior

(VI.8.b.B, p. 298). The human being experiences himself or herself as a person oriented to God in an event. It is the absolute event of salvation, none other than the event of what Rahner calls the "absolute savior." It is the event of God's self-communication. In this event, we see ourselves affirmed by God, affirmed in God's offer to us of the divine self, an offer we accept. It is a "historical" event, and distinct from the mere offer of transcendence. Why? Because the mere offer of transcendence, Rahner says, cannot be of final validity. The eschatological event of salvation is made effective when God's offer is accepted.

The event of salvation is not the fulfillment of the human race in the immediacy of the beatific vision. That fulfillment comes much later, Rahner says, at the "end of time." The event of salvation instead takes place in time. It comes as people accept God's offer of the divine self. Although the event occurs "in time," says Rahner, it is irreversible. God has offered the divine self, and that offer cannot be retracted. To be sure, the future of each individual remains open. Individuals can reject God's offer. But the offer has begun a dynamism in history that is God's own.

When Rahner asserts that humanity experiences its basic orientation to God in the event of salvation, he refers specifically to Jesus Christ. The assertion presupposes two things about Jesus himself. First, it presupposes that Jesus understood himself as the absolute savior. Second, it presupposes that Jesus did in fact reach "historical fulfillment" as the mediator of salvation. Under the next heading, Rahner explores what these presuppositions mean.

C. The Connection between this Reflection and the Church's Doctrine of Incarnation

(VI.8.b.C, p. 299). Rahner begins by explaining two terms, "absolute event of salvation" and "absolute mediation of salvation by a man." He says that these two terms mean what the church expresses in the doctrines of incarnation and hypostatic union. The "absolute event" is the incarnation. The "absolute mediation" is the hypostatic union. The term "absolute" means complete and unsurpassable.

Rahner then goes on to say what he means by revelation. It is a free act of God—an act that has its origin in God. By calling it a free act, Rahner suggests that revelation is more than the "facts of revelation" conveyed in the Bible. Revelation exists, he says, within an infinite realm of possibilities. Therefore every revelatory event "is always surpassable and conditional, and exists with the qualification that something new might happen" (p. 300). In other words, what the church acknowledges as revelation is not the sum of revelation. Within God's providence, there is the possibility of something more.

But the incarnation, Rahner says, is not a surpassable event. Although the history of salvation is by no means finished, the event of Jesus Christ is absolute and eschatological. Why? Because it is not merely an event that has its origin in God. No, the incarnation is the gift of God's own self. It is not merely an event in history, but is rather God's own history. About the incarnation, Rahner says, "God must live out its history as his own history and retain it permanently" (p. 301). In short, the incarnation has "determined" God once and for all.

From a human point of view, the incarnation means our salvation. It means that the man Jesus of Nazareth, who preached the kingdom and died in obedience to God's will, showed himself to be the one whose life and words were affirmed by God. When we encounter this man, we realize that the transcendental offer of God was, at least in Jesus, fully accepted. Further, we realize that we can also hear God's offer and respond to it as Jesus did. This "Christology from below," says Rahner, is at one with the classical Christology of the church. The man Jesus is none other than the one by whom God intended from all eternity to reconcile us to the divine self.

D. ON THE RELATIONSHIP BETWEEN ASCENDING CHRISTOLOGY AND THE QUESTION OF ETERNAL, DIVINE SONSHIP

(VI.8.b.D, p. 301). Rahner tells us that his ascending Christology is able to reach a Christology of eternal and divine Sonship. In other words, there is no contradiction between the two Christologies. Rahnerian ascending Christology begins with the humanity of Jesus. In the man Jesus of Nazareth, God affirmed the complete and unsurpassable response to the divine self-communication. Jesus, who enjoyed a hypostatic union with the divine Word, mediates salvation in a complete and unsurpassable way.

Undoubtedly, says Rahner, we probably would not derive the Christology of divine Sonship by ourselves. It would be inexplicable without the biblical record, especially the first chapter of the Gospel of John. But the classical Son Christology, says Rahner, is contained in the absolute-savior Christology he has outlined.

How is the high Christology of eternal Sonship contained in the ascending Christology that begins with Jesus of Nazareth? We find it there, says Rahner, because we experience the self-expression of God in history. We experience it in a human being, in Jesus. Once we experience God's self-communication in a concrete human being, we also experience the self-expression of God in its eternal possibility. We can suppose that a Son- and Logos-Christology are implied in the notion of an absolute savior. They are not added as something extra. If in the man Jesus of Nazareth, we meet one whose life and death were affirmed by God, then we can suppose that this man's life and history were intended by God from all eternity. Further, we can suppose that we, like Jesus, can also respond to God's offer.

(c) Specific Dogmatic Problems

(VI.8.c, p. 302). This subdivision takes up three problems. The first is that of the "consciousness Christology," which Rahner says is a quite legitimate way of talking about the unity between the self-consciousness of Jesus and his very being as one with the Father (A). The second problem is that of the "preexistence" of the eternal Word and the compatibility between it and the finitude of Jesus. Rahner's solution is to say that the preexistent God is wholly present in the man Jesus (B). The third problem is that of the "death of God." The death of Jesus, Rahner says, is essential to what God wants to be. In death, we encounter the fate of Jesus, who was one with God (C).

A. THE POSSIBILITY OF AN ORTHODOX "CONSCIOUSNESS CHRISTOLOGY"

(VI.8.c.A, p. 302). An orthodox consciousness Christology (in contrast to a heretical consciousness Christology, p. 178) would mean that we understand Jesus as having a consciousness of oneness with the Father. In his being and his consciousness he understood his origins to be in God. Jesus was one, Rahner says, who "accepts himself from the Father and who in all of the dimensions of his existence has always given himself over to the Father totally; in this surrender he is able to accomplish due to God what we are not able to accomplish" (p. 303). His consciousness of the Father did not evolve or come to him gradually. From his earliest years, Jesus knew himself to be one with the Father.

The heretical consciousness Christology of the early twentieth century, says Rahner, was "a kind of modern edition of the Nestorian 'trial and probation' Christology" (p. 302). Nestorius believed that the man Jesus became the Christ by overcoming trials of strength and by proving himself. It held that Jesus' especially intense trust in God is all that is meant by Christology. Today we would call it a form of rationalism.

Classical Christology, by contrast, is an "ontic" Christology of nature and hypostasis. This ontic Christology can be quite properly combined, Rahner says, with an "ontological" Christology. An ontological Christology insists upon the identity in Christ of being and consciousness. It reaffirms the insight of Thomism that being and consciousness are the same thing. Rahner summarizes it this way: to the degree that Jesus was "present to himself" in knowledge and freedom, he opened himself to the whole of reality, especially to his oneness with the Father.

B. THE PROBLEM OF PREEXISTENCE

(VI.8.c.B, p. 304). Some people question whether orthodox Christology needs a preexistent Christ. Not Rahner. He says that if Jesus is the absolute offer of God's own self, "Then the one who expresses himself and offers himself, namely God, is 'pre-existent'" (p. 304). The preexistent God is wholly present in the man Jesus. What remains to be explored, however, is the title "Son of the Father." When Jesus uses this title, does "Son of the Father" simply mean that he is identical with God? This is a problem for biblical exegetes. The ordinary believer, however, need not doubt the preexistence of the Word who expresses the divine self in Jesus.

C. THE DISCUSSION OF THE DEATH OF GOD

(VI.8.c.C, p. 305). Rahner then turns to the death of God's Son on a cross. In light of Rahner's discussion of the *communicatio idiomatum* (p. 290), we can understand how death can be predicated of God. It is a predication of unity (God "tasted" death), not of identity (God was dead). But Rahner does not want his readers to dismiss the language of the death of the Son. "If someone says that the incarnate Logos 'merely' died in his human reality," says Rahner, "and implicitly understands this to mean that this death did not touch God, he has only said half of the truth and has left out the really Christian truth" (p. 305). In Jesus' life, including his death on the cross, we find God's own destiny.

Just as Jesus' life expressed who God is, Rahner states, so Jesus' death expressed God as God is and wants to be in relation to us. We can speak of a "death of God," really and truly, "in his [God's] being and in his becoming in the other [i.e., Jesus] of the world" (p. 305). Hence we share the destiny of God in the world. We "know" and "have" God by encountering God in the experience of death. It is the experience where God meets us in a radical way. So Rahner says, "The death of Jesus belongs to God's self-expression."

9. The Personal Relation of a Christian to Jesus Christ

(VI.9, p. 305). Part 9 probes the concrete life of the Christian believer. The Christian is always in the process of becoming a Christian, Rahner says, a process that takes place not primarily by intellectual reflection but by responding to God's invitation (A). The Christian's relation to Jesus Christ is identical with his or her life-work and destiny, that is, the way one accepts God's offer of life and lives it freely and responsibly (B). In the way we respond to one another, we express our relation to God's Word and to the Father himself (C). God intends us to love, not in the abstract, but in the concrete. When we love one another, we express what God wants, namely, the human love for God (D). When we make choices, when we commit ourselves to this or that, we are committing ourselves to a direction in life. We commit ourselves to the fate that we hope God will affirm at the moment of our death (E).

A. THE NEED FOR AN "EXISTENTIELL" CHRISTOLOGY

(VI.9.A, p. 305). "A person is always a Christian in order to become one," says Rahner. He means that the Christianity we know, even in our Baptism as children and also in the kind of "social Christianity" we experience in family and community, is a Christianity we still need to appropriate as our own throughout our entire lives. This is the meaning of "existentiell." When we appropriate the faith as our own, we realize it, we make it real, we bring it to actualization, and it becomes "existentiell."

An existentiell Christology is not, however, a Christology that necessarily comes to full reflection and expression. Even an anonymous Christian can have an existentiell (i.e., a real, deeply held, and fully-embodied) Christology insofar as that person obeys an orientation in grace toward God. An existentiell Christology is an expression of Christian existence, an entrusting of oneself to the development of a personal relationship with Jesus Christ.

B. INDIVIDUAL, CONCRETE RELATIONSHIP TO JESUS CHRIST

(VI.9.B, p. 307). In each individual, even in those who do not know Jesus Christ, there is at least a possible relationship to him. This relationship is identical with each person's life work and destiny. Whenever an individual entrusts him- or herself to God, a relationship develops. In this relationship, the individual does not entrust an abstract human nature, but rather his or her own self. This is the self for which each human being is responsible. For the non-Christian, the relationship to Jesus Christ will not be personal and intimate. But the God to whom human beings entrust themselves is the very one who has first turned to them concretely in Jesus Christ.

C. A THEO-LOGICAL REFLECTION

(VI.9.C, p. 308). Viewed from the standpoint of a theology from above, Jesus Christ is the icon of the Father. When we treat another person with kindness, we are expressing our relation to Jesus Christ and thus to the Father. From the standpoint of a theology from below, our relationship to Jesus makes our every interaction with another person salvific. Jesus Christ is not only the eternal Logos, but also the "first fulfillment" of humanity. He was the first to fulfill the promise which life with God holds for every person.

D. THE UNITY BETWEEN THE LOVE OF GOD
AND CONCRETE LOVE OF NATURE

(VI.9.D, p. 309). Love for our neighbor is the actualization of Christian existence. In love of neighbor, we express our acceptance of God as the neighbor's ground and the neighbor's ultimately mysterious partner. Love wants to be faithful, and love in the human being actualizes a spiritual existence. This is the existence that is taken up into eternal life by means of one's death. Death is thus a fulfillment, not a conclusion. When we love our neighbor, we are loving in the way God deserves to be loved, namely, loving in the concrete.

E. THE RISK OF ENCOUNTER

(VI.9.E, p. 310). One has to take a risk in order to encounter Jesus personally. This is the risk of finding whether, when he or she speaks the name of Jesus, the person means only an abstract idea of an infinite God. The

Christian life is not about satisfying universal norms, but rather about discipleship and participation. These initiate us into Jesus' death and resurrection.

10. Jesus Christ in Non-Christian Religions

(VI.10, p. 311). Jesus is limited in time and space, Rahner says. Non-Christians find it scandalous when Christians claim that Jesus has universal salvific significance for all times and peoples. Rahner takes up this question from the view of dogmatic theology. He asks how the Christian theologian (rather than the historian of religion) is to understand the significance of Jesus Christ for all people (A). He presupposes God's salvific will for all people and the positive role played by non-Christian religions (B). Making his question narrower, Rahner then asks how Christ is "present" in the faith of non-Christians (C). Christ is present through his Spirit, the very Spirit who was the "efficient cause" of Christ's incarnation and cross, so that Christ himself might be the "final cause" of God's self-communication to humanity. Just as the two causes are united, so the explicit Christology of Christians is united with the implicit Christology of the non-Christian responding to God's transcendental call (D). All humanity, insofar as it seeks an absolute savior, embodies a searching Christology (E). This is a search for the memory of God's word. People have encountered this word in the many "saviors" sought and found throughout human history. All of these memories express a hunger for the absolute savior we encounter in Jesus Christ (F).

A. THE QUESTION WITHIN THE LIMITS OF A DOGMATIC REFLECTION

(VI.10.A, p. 312). A history of religion looks at Jesus Christ in an "a posteriori" fashion—namely, from the viewpoint of history. In that history, Jesus Christ is not the only religious figure of universal significance. The Christian dogmatic theologian, by contrast, looks at Jesus Christ in an "a priori" fashion. The dogmatic theologian looks from the viewpoint of those binding sources of faith (the Old Testament and the New Testament) that arose without immediate contact with most non-Christian religions. Such a dogmatic theologian begins with the testimony of Christ's universal significance.

Given this significance, it is a fair question to ask how Christ is salvific for all. In asking this question, the Christian presupposes that non-Christians are people of good will. Their own religious beliefs testify to their good will, and God's Word may be at work in those beliefs themselves. If Christ has significance for the entire history of salvation, says the Christian, then his significance must have a place where human beings have an explicitly religious, but non-Christian, faith.

B. Two Presuppositions

(VI.10.B, p. 313). In order to describe the role of Christ in non-Christian religions from a dogmatic theological standpoint, Rahner presupposes two things. First, God has a universal and salvific will that is present in the world. One sees a testimony to this universal and salvific will in the Letter to the Hebrews. Rahner treated this point in chapter V (p. 153ff.). There he speaks of the possibility of a genuine history of revelation outside the Old Testament and the New Testament. Here he speaks of the elevation of human transcendental experience in grace. He says that this elevated transcendental experience, along with the supernatural object of that experience, are indeed supernatural revelation.

But does the notion of transcendental revelation as it may exist among non-Christians actually "reach" Christ? Rahner asks that question here. If the non-Christian's experience does not reach Christ, then his or her faith lacks a Christological character. But if it does reach Christ, if it does have a Christological character, then non-Christian religions may well have a positive significance, even for Christians. That is Rahner's first presupposition.

The second presupposition is that, when a non-Christian attains salvation in faith, hope, and love, then the non-Christian religion plays a role in his or her justification and salvation. If this were not the case, if the non-Christian religion had no significance, then we would be guilty of viewing salvation in an a-historical and a-social way. To postulate special revelations (e.g., a special vision of Christ conceded to the non-Christian) is arbitrary and improbable. The human being is social, and his or her decisions are mediated by social and historical life. The decision to respond to God's call to transcendence must be mediated by the non-Christian religion.

Dei Verbum 3 (Vatican II's Constitution on Revelation) passes over the interval between Adam and Moses "too quickly," says Rahner. He suggests that the religions of this vast and ancient period kept alive "man's relationship to the mystery of existence" (p. 315). To be sure, the ancient religions may have kept alive the transcendental relationship in an incomplete and possibly depraved way. But they did play a role in the history of salvation. We cannot do justice to these ancient religions, for we do not know much about them. But we may suppose that they have had a positive function.

C. Christ and Non-Christian Religions

(VI.10.C, p. 315). The two presuppositions—namely, that of God's salvific will and that of the positive role played by non-Christian religions—

prepare the way for Rahner's next question. How, he asks, is Christ present in non-Christian religions from the viewpoint of dogmatic theology? How is Jesus Christ operative in the faith of individual non-Christians? To that question, says Rahner, he will confine himself. A broader question, how Christ is present in the religions themselves, is a topic for historians of religion.

D. THE PRESENCE OF CHRIST IN THE HOLY SPIRIT

(VI.10.D, p. 316). Rahner begins this highly compressed section by asserting his thesis. It is that Christ is present in non-Christian believers by means of his Spirit. Even traditional dogmatic theology would affirm that the Spirit of grace and justification, present in the non-Christian, is the Spirit of Jesus Christ, the Spirit who proceeds from the Father and the Son. This Spirit is present, according to Christian tradition, "in view of the merits of Christ" (p. 316).

Then Rahner proceeds to point out the two difficulties that this thesis entails. First, he says, the whole question of Christ's merits can be misinterpreted. People can mistakenly believe that Christ's death changed the supposedly immutable will of God.

Second, there is even a problem when one retreats from the theory that Christ's death "influenced" God. The supposedly easier claim is that the sufferings of Christ are connected with the grace of the Spirit, as in our prayers of petition. We say that the prayer of petition does not "cause" God to hear us, but is rather "the moral cause of the reality which is given by God in hearing it" (p. 317). In other words, God "hears" us by creating humanity capable of petitioning God. This is problematic, because the moral cause (our prayer) is later than the effect (God's creation of a humanity able to pray). To sum up, our prayer comes after God has created a world in which creatures communicate with God. Who would pray for a reality, Rahner asks, that has already taken place?

After laying out the two difficulties, Rahner answers them. He says that incarnation and cross are the "final cause" of God's self-communication. They are the final cause of what we name the Spirit, the Spirit that proceeds from Father and Son. Incarnation and cross are "causes" (see p. 283) in the sense that they have as their goal or entelechy the communication of Spirit. In the incarnation and the cross, the communication of the Spirit becomes tangible and irreversible. So the event of Christ is the final cause of the communication of Spirit, the Spirit of Jesus Christ. This Spirit is intrinsically related to Christ. Their intrinsic relation must be distinguished from extrinsic relations, as if Christ were not essential, as if the relation were merely an intention of God that transcends the world and history. Because of Christ, we know the Spirit of Christ.

Of course, says Rahner, the opposite is also true. Spirit is the *efficient* cause of incarnation and cross. God's Spirit moved Jesus' entire life. The Spirit of the Lord was upon him. Final and efficient causes are united if distinguishable. The justifying faith brought by the Spirit (as *efficient* cause) comes to be in the Spirit of Jesus Christ (the *final* cause). By means of his Spirit, Christ sanctifies and justifies people of all faiths.

E. THE SEARCHING "MEMORY" OF ALL FAITH IS DIRECTED TOWARD THE ABSOLUTE SAVIOR

(VI.10.E, p. 318). The faith of all religions, insofar as it is a faith brought by the Spirit of God, is a justifying faith. It justifies in that it enables the believer to participate in the justice to which God invites everyone. This justifying faith, says Rahner, is "the searching memory of the absolute savior" (p. 318). It is a searching memory in the sense of the Platonic *anamnesis* or the Augustinian *memoria*. Although the non-Christian cannot be said to explicitly remember Jesus Christ, he or she has had a transcendental experience of hearing God's Word and responding to it. So the inexplicit memory of every person who has responded to God's transcendental call is a memory of God's Word, a memory of the absolute savior, Jesus Christ.

What does it mean to call this memory a "searching" memory? Rahner answers in this way: "We can find and retain something which encounters man in history only if there is present in the finding and retaining subjectivity of man an a priori principle of expectation, of searching, of hoping" (p. 319). It is memory because it causes us to *expect* something. We have been given reason to expect that the God who calls us may have called another who responded to God's call in the fullest possible way.

Rahner develops this in yet another way. He says that there is something in the structure of history itself that enables people to realize that their free decisions shape history. In their decisions, they move the course of history from a contemplation of mere possibilities to the actualization of something final and definitive. The structure of history invites us to search history for an event in which salvation has become tangible. What memory anticipates is the absolute savior.

F. THE QUESTION ABOUT THE CONCRETE HISTORY OF RELIGION

(VI.10.F, p. 321). Can we demonstrate the existence of a "searching memory" in mythology or history? This is a question for the historian of religion. The historian can show how humanity's searching memory for an absolute savior has been projected on historical figures (for example, the "divine" Caesars or Alexander the Great), who are then acknowledged as saviors. Dogmatic theology can recognize that human beings in their search for an absolute savior create such savior figures.

· VII ·

Christianity as Church

In this, the second longest chapter, Rahner shows that the church belongs inextricably with Christianity itself. Part 1 explains that the church is not the primary truth of Christianity, but still fundamental. Part 2 of the chapter explains what it means to say that the church was founded by Jesus Christ. Jesus did not personally authorize all the explicit features of later Christianity, but he gave them to the church as possibilities. Part 3 shows the relation between the church and the New Testament. Rahner synthesizes the various New Testament portraits of the church, showing the church as a structure, as a college of various local churches, and as a unity in Christ. In part 4, Rahner outlines what he calls the "fundamentals of the ecclesial nature of Christianity." The Christian church can be said to be autonomous and a divine law unto itself. For that reason, it belongs to the necessary historical and social mediation of salvation. Part 5 offers, in twenty-four pages, an "indirect" method for showing the legitimacy of the Catholic Church. Rahner begins the method by offering three "norms" for authentic Christianity: it has existed from the beginning until Reformation times; it expresses itself in a concrete form compatible with the gospel; and it operates in an authoritative way independent of the believer. These norms undergird Catholic Christianity. In part 6, Rahner argues that the formation of the scripture is a "fundamental moment" in Christian tradition, but not a separate source of truth alongside of tradition. Part 7 defines the church's teaching office. It helps the church to persevere in the truth. It does so by confronting Christians with the challenging demand of Christ to believe, that is, to enter into a living relationship with God. Part 8 suggests that ecclesial life is necessary but limited. Just as we are bound to our families, even in recognizing their limitations, says Rahner, so we are bound to the church.

1. Introduction

(VII.1, p. 322). In this first part, Rahner claims that the ecclesial aspect of Christianity is not an adjunct to personal faith in Jesus Christ. No, faith

117

concerns the whole human person, whose nature is interpersonal. The ecclesial nature of the church corresponds to the interpersonal nature of human beings (A). The ecclesial dimension is not, however, the primary dimension of Christianity. There is a hierarchy of truths, and ecclesial consciousness is subordinate to higher truths (B). Rahner explains that he does not intend to offer a full justification for believing that Catholic Christianity is the one church intended by Christ. Instead, he wants to show why Catholic Christians may confidently trust in the church handed down to them.

A. The Necessary Institutional Mediation of Religion and Its Special Nature in Christianity

(VII.1.A, p. 322). What is the church? Rahner calls it "The historical continuation of Christ in and through the community of those who believe in him, and who recognize him explicitly as the mediator of salvation in a profession of faith" (p. 322). Then he makes three initial observations.

First, Rahner acknowledges that the period since Jesus can be called "the period of the church," because after Jesus the hope of humanity acquired a new and eschatological character. But then he qualifies his observation, perhaps out of fear of sounding triumphalistic. He insists that even the period before Jesus was "encompassed by God's salvific will" (p. 322). The self-communication of God predated the church.

Second, he remarks that the Christian understanding of religion is necessarily ecclesial. Human beings, he says, are "co-determined" by interpersonal communication. Such communication belongs to the church as well, for religion concerns the whole of human existence, even the interpersonal.

Finally, he notes that many thinkers in the nineteenth century lost sight of this "institutional" aspect of the church. They thought they could appropriate religion in a private kind of interiority. But today we acknowledge that an individual cannot discover personhood by looking for it as something contrary to his or her social nature. Human beings live an interpersonal life.

B. The Doctrine of the Church Is Not the Central Truth of Christianity

(VII.1.B, p. 324). One could easily find in the Catholicism of recent centuries a kind of "militant ecclesiality" which expressed an extreme reaction against individualism. This extremism proclaimed that belonging to the church is "the most specific and central thing about Christianity" (p. 324). Rahner rejects this view. He notes that many dimensions of Christianity—such as the Sermon on the Mount, love, and the freedom of the spirit—might be considered "suspect" in such a militantly ecclesial climate.

Against this militancy, Rahner (quoting the Vatican II Decree on Ecumenism, no. 11) reminds readers of the doctrine of the hierarchy of truths. There are many truths in Christianity, and not all of them are equally foundational. The doctrine of God, for example, is more fundamental than ecclesial consciousness.

C. THE DIFFICULT QUESTION ABOUT THE CHURCH

(VII.1.C, p. 324). The difficult question is, "Why [do] we believe that our concrete church is *the* church of Jesus Christ"? (p. 324). It would be difficult to answer this question, says Rahner, so as to do full justice to the traditional assertions about the church in Catholic theology. To answer the question fully, one would have to (1) analyze the treatment in Matthew 16 of the apostolic office, and (2) show why an episcopacy with apostolic succession belongs to the church which Christ intended. Rahner says that such an answer is beyond the scope of *Foundations*.

His intention is rather to reflect, as a Catholic Christian, upon his membership in the church. He wants to show that he and other Christians have no reason to cast doubt on the church handed down to them in their existentiell situation.

2. The Church as Founded by Jesus Christ

(VII.2, p. 326). In this second part of chapter VII, Rahner raises his fundamental, pastoral question: with what right can a Catholic Christian confidently assert that his or her church is the church intended by Jesus Christ? The issue is not whether Jesus intended a church, but rather what features he intended (A). In order to answer this question, Rahner lays out three minimal presuppositions: Jesus proclaimed a historical event (i.e., the kingdom of God); he drove a wedge between his followers and the Jews; and he foresaw his death (B). The major difficulty is proving that Jesus intended a church, because the church cannot establish a relation to Jesus on its own (C). In order to resolve the difficulty, Rahner lays out some basic principles, the first of which is that Jesus intended God's Word to remain as a permanent presence in the world (D). Next, he applies his principles to the question of continuity. We do not have to show that Jesus authorized all the explicit features of later Christianity, but only that they were possibilities given by Jesus (E). Finally, Rahner lists the four concrete historical acts by which Jesus can be said to have founded the church, namely, his gathering of disciples, his teachings which they maintained, the power he bestowed on them to continue his work, and the position he granted Simon Peter (F).

A. THE QUESTION

(VII.2.A, p. 326). "Is *my* church the church intended by Jesus Christ?" The question is fundamental, says Rahner, because it focuses on the connection between Jesus Christ and the church. Rahner rejects the nineteenth-century view that the church is merely a spiritual community without an institutional dimension. Anyone who advocates the unity of the churches, he says, must reject that view.

But Rahner is not opposed to at least entertaining the question of whether Jesus, with his imminent expectation of the kingdom in a temporal sense, intended to found a church. He allows the question but answers it by expressing what he takes to be a scholarly consensus. Most scholars recognize, he says, that "something like the constitution of the church is found soon after Easter" (p. 327). The disciples continued to gather and developed a public ministry.

The fundamental debate is not *whether* a church was intended, but rather *what* features belong to it. Did Jesus intend the primacy of Peter, the role of the Twelve, and the apostolic succession? In addition, there is a still more essential question: was there, in New Testament times, one church among the many which could claim to be *the* church intended by Christ?

B. PRESUPPOSITIONS FOR THE "FOUNDING OF THE CHURCH" BY JESUS

(VII.2.B, p. 327). In order to contend that Jesus founded the church, Rahner insists upon three presuppositions:

The first is that Jesus did not intend to teach universal religious ideas so much as he meant to proclaim a historical event. The event was the breaking-in of God's kingdom. It had been achieved in his person.

The second was that his teaching drove a wedge between his followers and the Jews. Why? Because he offered salvation to everyone, not just to his own ethnic group or to an isolated sect (like the Essenes).

The third was that Jesus foresaw his own death. He also foresaw that, through his death, the closeness of God's kingdom would reach a victorious fulfillment. Moreover, he foresaw that there would be a period of time between his death and the arrival of God's kingdom. During that period, faithful Christians would have to wait.

Unless one accepts these minimal presuppositions, one must believe that Jesus acted unreasonably up to and during his passion. It would have been unreasonable for him to believe that he could teach universal ideas without dying, that he did not have to proclaim salvation to all, and that there was no need to promise the kingdom. The fact that Jesus taught, proclaimed, and promised what he did is evidence that he intended a church.

C. The Thesis and Its Problem

(VII.2.C, p. 328). The meaning of the thesis "Jesus founded the church" is that the church has its origins in Christ. The church does not establish a relation to Jesus "autonomously and by itself." Rather, the establishment of the church is "an act of Jesus and not primarily an act of the church itself" (p. 329).

Rahner concludes this short article with a series of questions: could Jesus have intended that his narrow circle of disciples "would ever continue with essentially the same function in what we see in the church later as bishops?" (p. 329). Could Jesus foresee a juridical organization? Could he foresee the privileged position he bestowed on Cephas as a permanent institution? In this section, Rahner provides no answer—but he does in article E (below).

D. The Attempt to Respond: The Principles Involved

(VII.2.D, p. 329). Rahner wants to clarify the sense in which one can say that Jesus "founded" the church. In order to do so, he lays out some basic principles, principles that lead to a minimal but affirmative assertion.

First, he says that Jesus, as absolute savior and God's self-communication, intended God's Word to be a permanent presence in the world. Jesus would not have been who he is "if the offer of himself which God made in him did not continue to remain present in the world in an historically tangible profession of faith in Jesus" (pp. 329-30). Insofar as faith in God's self-communication has its origins in Jesus, the church has its origins in him.

Second, the faith of the church is a public profession. It is the faith of a community. Since faith is communal and has its origin in Jesus, the church has its origin in him.

Third, the faith that forms community must have a history and be part of salvation history. In this history, every later epoch continues to have its origin in an earlier epoch, even when it diverges from it. "In order that a historical decision in one epoch be binding for later epochs for the sake of preserving historical continuity, all that can be seriously required is that this decision lay *within* the genuine possibilities of the church's origins and does not contradict these origins" (p. 331). The church belongs to the basic history of Christian faith.

E. Application to the Problem of Continuity between Jesus and the Church

(VII.2.E, p. 331). Having accepted the principles articulated by Rahner in the previous article (namely, the principles of the believers' faith, of their public profession, and of the nature of historical continuity), one can then draw important consequences.

First, we can assert that the church was founded by Christ if we can say that later decisions of the church, now termed "binding," were at least possibilities given through Jesus.

Second, we do not need (according to Rahner's method) to trace back to the sayings of Jesus concrete structures such as a permanent Petrine office or a monarchical church constitution.

If it is fair to grant these two consequences, then we can grant that the church developed freely "from out of her origins in her full *essence*" (p. 332).

F. THE ACTS OF JESUS WHICH FOUNDED THE CHURCH

(VII.2.F, p. 332). Can we point to definite acts of Jesus, acts which biblical scholarship can show belonged to the historical Jesus, acts that did in fact "found" the church? Relying mainly on the work of New Testament exegete Rudolf Schnackenburg, Rahner notes four such acts:

First, Jesus did gather around him disciples, who in turn assembled a "people of God." The significance of the Twelve was to recall the twelve tribes, and so to indicate Jesus' claim upon all of Israel, an "eschatological Israel" (p. 333).

Second, the Christian community stayed together after Jesus' death. The members believed themselves to be the Elect. He had introduced them to "the mystery of his suffering." They were encouraged to endure persecution. The community was intended by Jesus to be a community that called all to *metanoia* (conversion) and faith.

Third, there was an "ecclesiological mandate" in the sayings of Jesus, according to theologian Anton Vögtle. The mandate bestowed Jesus' powers on his disciples in order to continue his work.

Fourth, the "Cephas-sayings" of Jesus founded the tradition by which Simon was called Cephas or Peter (Matt. 16:18f.). The meaning of these Cephas-sayings is that "Jesus wants to found his community of salvation on Simon and on his person as on a rock." The saying about the keys means that "Peter is given power to grant admission to the future kingdom" (p. 334). Beyond these basic four provisions, says Rahner, all is left to the Spirit, to the Spirit-led history of the church, and to the history of the original church.

3. The Church in the New Testament

(VII.3, p. 335). What were the characteristics of the original Christian community? It was distinct from Judaism from the start, says Rahner, possessing its own cult, reaching out to the Gentiles, and viewing itself in eschatological terms (A). Then Rahner gives an overview of the portrait of the early church in various New Testament documents. First, he looks at the Lukan and Matthaean portraits. The Lukan is marked by its recasting of world history in Christological terms, and the Matthaean portrays Christianity in ecclesial terms (B). Paul's letters regard the church in terms of its link to the traditions about Christ, to the Jerusalem community, and to aspects of the church echoed in the rest of the New Testament (C). In 1 Peter, Hebrews, the Johannine Letters, and the book of Revelation, we find a variety of ecclesial elements: the priesthood of believers, a community united in a common sacrifice, a sacramental and eschatological community (D). Finally, Rahner presents a synthesis of the New Testament ecclesial portraits, according to which the church is a structure, a college of various local churches, and a unity in Christ (E).

A. ON THE SELF-UNDERSTANDING OF THE ORIGINAL COMMUNITY

(VII.3.A, 335). How did the earliest Christians understand themselves? Rahner asserts that they first called themselves "the saints" and perhaps the "community of God." They did not see themselves as community within Israel, but rather as a community assembled by Jesus, assembled and called by him. It had its own cult (apart from Jewish worship) and eventually extended its mission to the pagan world. The Pentecost experience defined for the community its nature as "eschatological" and showed itself to be a community "obligated" to holiness in life. Even the earliest Christians distinguished themselves from Israel.

B. ON THE THEOLOGY OF THE CHURCH IN LUKE AND MATTHEW

(VII.3.B, p. 336). Luke's special contribution to a theology of the church was that he defined a "period of the church" between the ascension and the parousia. There is, for Luke, a period of history belonging to Israel, belonging to Jesus, and belonging to the church. Only because of the disbelief of Israel, Luke suggests, did the church take up a mission to the pagan world.

Matthew's special contribution is a theology of the church. Schnackenburg called Matthew the "ecclesial gospel." In Matthew, the call of Jesus "does not merely address the individual in the interiority of his conscience," Rahner says, "but rather it really builds church communities around Jesus" (p. 337). In Matthew we find a distinct law of Christ, a cult, and leadership in Peter and the Twelve.

C. ON THE PAULINE THEOLOGY OF THE CHURCH

(VII.3.C, p. 337). Although Paul was not particularly concerned about drafting a "church constitution" for later times (when his direct apostolic mission was over), nevertheless he preaches a doctrine that has several ecclesial elements. For example, Paul respects the principle of tradition, seeks the approval of the Jerusalem community, and has respect for "the church in its totality with its antecedent structures" (p. 338).

How did he understand the "church in its totality?" It was a church (1) composed of Jews and pagans (Eph. 3:4, 6), in which (2) the unfinished role of Israel in salvation history was recognized (Rom. 9-11), a church (3) founded sacramentally on Baptism and Eucharist, (4) recognized as a single entity composed of smaller, localized churches, and (5) both a cosmic reality and a heavenly presence expressed in terms of the "body of Christ." In short, Paul understood the church as broader and as more inclusive than the various local churches he had helped to found.

In the Pastoral Epistles, we find an image of the church with a strong institutional stamp. This image, however, does not contradict the eschatological image of the church reflected in the earliest letters of Paul.

D. OTHER NEW TESTAMENT ECCLESIOLOGIES

(VII.3.D, p. 339). In this brief section, Rahner looks at four texts significant for New Testament ecclesiology. The first is 1 Peter 2:4-10. It is remarkable for its strong emphasis on the church as a spiritual house, erected on the Holy Spirit, with Christ as cornerstone. In 1 Peter also we see a holy priesthood of all Christians offering spiritual sacrifice.

The second text is the Letter to the Hebrews. Its foundation is the Old Testament idea of a pilgrim People of God (an image drawn from Exodus). It also presents the church as an eschatological community, destined to enter heaven because Christ has entered there. The church is both a "heavenly Jerusalem" in anticipation and the place of temporal struggles and trials.

The third text is the collection of Johannine letters. They present the "church" (without ever using the word *ecclesia*) in terms of its sacramental life and its foundation in the Holy Spirit. It looks to the future when the scattered children of God will form one flock.

Finally, the book of Revelation reminds the persecuted church of its eschatological dignity. The great beast persecutes the church because it is the bride and the lamb. From the flock of the redeemed in heaven, it draws strength to continue struggling and its assurance of final victory.

E. UNITY AND VARIETY IN THE NEW TESTAMENT IMAGE OF THE CHURCH

(VII.3.E, p. 340). A brief overview of the New Testament texts related to the church suggests that the church has not one but many levels. There seem to be, however, a number of common aspects: (1) a marked institutional structure with various offices; (2) an interconnection among the various churches; (3) an inner life variously described as being on pilgrimage, as being one body, and as being composed of witnesses to the truth of Christ. Rahner concludes that, contrary to older opinions in New Testament research, Paul's view of the church is not incompatible with that of the original community or with that of the so-called early Catholicism of Luke and the Pastoral Letters.

Although it is true to say that the same image of the church did not prevail everywhere, nevertheless one does not have to prove a single image of the church to maintain the thesis of unity. It is also true that not all of the elements of what traditional Catholic theology would call the "divine constitution of the church" were present until the beginning of the second century. For example, consider the formation of the New Testament canon, which was not complete until then.

But despite the fact that we see a development in the church, even in the apostolic period, still we need not conclude these developments were arbitrary or false. Rather, they give us insights, says Rahner, into the different ways we might structure today's church.

4. Fundamentals of the Ecclesial Nature of Christianity

(VII.4, p. 342). In this brief part, Rahner makes an argument for the ecclesial nature of Christianity based on his transcendental theology. God's transcendental call to human beings is not just a call to individuals, but to the essence of humanity—including humanity's communal and social dimension (A). The essence of humanity is addressed only by a religion that comes from God and is not a merely human projection. Because it comes from God, religion is autonomous, a divine law unto itself, and it possesses authority (B). The church belongs to the necessary historical and social mediation of salvation. To think that the Christian individual can dispense with religion and its social dimension is an illusion (C).

A. CHRISTIANITY IS NECESSARILY CHURCH

(VII.4.A, p. 342). "Christianity must be constituted as a church." That is Rahner's central thesis. In saying that, he does not mean that the church must necessarily be constituted in this way or that. He means rather that joining with others belongs to the very "religious existence" of humanity. The church is not just a religious organization, but it helps constitute the human being's relation to God.

To be sure, the person who does not belong to a church does not thereby "lose" salvation. Indeed, such a person can have an ultimate and decisive relation to God. But church is the norm, says Rahner. Ecclesial Christianity is "the full and historical actualized Christianity of God's self-communication" (p. 343).

The rightly understood idea of church is one that springs from God's supernatural self-communication in Jesus Christ. This self-communication is not a relation between God and the isolated individual but is rather a communication between God and the essence of humanity. That essence includes communal and social intercommunication.

B. THE AUTONOMOUS CHARACTER OF THE CLAIM OF JESUS CHRIST'S MESSAGE

(VII.4.B, p. 343). An element of what Rahner calls "the authoritative" belongs to the essence of the Christian religion. The call of God is not a merely transcendental affair but comes in history. Religion becomes historically real not just when an individual accepts it in accord with his or her private mentality. No, it becomes real when the Christian adopts it as the religion of God, given by God to those who will treasure and conserve it. Religion must be acknowledged as a reality independent of the recipient— if it is to be something not merely at the recipient's disposal.

To be sure, the objective, the authoritative, the institutional aspect of religion cannot take the place of Christianity's personal dimension. One must realize one's faith subjectively. Still, there is something in religion that obligates the individual, Rahner says. Religion is necessarily objective and one can orient oneself to it.

Religion must, in the end, be a "norm" for one's subjectivity. Christianity is the religion of a jealous God who makes demands on a chosen people. Without the autonomy of religion, a people is "abandoned" to its own poverty, problems, and the potentiality of distorting religion. The mission, mandate, and proclamation of the church "make the reality of salvation present for me" (p. 344).

C. THE NECESSARY HISTORICAL AND SOCIAL MEDIATION OF SALVATION

(VII.4.C, p. 345). History itself has salvific significance, says Rahner. Salvation does not take place merely in a subjective and transcendental interiority. For that reason, salvation must be mediated in history and society. The church belongs to the salvation history of God's grace. It is "the categorical concreteness and the mediation of salvation and grace" (p. 345). It expresses the transcendental.

It is an illusion, Rahner says, to think that human beings can organize themselves in a "reasonable" and "social" way and, at the same time, can abstain from any particular worldview. Even supposedly secular states make use of ideology and embody a particular worldview. In short, the social and the human dimensions of humanity are inextricably linked. So for Christianity to affirm that the Christian individual is also an "ecclesial being" with allegiance to a social view of Christian faith is not an incomprehensible statement. It reflects the fundamentally social nature of the human being.

5. An Indirect Method for Showing the Legitimacy of the Catholic Church as the Church of Christ

(VII.5, p. 346). Rahner's indirect method is not to try to solve the many historical questions about the division among the many branches of Christianity (A). His aim is rather to lay down some general principles about the necessity of Christianity being ecclesial, then apply them to his own Roman Catholic tradition (B). He starts by asserting the unity of the churches in the apostolic age and then argues that even Evangelical Christians will admit that there existed some continuity between early Christianity and the Reformation (C). He then notes, on anthropological grounds, that it is legitimate for an adult to trust the faith handed down by earlier generations—and that Catholic theologians should acknowledge a certain legitimacy in the Protestant Christianity handed down to faithful people outside Catholicism (D). One must be satisfied that one's church is "Christian," but one need not become a theologian to reach that satisfaction (E). Next, Rahner tries to distinguish this basic principle from what he calls "ecclesial relativism." His first norm is that the church of Jesus Christ had to exist until Reformation times, however unfaithful individual Christians were (F). His second norm is an appeal to experience: Rahner claims to have found the reality of Christian faith in Roman Catholicism (G). His third norm is that for any church to call itself Christian, it must exist in an authoritative way independently of the believer (H). When Rahner seeks his three norms, he finds them in Catholic Christianity (I). Moreover, he argues that the continuity between the church after the Council of Trent and the earliest church is stronger in Roman Catholicism than in any other branch of Christianity (J). Rahner then looks at the three *solas* of Evangelical Christianity (*sola gratia, sola fide, sola scriptura*) and asks what the Catholic can learn from them (K). He believes that these have helped all Christians to "crystallize" what is most essential about the faith (L). The divisions among Christians are interpreted as God's effort to purify the faith (M). There is more that divided Christians have in common than that which separates them (N).

A. INTRODUCTION

(VII.5.A, p. 346). The normal method of fundamental theology, namely, to offer a direct historical proof that the Roman Catholic Church is the church of Christ, involves many difficult historical questions. Rahner says that this normal method is not practical and feasible for most Catholics. So he proposes an "indirect" method. He promises to show first the formal principles of his method and then to apply those principles to the Catholic Church.

B. ON THE NECESSITY OF CHURCH

(VII.5.B, p. 347). Church is "necessary" because (1) the human being is a historical and social being, and because (2) "Christianity claims the whole person for the salvation of the whole person" (p. 347). It is an authoritative religion because Christianity is more than an affair of pious and subjective dispositions. In addition, it makes a claim that is the concretion of God's demands. They are demands made by Jesus and his church. So the church is, first of all, necessary. The ordinary Christian believer necessarily belongs to a concrete and historical church.

C. THE CHURCH OF JESUS CHRIST MUST BE ONE CHURCH

(VII.5.C, p. 348). In addition to being necessary, the church of Christ is one church. It is not just a group of Christians forming pious communities, but comes objectively and with authority as the representative of Christ. The New Testament, and especially the writings of John and Paul, presupposes this unity. To be sure, the church exists wherever there is true Eucharist, Baptism, and gospel. But the existence of these three presupposes the one church.

We do not have first individual communities or churches that later combine for ideological reasons into a single church. No, the single reality that is church comes first and manifests itself in the various communities. This is Paul's basic teaching, and Rahner puts it this way: "one and the same people of God filled with the Spirit of God becomes manifest in every local community" (p. 349). Although the various churches of early Christianity were spread out and apparently independent, they had common features. Rahner lists them as follows: they were founded by those who carried out the mission of Jesus; they were led by an apostle (even if he was not present); they exchanged letters; and they were built upon Peter as the rock.

Even Protestant Christians recognize that the oneness and unity of the church is not for Christians to decide as they will. While there remains much disagreement about how the Christian church is to be one, nevertheless the conviction exists that there ought to be one church, and that its unity has not yet been sufficiently realized.

D. LEGITIMATE CONFIDENCE IN ONE'S OWN ECCLESIAL COMMUNITY

(VII.5.D, p. 350). Individual Christians have a right to assume that their ecclesial existence is legitimate. To be sure, individuals can and do break out of the situation of their existence, encounter an "existentiell revolution," and conclude that the religion of their parents is inauthentic. But this is not the norm. No one can project the totality of his existence in an absolutely new way. The norm is to presume the legitimacy of the ecclesial situation bestowed by history. One trusts one's parents, accepts one's culture, and presumes the legitimacy of received values.

If this is true, then "it makes things more difficult for Catholic fundamental theology as an apologetic for the Roman Catholic Church which is also intended for other Christians" (p. 351). How is Catholic theology to "come to terms with the fact of this real and genuine Christian experience which comes from other ecclesial denominations"? (p. 351). Every genuine Christian experience, including the experience of Protestant Christians, "must be regarded as an experience of the power of our existence which is really grounded in the mystery of God" (p. 351). One cannot dismiss Protestant Christianity because it is not Roman Catholic.

E. CRITERIA AND PRESUPPOSITIONS

(VII.5.E, p. 352). All Christians find themselves in a concrete experience of Christianity, in a specific Christian church. Good conscience demands that they examine whether this church contradicts the basic substance of Christianity. Further, Christians must judge how closely their church stands to the origins of Christianity in its ecclesial constitution. To be sure, ordinary Christians do not have to master all the exegetical, historical, and dogmatic questions of technical theology. But they must be satisfied that their church is truly Christian—however incomplete the basis for reflection is.

F. THE CRITERION OF CONTINUITY WITH THE ORIGIN
AS A DEFENSE AGAINST ECCLESIOLOGICAL RELATIVISM

(VII.5.F, p. 352). We can rely on the concrete Christian church that has come to us, says Rahner, "*if* it has the closest possible historical approximation to the original Christian church of Jesus Christ" (pp. 352-353). The goal of all Christians is to affirm that their own church is indeed "the church of Christ."

Although many people today would say that the church to which they belong (or want to belong) is "a question merely of historical accident and individual taste," Rahner disagrees. Such a view was completely foreign to the sixteenth-century Reformers. They presumed that the true church of Jesus Christ *had* to exist somewhere. The Catholic Church could not be the true church, they agreed, because it lacked the basic elements of the

Augsburg Confession. In it they found no genuine preaching of the gospel, no legitimate authority, and no correct administration of the sacraments of Baptism and Eucharist.

Ecclesial relativism presupposes either that the true church of Christ as he willed it does not exist or that it exists to such an extent among all the divided churches "that it does not really have to be brought about" (p. 353).

Against this relativism, Rahner proposes what he calls his *first* norm. It is that the Christian church began with Jesus Christ. The church of the intervening centuries, however depraved and unfaithful, supplied continuity from the time of Jesus to Reformation times. No Protestant Christian, says Rahner, will argue that the Christian church began with the Reformation. Many Protestants will assert that their own churches have a concrete, historical continuity with the church of original Christianity.

G. The Criterion of Preserving the Basic Substance of Christianity

(VII.5.G, p. 354). The *second* norm or principle in Rahner's indirect method of justifying Catholic Christianity is that the "basic substance" of Christianity "may not be fundamentally denied in concrete Catholicism" (p. 354). With this norm, Rahner departs from traditional ecclesiology. He does not want to argue, he says, that the basic substance of Christianity is guaranteed by the structures of Roman Catholicism. Instead he argues that he, in his concrete experience of faith, has experienced the reality of Christianity. His concrete experience as a Roman Catholic "does not contradict the basic substance of Christianity" which he has found in his own existence.

The true church can exist only where the gospel is preached in its purity, according to the Augsburg Confession. That confession (Rahner says) is perfectly correct. An ecclesial community that denies a basic principle of Christianity cannot be the true church of Christ. So Rahner appeals to the Holy Spirit. He says that the Spirit bears witness to the reality of his own Christian experience.

H. The Criterion of Objective Authority

(VII.5.H, p. 355). Rahner's *third* norm or principle is that "the religious community of church must obviously exist as a reality which is independent of my subjectivity" (p. 355). The church has an authority that stands over the believer and articulates a Christian reality that can never be reduced to an individual's interpretation. Without a doubt, every objective reality is mediated in one's own conscience. For me to perceive a Christian teaching as true, it must be true for me. But this does not alter the Rahnerian postulate: "Christian religiosity is not yet religion unless it includes the concrete and social reality of a church which is independent of me" (p. 355). An authentically Christian church has an authority that is greater than one's own subjective judgment.

I. THE SPECIAL APPLICATION OF THESE CRITERIA IN OUR SITUATION

(VII.5.I, p. 356). In this section, Rahner lays the basis for his application of the three norms, that is, continuity, subjectivity, and objective authority. First, Christian truths do not all have the same existentiell and salvific significance, says Rahner, because there is a hierarchy of truths. The acknowledgment of this hierarchy, referred to in the Vatican II Decree on Ecumenism (*Unitatis redintegratio*, no. 11), means that some truths of the faith are more foundational than others.

Next, Rahner says that "other Christians" live in grace, are filled with Spirit, are justified, and so on. To an extent, they are already united with Roman Catholics. Finally, he says that only Evangelical Christianity (i.e., the Protestantism that remains close to its pre-Reformation roots) can be a question for Roman Catholics. Evangelical Christianity belongs, says Rahner, to the Roman Catholic's own history. By contrast, the forms of Christianity that have severed their relation to the pre-Reformation church do not belong to the history of Roman Catholicism.

J. THE HISTORICAL CONTINUITY OF THE CATHOLIC CHURCH

(VII.5.J, p. 357). Rahner's basic conviction is that the Catholic Church most decisively accords with his three norms or principles. "It possesses in the concrete a closer, more evident, and less encumbered historical continuity with the church of the past going all the way back to apostolic times" (p. 357).

To be sure, Rahner refuses to establish this connection by means of a detailed investigation. He says that such an investigation is beyond the scope of *Foundations*. He believes that such an investigation is unnecessary. "The historical continuity between the post-tridentine and post-Reformation church and the ancient church is greater, more evident and less ambiguous in the Catholic church," he says, "than in the other ecclesial communities, including those of Evangelical Christianity" (p. 357).

Rahner insists upon the Petrine Office, which provides continuity with the "Roman episcopacy" of the ancient church. It is hard for the Evangelical church to declare, he suggests, that this feature is superfluous or unChristian. It is fundamental. On the other hand, Evangelicals rightly insist on justification by faith, gospel, Baptism and Eucharist. These too are fundamental. And no one can deny that the Roman Catholic Church of the Middle Ages showed "massive tendencies" in its life, practice, and mentality that contradicted the central concerns of Evangelicals.

Having conceded that, however, Rahner makes a case for confidence in

today's Roman Catholic Church. The contemporary Catholic does not have
to admit, he says, that the church of the Middle Ages taught something
"which was so contrary to the real and basic concerns of the reformers"
(p. 359) that its teaching would force him or her out of the Catholic Church.
Even in the medieval church, the essence of Christianity was still present.

K. The Criterion of Preserving the Basic Substance in the Light of Reformation Controversies

(VII.5.K, p. 359). Rahner proposes to examine the three basic "onlys" of
the Reformation—only grace, only faith, and only scripture—in order to
show that membership in the Catholic Church is possible for the conscien-
tious Christian.

(i) *Sola Gratia: By Grace Alone*
(VII.5.K.i, p. 359). In this section, Rahner aims to show that the Evangelical linchpin, the doctrine that we are saved by God's grace alone, is no
less a linchpin for Roman Catholics. To be sure, Catholics reject predesti-
nation in the name of human freedom. But Protestants insist on human freedom as well. All Christians must freely accept that their salvation is God's
initiative. Humans contribute nothing to salvation that is not, first and fore-
most, God's free gift. In that sense, Protestants and Catholics agree.

(ii) *Sola Fide: By Faith Alone*
(VII.5.K.ii, p. 360). *Sola fide* is the subjective side, Rahner says, of the
Sola gratia doctrine. The response to God's grace is not a "work" of human
beings, but "faith" in Paul's sense. Faith is, of course, based on interior hope
and must be fulfilled by love. Scholastic theology may have distinguished
these, Rahner admits, in a "somewhat schematic" fashion. But they remain
interconnected. To this Evangelical theology cannot object.

(iii) *Sola Scriptura: Scripture Alone*
(VII.5.K.iii, p. 361). The third basic *sola* is one against which Catholics
may object. Catholics insist that the gospel comes from scripture and tradition, and not from scripture alone. Rahner starts from the concrete position
of scripture studies in Evangelical Christianity today. Evangelicals will
grant, he says, that scripture is a product of the church. It is based on the
preaching of the living church, and so is the "result" of tradition. One cannot explain the formation of the canon without reference to the relation
between scripture and tradition.

Rahner then asserts that Evangelical Christianity has abandoned the
principle of the "verbal" inspiration of scripture. The doctrine of verbal
inspiration views scripture as "the one and only product which comes
immediately from God independently of any historical . . . process of

becoming" (p. 362). Because this principle has been abandoned, he says, one cannot "still maintain the principle of scripture alone in the sense which it had at the time of the reformation" (p. 362). Scripture is a product of human history as well as divine authorship.

Finally, Rahner argues that the principle of scripture as a *norma non normata* (a norm which is not mediated by others) can still be affirmed by Catholics. It is affirmed in two ways: first, in the sense that the church "does not receive any new revelation over and beyond this scripture" (p. 363); and second, that the task of the church's teaching office is "to remain within the ultimate and eschatological revelation which has been handed down" (p. 363) in scripture.

The substance of faith is immutable, but it can develop. Developments need to be judged by an objective authority, and the Catholic Church claims that it can give a basic interpretation of scripture that is binding on individual Christians. God's word in scripture is capable of forming faith, but it does so (the Catholic believes) in the preaching of the concrete church. The norm for the teaching office in the Catholic Church is not its own subjective view, but scripture itself. The ecclesiastical magisterium (says Rahner), "does not receive any new revelations" (p. 365).

L. The Three Reformation "Onlys" and Catholicism: The Result

(VII.5.L, p. 365). The three Reformation "onlys" should not lead one out of the Catholic Church, says Rahner. On the contrary, they have a central place in Catholicism. Other Evangelical theologies (e.g., Rudolf Bultmann's theology of demythologizing) may well lead one out, but not the core teachings of the Reformers, because they embraced the traditional creeds.

M. The Positive Significance of Evangelical Christianity for the Catholic Church

(VII.5.M, p. 366). Evangelical Christianity has significance for Catholic Christianity. It has crystallized the Christian faith, reduced it "to the ultimate, to what is most specific, to the animating power, and to that which gives Christianity its ultimate meaning" (p. 367). Thanks to the "goad" of the Reformation, there has been a "corrective influence" on Catholics. Evangelical Christianity belongs to the historical moments that have had a powerful and beneficial impact on Catholicism.

N. The Fundamental Unity of Christianity and the Question about the "Meaning" of the Division

(VII.5.N, p. 367). Why did God allow the division of Christianity? In order to answer this question, Rahner lays down two important assumptions: first, that Christians are united in a more radical sense than they are divided; and second, that the majority of Christians exist in a "guiltless" relation to their own churches and to other churches.

Having said that, Rahner concludes that the division among the Christian churches was allowed by God in order to make the reality of Christianity more clearly seen. Without the division, we would not experience the truths of Christianity as clearly as we do. "We have to force each other," Rahner says, "mutually to be and to become as Christian as possible" (p. 369). This, he hopes, will help those from different churches to develop a theological unity, each working from within different traditions.

6. Scripture as the Church's Book

(VII.6, p. 369). This section begins with a hermeneutical discussion. Scripture is not the immediate Word of God, says Rahner, but is understood as such when human beings hear it as God's Word in an experience of grace (A). In the Christian church, the scriptures function as the link between God's decisive act on behalf of the world and the life and proclamation of Jesus (B). The church of the apostles can be said to have objectified itself in scripture, and we turn to scripture to know that early church (C). Although it was not the recognition of scripture by the church that made it inspired, nevertheless we can say that the essence of scripture is derived from the essence of the church (D). God is the author of scripture, in the sense that God inspired it by inspiring the church (E). Scripture is inerrant in that it cannot lead us away from God's truth, but scripture must be correctly interpreted (F). The teaching office of the church, far from being "above scripture," is bound to the scripture as the sign of its origins and of the transcendental truth to which it is committed (G). The formation of the scripture is a "fundamental moment" in Christian tradition, not a separate source of truth alongside of tradition (H).

A. Some References to Earlier Discussions

(VII.6.A, p. 370). Rahner begins by reminding readers of the relation between transcendental and historical reflection. This is a theme which, in Rahner's hands, subordinates the historical words of scripture to the transcendental Word of salvation history. According to this transcendental word, God invites the human being to hear God in the intimacy of his or her conscience and to respond in a free decision. Salvation history reaches its goal and climax, Rahner concedes, when it becomes a theme in explicit revelatory language. But scripture can only be understood as the Word of God when it becomes, in an experience of grace, a communication from God to the hearer.

B. THE CHURCH'S BOOK

(VII.6.B, p. 371). The scriptures remain normative for the church. They bind the church to its origins. Moreover, the scriptures bind God's transcendental turn to the world along with the proclamation and life of Jesus. Finally, the scriptures express the early church as it understood itself. Without the scriptures, says Rahner, we would not be able to understand inspiration or the church itself, which holds the scriptures to be inspired.

C. THE APOSTOLIC AGE

(VII.6.C, p. 371). The apostolic age "ended" with the writing of the final books of the New Testament, circa 110–130. The apostolic age is normative for defining the canon of scripture. But the canon, by means of a hermeneutical circle, defines what we know the apostolic age to be. So Rahner concludes that the apostolic age objectified itself in scripture, and now the scripture "has" the character of the apostolic age.

D. THE FORMATION OF THE CANON

(VII.6.D, p. 372). Rahner insists that the canon of scripture was recognized and constituted by the early church. Having said that, however, he cautions us. One cannot say that the church's recognition of scripture is what made it inspired and canonical. Vatican I denied this, and Rahner denies it as well. But the origin of scripture took place within a circumscribed series of moments. They are akin to the formation of the church, and the essence of scripture is derived from the essence of the church, even though the two do not coincide in time. The formation of the canon "belongs to" the formation of the church.

E. THE INSPIRATION OF SCRIPTURE

(VII.6.E, p. 374). The traditional teaching of the church is that God is the "author" of scripture. Is there a sense, Rahner asks, in which we can understand this in a way that is not mythological? We cannot understand it adequately if we try to save, by means of psychological theories, the notion of God as the "literary" author. That reduces the human authors to the status of being merely secretaries of the divine.

A word *about* God, even such a word caused by God, would not be a word *of* God unless God truly offers it. To be God's own self-expression, the word would have to be "effected by God" and "borne by grace" in a process of our hearing it, a process "borne by God's Spirit" (p. 374). God is the "author" of scripture in that God inspired it, inspired it by founding the church.

"The human authors of Holy Scripture work exactly like other human authors," says Rahner, "nor do they have to know anything about their being inspired in reflexive knowledge" (p. 375). God is the author of scripture in that God willed the church, whose human authors wrote the biblical books.

F. THE INERRANCY OF SCRIPTURE

(VII.6.F, p. 375). Vatican II stated that the scriptures teach "with certainty, with fidelity, and without error the truth which God wanted recorded" (Constitution on Divine Revelation, *Dei Verbum*, art. 11, as cited in *Foundations*, p. 375). But inerrancy must not be understood, Rahner warns, in connection with the discredited idea of verbal inspiration. *Dei Verbum* leaves open the question of the identity of the truths which God placed in the scriptures "for our salvation." It leaves us to ask whether that phrase is meant to explain the truths (i.e., they are truths "for our salvation") or to restrict them (inerrancy does not extend beyond those salvific truths).

Rahner affirms unambiguously that the scriptures objectify God's offer of salvation. They are inerrant in that they cannot lead one away from God's truth. But all scripture must be interpreted in the context of its genre, and further we must distinguish between the "correctness" of a saying and the "truth" it conveys. A saying may be correct in its biblical context and erroneous at the same time. It may be historically, scientifically, or even morally flawed, and yet may still contain a truth.

Just as the "analogy of faith" suggests that we must interpret the teachings of the church in their proper context, so the "analogy of scripture" holds for interpreting individual verses. The meaning of the scriptures depends on the context in which they are placed.

G. SCRIPTURE AND TEACHING OFFICE

(VII.6.G, p. 377). The magisterium does not stand "above" scripture, says Rahner. The magisterium is, first of all, bound to the faith of the early church which gave rise to scripture. Second, the consciousness of the early church is "objectified" in scripture. The magisterium, far from being above scripture, aims to witness to the truth of scripture.

H. SCRIPTURE AND TRADITION

(VII.6.H, p. 377). Scripture is the "objectification" of the original church's consciousness of faith. As an example of this consciousness of faith, Rahner points to the formation of the canon. The canon could not be established by scripture alone. The formation of the canon is, Rahner says, a "fundamental moment" in tradition. However, tradition is not, alongside of scripture, a second source of the gospel with a separate content. Even Evangelical Christian leaders recognize that scripture objectifies the original church's living consciousness. They freely confess, says Rahner, that scripture testifies to a legitimate pluralism in the church's unity, a pluralism in the one church's "single and living consciousness of the faith" (p. 378). Tradition and scripture both express the living consciousness of the original church.

7. On the Church's Teaching Office

(VII.7, p. 378). The church's magisterium confronts the believer with a problem. It is that the magisterium as such did not exist in the Old Testament or before the church came into being (A). So how are we to interpret it? Rahner asserts that the magisterium is part of God's will in proclaiming truth and establishing a church (B). The church perseveres in the truth because it participates in God's offer of the divine self in truth and love (C). The issue is not "whether" the church perseveres, but "how." It perseveres by confronting the Christian with the challenging demand of Christ to believe (D). Faith aims, not at the formulation of propositions arranged in a hierarchy but at a living relationship to God (E). The importance of propositions cannot be avoided, however, and Rahner asks if the Catholic Church, by defining doctrines in an infallible way, raises an insuperable obstacle to the reunion with Evangelical Christians (F). To answer, he first asserts that the ascription to the pope of infallible teaching authority is fundamentally no different than the time-honored ascription to the whole church of infallibility (G). Finally, Rahner affirms that the doctrines of the Immaculate Conception and of the Assumption of Mary assert nothing other than the Mary has realized the promise in which every Christian hopes (H). The so-called new doctrines are not new, but developments of ancient Christian teaching.

A. THE PROBLEM OF THE UNIQUENESS OF AN "ECCLESIAL TEACHING OFFICE"

(VII.7.A, p. 378). The problem of the teaching office lies in the fact that it did not exist in Old Testament times or before the church of Christ. Indeed, the official teachers of Old Testament times were acknowledged capable of falling away from God, and in fact did not recognize Jesus Christ.

For Catholic Christians, it cannot suffice to proclaim that God endowed the episcopate (with Peter and his successors as the head) "with formal authority of a fundamental kind" (p. 379). A formalization of this kind does not explain anything about the relation between formal teaching authority and the essence of the church.

B. The Christological Reason for the Teaching Office

(VII.7.B, p. 379). The fundamental reason for the teaching office begins with Jesus Christ. In Christ, God's self-communication became tangible and irreversible. The historical manifestation of Jesus' coming includes the rise of the church and its teaching office. That is the real reason for the authoritative magisterium. In the church, God expresses the divine truth and love. God encompasses human freedom with grace in such a way that "man's freedom as a whole really accepts this truth and preserves it" (p. 379). By extension, the Catholic community accepts and preserves the magisterium as an extension of God's own truth. The teaching office belongs to God's activity of proclaiming the truth.

C. The Church and Perseverance in the Truth

(VII.7.C, p. 379). The church is "the ongoing presence and the historical tangibility of this ultimate and victorious word of God in Jesus Christ" (p. 379). Its task is to "found" or to usher in the "eschatological age." To do so, it must truly "participate" in God's offer of the divine self as truth and love. By participating in God's offer, the church can never lose the truth and love which belong to God. How can the church be preserved in truth? Because in Christ, God has (1) "encompassed every conceivable rejection" and (2) has "redeemed man's freedom and his history" (p. 380). It is not a human accomplishment, but God's grace, that is, God's desire to maintain the victory of Christ. God has made a gift of the divine self and enables us to remain faithful—to call one another to faithfulness.

As for disputes between Catholic and Evangelical Christians, Rahner says that the issue is not *whether* the church of Jesus Christ can lose the truth, for it cannot; the question is rather *how* God triumphs and makes the divine presence victorious. If the Catholic professes that the church has a hierarchical structure, then the Catholic cannot allow himself or herself to be put into the dilemma of having to choose between God's truth and the structure of the church. The dilemma is "impossible," says Rahner, because the church's teaching authority speaks in the name of Christ, not merely from its own subjectivity but because it was "sent" just as Christ was. Because the church was sent by Christ to found the eschatological age, the church "as a whole" cannot lose Christ's truth and love.

D. Teaching Authority according to the Catholic
   Understanding of the Church

(VII.7.D, p. 381). What does it mean that the church "perseveres in" and "can never lose" the truth? Rahner says that, when the church confronts the believing Christian in its teaching with "an *ultimate* demand in the name of

Christ," then "God's grace and power prevent this teaching authority from losing the truth of Christ" (p. 381). This teaching authority does not offer any new revelation, but "simply interprets, develops and actualizes in ever new historical concretions the message of Christ" (p. 381). It is the "organ" and "embodiment" of the church's understanding of faith.

It must be said, however, that the teaching office speaks with all of its authority "only in relatively rare instances" (p. 381). Usually, the pronouncements of official teachers are "provisional and limited exercises" of the real authority which exists in the total consciousness of the faith. The obligation of the individual Christian to obey this authority "varies a great deal depending on the level of the authority exercised" (p. 381). Evangelical Christianity has a teaching authority too, but it does not declare itself absolute and ultimately binding.

E. The "Hierarchy of Truths" and Its Subjective Appropriation

(VII.7.E, p. 382). When we speak of a hierarchy of truths, we mean that each of the truths of faith, while all are revealed, have a "different relationship to the real core of faith" (p. 382). While each truth can be stated as a proposition materially distinct from every other, they are grasped altogether. The Christian accepts them altogether, not as a series of acts which we take one at a time or accept each individually. The act of faith does not aim at human propositions but at a relationship to God.

When we appropriate the truths of faith, we do so in a way that each truth has a "different" relationship "to the core and to the substance of Christian faith" (p. 383). One finds one's own understanding of the faith within a community. "But this does not mean, however, that he [the believer] is required to assimilate the faith in all of the differentiated nuances which it has objectively and has acquired in history" (p. 383). Rather, one lives in the implicit faith of the church and need not be concerned about details which do not touch the believer in the concrete.

Indeed, the details can distract one from the heart of the message. "We even have to say," Rahner asserts, "that many times it would be better if Christians knew less about certain details of the Catholic catechism but had really grasped the ultimate and decisive questions in a genuine and profound way" (p. 383). Faith depends less on external and formal teaching than on the interior reality of what is believed.

F. The Question of the Post-Tridentine Development of Dogma

(VII.7.F, p. 384). Has the Catholic Church raised insuperable obstacles to reunion with Protestant Christians by its explicit dogmatic teachings since the sixteenth century? Have doctrines about the teaching authority of the pope, the Immaculate Conception of the Blessed Virgin Mary, and

Assumption of Mary into heaven been offered as "new" revelations? Certainly, an Evangelical would have to accept these doctrines if he or she wanted to be a Catholic, and they go beyond what was disputed at the time of the Reformation.

G. THE PRIMACY AND TEACHING AUTHORITY OF THE BISHOP OF ROME

(VII.7.G, p. 384). To answer the questions about the post-tridentine development of dogma, Rahner asserts that the doctrine about the authority of the church is not new. The doctrine of the infallible teaching office of the church was held before the Reformation, he says, although it was not always ascribed explicitly to the pope. The question of today is not about the authority of the church per se, but rather about the authority of the pope.

Rahner begins his answer to the question by noting two qualifications to papal authority. First, it is not the authority of a private person but of an office. Second, by virtue of this office, the pope may exercise an infallible teaching authority in the interpretation of revelation, that is, of scripture and tradition. So infallible teaching is exercised in a public and official manner in the interpretation of revelation.

Having asserted these qualifications, Rahner states that the exercise of papal authority is nothing other than an ascription to the pope of an authority believed throughout Christian history to be present in the church and in ecumenical councils. To assert this about the pope is (theologically speaking) no more difficult than to assert it of the whole church or of ecumenical councils, says Rahner, and "more natural and sensible from a human point of view" (p. 385). It is more natural and sensible if we regard the pope as "acting as the head of the church and as the person who represents the whole college of bishops" (p. 385). Democratic considerations, says Rahner, are "out of place for the church and for the issue in question" (p. 385).

He goes on to say a few more things relevant to the question of democracy. "We are not dealing here with a collective discovery of truth," he says, "where basically and by the very nature of the case more people really do have a greater chance to discover the truth than an individual has" (p. 385). It is not a matter of intelligence or education, but of the gift of the Spirit. It is no more difficult to say that a person can discern and express the truth than to say that a society of church can discern and express it.

Hence the Catholic Church cannot be said to have erred when it declared that the primacy and power of the pope belong to the essence of Christianity. Indeed, Rahner suggests that Evangelical theology is in error. For such theology does not deny solely that the pope can oblige the Christian conscience. It also denies that no council or tangible authority can oblige the conscience. Prior to the Reformation, an authority akin to the authority of scripture was ascribed to ecumenical councils. The Reformation churches deny even that—a far greater and more significant denial than the denial of post-tridentine developments. One cannot rightly protest against papal primacy, Rahner concludes, in the name of a generalized "Christianity," because Christianity all along has presumed the unity of the churches under a concrete head.

H. THE "NEW" MARIAN DOGMAS

(VII.7.H, p. 387). In order to understand the Immaculate Conception and Assumption of Mary, one must believe in the incarnation of the eternal Word in human flesh. That is Rahner's starting point. Mary is not just a character in the biography of Jesus, he says, but one who has "an explicit historical role in the history of salvation" (p. 387).

To be sure, says Rahner, there is no explicit testimony to the Marian dogmas in scripture or in the explicit tradition of the first centuries. Rahner chooses not to explore the emergence and development of the Marian dogmas. But he affirms that they reflect what most Christians believe about salvation and eschatology.

At their heart, the Marian dogmas state "that Mary is someone who has been redeemed radically" (p. 387). She was redeemed as one who helped to "realize" the salvation of the world, who bore the fruit of salvation, and who "received" salvation. Evangelicals may protest that the Immaculate Conception undercuts or denies the universality of original sin. But Rahner replies that it is quite biblical to affirm that Adam's sin has been "transcended and encompassed by God's salvific will and by the redemption of Christ" (p. 387).

All of us are sanctified and redeemed insofar as we have our origin in Christ, just as we are sinners because of our origin in Adam. The Immaculate Conception proclaims that the Mother of God "was conceived and willed from the beginning by God's absolute salvific will as someone who was to receive salvation in faith and love" (p. 388). She was the first to be redeemed.

And what of the Assumption? It says about Mary, claims Rahner, what we profess about ourselves in the creed when we refer to the resurrection of the body and eternal life. The Assumption proclaims that the fulfillment of Mary's life—the resurrection of her body and her eternal life—took place with her death, with her own eschatology, and with her very person as "the most radically successful instance of redemption" (p. 388). What we profess about Mary, says Rahner, is what we profess about our hope for ourselves.

8. The Christian in the Life of the Church

(VII.8, p. 389). In this brief section, Rahner starts by affirming the ecclesial life of the church as the realm of our Christian existence. Just as we are bound to our families, even in recognizing their limitations, so we are bound to the church (A). Ecclesial existence is necessary for the Christian, but the Christian acknowledges that there is a difference between ecclesial and divine laws (B). While rejecting subjectivity and situationalism, Rahner affirms that church law is relative, while divine law encompasses church law and is absolute (C). The church is not one among other groups competing for people's allegiance in a pluralistic society, but the place where faithful people recognize that God offers the divine life to all, and where they revere that divine life in its many forms (D).

A. On the Ecclesial Nature of a Christian

(VII.8.A, p. 389). Does one become a Christian by gaining a sudden religious enthusiasm or by experiencing what no one else has experienced? No, Christianity comes to the individual through history, Rahner says. By that he means from a people, from family, from the Holy Spirit objectified in the concrete and the particular. It comes from a profession of faith, from a cult, from a community.

The church exists because, without it, Christianity (if it existed at all) would be incomplete. It would be only a soul without a body, a transcendental essence without a historical constitution, an individual without any possibility of intercommunication.

This does not mean, however, that one must have illusions about the church. One loves the church, not for what it might be, but for what it is. That love makes a claim on us. Just as love for one's parents is binding (despite the fact that we see their finitude and limitations), so love for the church is binding. We accept the church as the realm of our Christian existence, even with the church's failings "and perhaps even false developments" (p. 390). We are obliged, says Rahner, to recognize the church as the assembly that we ourselves constitute, even with its failures. The church manifests itself in us, a people enmeshed in guilt.

B. On Law and Order in the Church

(VII.8.B, p. 391). Catholics understand the hierarchical structure of the church as a necessity of labor, of functions, and even of rights. This understanding should not be seen merely as a pragmatic concession. "There has to be in the church a holy order, a holy law, and hence also a power which may and must be exercised juridically by one person in relation to others"

(p. 391). There is a legitimate power to lead and govern. In every Christian community, the individual has an obligation in conscience to church authority.

Undoubtedly there is a difference between a "divine law" and the claims made by the church upon the conscience of the Catholic Christian "on the basis of its power to govern" (p. 391). Church law is mutable; divine law is not. "It is also subject to the criticism and to the desires for change on the part of the faithful" (p. 391). The church stands under the divine law. Church laws are addressed to the conscience of individual Catholic Christians, whose relationship to church laws is "much looser and much freer" than their relationship to God's laws.

How are we to distinguish between church laws and divine laws? Rahner does not treat this in detail, but he gives an example. Keeping the Sabbath holy is a divine law. The church's command to attend Mass on Sunday differs from the third commandment and "cannot be traced back" to it. Church law does not bind the conscience in the same way that a divine command is binding.

C. Levels of Relativity in the Law

(VII.8.C, p. 392). In this section, Rahner adds precision to his earlier remarks about church law. He states that church laws demand loyal obedience and have a right to make that demand. But there is a "discrepancy," Rahner says, between the individual conscience and "what is regulated and can be regulated by the church" (p. 393). There is "relativity" in the church with regard to its law.

To explain this Rahner says that some laws concern the church's social order. They are not "a divine law either of revelation or of nature" (p. 393). He gives three examples. First, the law that witnesses are required for the validity of marriage even when no priest is available. Does this law always hold? Second, the law that a person once married must prove the nullity of the marriage in order to marry again. What if there were no marriage but the person cannot prove it? Third, the law that only a bishop can ordain. Could not a priest in, let us say, a refugee situation, ordain another? Basically, Rahner is raising the possibility that one need not always and in every case follow the letter of the law when the Spirit counsels something else. The church's basic and transcendent principles must be maintained, even when a faithful interpretation of them puts one into conflict with the church's disciplinary laws.

Situational ethics has been rejected by the church, and Rahner is not proposing a "situational law." He does not intend to propose a theory that would deny objective law and subject it to capricious interpretations. The law proposed by Rahner is nothing other than the long-established princi-

ples of Greek philosophy, namely *epikeia* and the force of custom. Even the
sacraments, which are one instance of divine law, can be subsumed under
another instance of that law. The example Rahner gives is from the Council of Trent. It declared that, in spiritual (as distinct from sacramental) communion, the grace of justification is present, even when the sacrament is
missing. The law governing the actual sacrament is subsumed under the
doctrine of justification. The actual sacrament need not be present for communion with God to be real.

Does this relativity of church law deprive it of all power and validity?
No. It has power and validity, in short, true effectiveness, when it is recognized by the moral conscience of the individual. Until it is recognized by the
conscience church law is not the norm of conscience. But once recognized,
the law has power and validity. To be sure, the law remains relative. But a
law can be both authoritative and relative.

The limitations of our knowledge cannot always be overcome by the
greater intelligence of the church. We cannot simply state that, because our
knowledge is limited, we should adhere always to the letter of the church's
law. There are situations in which the letter of the law does not suffice. In
these situations, a person must proceed according to conscience and without hope of official church support. Universal laws cannot and do not cover
concrete instances completely. We can imagine a situation in which a person
simultaneously may be justified before God and a lawbreaker before the
church. The person remains subject to church law, and may well be pun-
ished for disobedience. But the law of the church recognizes that it must
leave room for the free moral decision of individuals.

Rahner reiterates that he is acknowledging the relativity of law, not
proposing a "situational" interpretation governed by subjectivity. Law is a
real expression of the church and of God's intention for it. But law can neither be simply identified with God's will and Spirit, nor dismissed in liber-
tinism.

D. THE CHURCH AS THE PLACE FOR LOVE OF GOD AND OF NEIGHBOR

(VII.8.D, p. 398). The church is, for the Christian, the place for the love
of both God and neighbor. In these two loves, one discovers one's true
essence, says Rahner; at the same time, these loves are a gift, and not one's
own possession. The church is the place where we have "the assurance and
promise" that God loves us.

When a person encounters God, he or she wants to experience God, not
only in the ultimate depth of conscience, but also in something tangible. The
church is the tangible place. Human love is something necessary to life, yes;
but "from a human point of view," says Rahner, human love "reaches a
dead end" and "comes to naught" (p. 399). It attempts to bridge the chasm

that divides people, but human love has no final guarantee of ultimate success. The ultimate success of human love exists in a process whose fulfillment lies in hope.

The pledge of this hope is sacramentally present in the church. "Interpersonal love can find ultimate success only if it takes place within the realm of God" (p. 399). It is "given in hope" and "present in the church" (p. 399).

E. THE UNIQUENESS OF THE CHRISTIAN OFFER OF MEANING
   IN A PLURALISTIC SOCIETY

(VII.8.E, p. 400). The church often seems to be no more than one among other groups in a pluralistic society, each competing for a claim on us, each offering a limited worldview. But Rahner says that the church transcends pluralistic life. It does so, first of all, because it does not offer an ideology, but liberation into the mystery of God. The church is not in competition with other groups, but a place where faith in the transcendental God is expressed.

Second, non-Christians are not living out their existence in opposition to Christianity, says Rahner. The Christian recognizes the non-Christian as the one to whom God has offered the divine self as freedom. Whenever one accepts one's existence with resolve and trust, confident that it has meaning, one is accepting God. Christians stand beyond pluralistic confusion without despising it. They affirm all people who hear God's word and who respond to it with good will.

· VIII ·

Remarks on Christian Life

This chapter has two parts. In part 1, Rahner describes the Christian life as a relationship between the life of inner freedom and adherence to Christian moral norms. When human beings accept reality, they freely accept its burdens and responsibilities (even the burden and responsibility of death) as a gift from God. The Christian acceptance of reality is not a passive resignation but active obedience to God. Part 2 treats the sacraments of the church. The sacraments are God's offer of salvation in the church. When Christians receive the sacraments, they are responding to the offer that God has made. The Christian life is not a special kind of life, removed from ordinary reality. Rather, it is life as it really is, the life that God has given.

1. General Characteristics of Christian Life

(VIII.1, p. 402). In this section, Rahner describes the relationship between the life of inner freedom and adherence to Christian moral norms. Accepting reality is the basis of freedom. When we accept reality, we freely accept its burdens and responsibilities as a gift from God (A). Hence our realism, Rahner says, is pessimistic. It acknowledges death, not just as the passage to eternal life, but also as a harsh fate that we all must endure (B). On the other side of death, however, is God's future. It belongs to every Christian who regards the future as God's gift to humanity (C). Life is a plurality, but it is God's plurality, and its unity and purpose lie with God (D). Christians recognize the difference between what they are and what they are called to be. For that reason, their acceptance of reality is not passive resignation but active obedience to God. We distinguish between this obedience to God and obedience to concrete moral norms. The moral norms are conditioned by time and they express (but are no substitute for) a transcendental encounter with God. Although they are secondary expressions, moral norms accord with an existential knowledge of God and deserve obedience (E).

146

A. THE FREEDOM OF CHRISTIANS

(VIII.1.A, p. 402). The "basic and ultimate thrust" of Christian life is not that the Christian is a special instance of humanity. Rather, Christian life is human life as it really is. Christian life accepts reality in its fullness. The Christian, even the anonymous Christian, "accepts without reservation the whole of concrete human life" (p. 402). People without implicit faith in God lack this acceptance. They want to escape the burdens and responsibilities of life that they claim to have been unjustly imposed on humanity. The Christian sees these burdens and responsibilities as part of humanity's common task.

Christian life is the life of freedom, says Rahner, freedom as openness to the whole of reality, including God. The person without freedom is not open. He or she wants to avoid reality, to escape the forces that determine our existence. To be sure, part of our task is the struggle to free humanity from forces that oppress us. God has given us gifts and abilities, and we use them well when we put them at the service of human liberation. But it is impossible to be free of all burdens and responsibilities. True freedom lies in the gift of God's own self, says Rahner, "throughout all the imprisonments of existence" (p. 403).

B. THE REALISM OF CHRISTIANS

(VIII.1.B, p. 403). Christian life is characterized by what Rahner calls "pessimistic realism." It is realism in its openness to the whole of reality. It is pessimistic because it sees existence "as dark and bitter and hard," that is, a "risk" that leads to death. The Christian is an existentialist in that he or she makes a decision about existence—a decision to accept reality. Reality includes the hope that God will triumph over the risks of this world with divine love.

The Christian realist knows that human existence has "to pass through death" (p. 404). Facing death means acknowledging the hardness and darkness of death. It means recognizing that death "is the only passage to the life which really does not die" (p. 404). Our pessimistic realism consists in accepting death and renouncing everything that would distract us from reality or substitute for it.

C. THE HOPE OF CHRISTIANS

(VIII.1.C, p. 404). Christian hope consists in the realistic belief that God's future—"the absolute and infinite future"—belongs to every Christian. It belongs to him or her in the sense that God offers that future as a grace and a gift. The Christian, Rahner says, "hopes for the infinite and therefore confronts the finite calmly" (p. 405). He or she is free of the illusion that the present is the whole of reality. The present is "encompassed by the holy mystery of eternal love."

D. CHRISTIANITY AND THE PLURALISM OF HUMAN EXISTENCE

(VIII.1.D, p. 405). The Christian is open to the pluralism of reality for two reasons. First, the Christian knows that pluralism is itself the creation of God. Second, the Christian knows that God is different from pluralism. Because reality belongs to God, one can open oneself to it "in real trust and without reservation." But because the pluralism of reality is not God, not the divine itself, the Christian knows that its unity and purpose lie "beyond the realm of his [God's] tangible reality." The pluralism of reality is not a system that humanity can control. Why should one give oneself up to such a pluralism, surrendering in trust and without reservation? Because in this pluralism, God communicates the divine self. To be sure, this communication is mediated. But it is nonetheless a true communication.

E. THE RESPONSIBILITY OF CHRISTIANS

(VIII.1.E, p. 407). One might protest against this line of thought. One might say that, if the basic thrust of Christian life is to accept human life as it is, then one denies the need for moral striving. Acceptance, one might say, is passivity. If this world is the best of all possible words, and if "whatever is, is right," then why try to improve oneself? Rahner replies that self-acceptance means accepting oneself as a moral being. To be human is to recognize the difference between what we are and what we ought to be. Only by accepting this aspect of being human does one become a Christian.

Accepting our humanity always means accepting it in what Rahner calls an "upward direction." We see the difference between what we are and what we should be, and we attempt to overcome the difference. Overcoming the difference means rising in response to God's Word. The decision for or against God is primary.

We must distinguish, as does Catholic moral theology, between objective moral norms and our subjective obligation to heed the word of God. The objective norm is binding, but it is historically conditioned. More important is the recognition of the difference between what one is and what one should be. Obedience to God in faithfulness is our primary obligation. Catholic theology recognizes that some individual moral norms "belong to a concrete reality which is different from God" (p. 408). These moral norms have only a relative value.

To be sure, one cannot disdain moral norms. To do so would be to make one's own judgment absolute. Such a judgment would then become a godless ideology. The Christian rejects such solipsism. But we must recall that God's word speaks to the human subject immediately. Hearing that word is essential to being human. Hence our subjective obligation of faithfulness to God is primary. Adherence to moral norms is secondary.

Ultimately, however, there is an "intrinsic unity between morality and religion" (p. 410). Although love for one's neighbor always transcends an ethic of laws, nevertheless those laws express that love. Rahner says that love is "the absolute sum of all moral obligations" (p. 410). To be sure, love for one's neighbor may be expressed today in different ways from those of the past. Those new expressions represent an authentically prophetic impulse, critical of the past and constructive of the future. But if love is the genuine love of true religion, then its expression is genuinely moral and cannot be opposed to moral norms.

Our Christian responsibility is to see reality for what it is. We are to acknowledge ourselves as God's creatures. We are sinful and weak, yes, but capable of confessing that sinfulness and of making the choices offered by God. That is what it means to say that we are simultaneously justified and sinners.

2. The Sacramental Life

(VIII.2, p. 411). In this section, Rahner presents a basic catechesis on the seven sacraments in the context of the basic sacrament, the church. He begins with what is basic about the church: it is the salvation history of human life made finally manifest, explicit, and irreversible. Within the church, which is the sign of God's efficacious word, God's gracious self-communication becomes tangible (A). Jesus instituted the sacraments in a way analogous to his founding of the church: he intended a church in which God's grace is tangibly sacramental (B). The sacraments in their public and ecclesial dimension—the *opus operatus*—are efficacious when they become the *opus operantis*, encountering humanity's openness and freedom (C). Baptism incorporates the believer into the church, initiating him or her into the death of Christ. Confirmation is the sign of the full maturation of Christian gifts for the church's mission (D). Holy Orders and Matrimony are signs of faithful people realizing their identity in the church, in one case by means of the love of the married couple and, in another case, by the service of the ordained minister (E). Penance is God's offer of forgiveness by means of the explicit reconciliation of the church. Anointing of the Sick is the church's holy word to the person in danger of death (F). Eucharist is a meal of thanksgiving and a continuation of the one sacrifice of Christ: we give thanks for what God has done by incorporating us into the life of the Son (G). Although each sacrament is different, together they offer God's Word to humanity, relate the believer to the church, help to realize the believer's role in the church, and unite us to God (H). The sacraments are God's offer of salvation in the church, and the reception of the sacraments is the response to the offer empowered by God (I). The Christian life is not a special kind of life but rather life as it really is, the life God has given, and the Christian reflects on it in an explicit way (J).

A. THE CHURCH AS BASIC SACRAMENT AND THE SEVEN SACRAMENTS

(VIII.2.A, p. 411). The transcendental relation between humanity and divinity is the right context for understanding the sacraments. It is not right to say that the seven sacraments are the only gifts of God, outside of which there is no grace. On the contrary, says Rahner, "The history of salvation and grace has its roots in the essence of man which has been divinized by God's self-communication" (p. 411). This is the proper context for understanding the sacraments. They are part of what Rahner calls "the process in which there becomes explicit and historically tangible the history of salvation" (p. 411). The history of salvation, we will recall, is coextensive with history as a whole (see p. 142). In the Judaeo-Christian history of revelation, the salvation that began with human history has become manifest. Sacraments and the entirety of the church "are only especially prominent, historically manifest and clearly tangible events in a history of salvation which is identical with the life of man as a whole" (p. 412). In the church, the process of salvation has become manifest as an object for reflection.

Salvation history entered into "its final, eschatological and irreversible phase" (p. 412) with Christ, the church, and its sacraments. In this history, God's eventual triumph is implicit, because Christians believe that the triumph cannot be undone by human beings. The sacraments signify the triumph of God. A Christian sacrament takes place "wherever the finality and invincibility of God's offer of himself becomes manifest in the concrete life of an individual through the church which is the basic sacrament" (p. 412). The church is a sign of salvation but is not salvation itself.

If the church and the sacraments signify (but may not be simply identified with) salvation, then how are they "efficacious"? Rahner says that they are efficacious because God is efficacious. "God's act of grace . . . continues to be definitively bound up with the acceptance of this offer" of grace (p. 412). The sacraments are efficacious because they manifest what God has done and continues to do—namely, to offer to human beings God's own life. In the seven sacraments, the church involves human beings with itself as the basic sacrament.

B. INSTITUTION BY JESUS CHRIST

(VIII.2.B, p. 413). Although it is problematic to trace the institution of the sacraments to their verbal institution by Jesus, nevertheless the sacraments can be understood in that way. The institution of the seven sacraments, says Rahner, is analogous to the institution of the church by Christ. We can show that Jesus envisioned the continuation of his teaching and ministry. We can show that the sacramentality of the church is implicit in the church's very essence. We can show that the seven sacraments are an interpretation of the church's sacramentality.

C. "OPUS OPERATUM"—"OPUS OPERANTIS"

(VIII.2.C, p. 413). Christians as a whole grasp a basic eschatology: the world is being redeemed, and the drama of salvation history has a happy ending. But one cannot know, as an individual, how God will judge "the secret depths of his own freedom" (p. 413). No one knows his or her destiny in advance. The individual cannot say "that he accepts with some absolute certainty the word and the offer which comes to him from God with absolute certainty" (p. 414). We are not in a position to judge our acceptance of God's Word.

To be sure, the Catholic admits that the sacrament is an *opus operatum*, a work of God that "causes of itself." God's offer has "an absolute unconditionality and certainty" (p. 414). But this *opus operatum* "encounters the still open word of an individual who responds with a 'yes' or a 'no,' and this is the *opus operantis*" (p. 414). The sacraments are not magic rites. They (1) do not coerce God, and they (2) "are efficacious only to the extent that they encounter man's openness and freedom" (p. 414). To profess belief in a sacrament as an *opus operatum* is to profess faith in God.

We falsely understand the sacraments as quasi-magic acts when we think that the sacraments exist in order to relieve us of an "ultimate and personal decision in faith, hope, and love" (pp. 414–15). In reality, they confront us with a decision about God.

D. THE SACRAMENTS OF INITIATION

(VIII.2.D, p. 415). Baptism has an individual salvific effect. It means that one's sins are forgiven, the glory of God's grace is communicated, and the capacity for faith, hope, and love is bestowed. But Baptism is not given primarily for individual salvation. Individual salvation can be achieved without the sacrament. Baptism is primarily an incorporation into the church. There, in the church, God's forgiveness has a human, tangible quality. There God's glory is recognized in communal worship. There one shares with others one's faith, hope, and love.

Along with the grace of the church, Baptism gives "a share in, and the mandate and capacity for participating in," the church. The church is the historical tangibility of God's grace in the world" (p. 416). Baptism requires that a person play his or her ecclesial role. In other words, one is obliged by Baptism to participate in the church.

Baptism is the more negative aspect, and Confirmation the more positive, in a single process of initiation. In Baptism, we die into the death of Christ. In Confirmation, we are empowered to give witness, to attain the fullness of Christian charisms, and to undertake a mission. Confirmation is "the grace of the church for its mission to the world" (p. 417).

E. THE SACRAMENTS OF THE STATES OF LIFE

(VIII.2.E, p. 417). Orders and Matrimony do not found two different states of life. It is not true to say that, because the married state and the celibate state are different, the two sacraments could not be administered to the same person. The two sacraments are rather two ways by which the church actualizes itself as the basic sacrament. The church is actualizing itself in relation to a person who is making a decision constitutive for his or her salvation. The church does not decide the person's vocation by administering the sacrament. No, it is the person who makes the decision.

Orders. Rahner then asks whether the sacrament of Orders, by which the church hands on its offices, is also a means of sanctification for the one who receives it. He answers as follows. God wants the church to be holy. If God wants the church to be holy, then God wants the church's officials to be holy. If they were unholy, then the church could not depend on them to help bring about the mission of the church.

But the church does depend on them. "The existence and continuation of sacraments" in general (although not the efficacy of any one celebration of the sacraments) depends on the holiness of ministers. Since God wills the holiness of the sacraments, then God must will a holy hierarchy. Thus the sacrament of Orders is also directed at the sanctification of the person who receives the sacrament.

Matrimony. Marriage is also a sacrament of a state of life. Since marriage is "an event of the grace and love which unites God and man" (p. 419), it is "a moment in the self-actualization of the church" (p. 419). The bride and groom "manifest that love which unites God and man" (p. 419).

Then Rahner asks whether the manifestation of love in marriage is essential to the church. Rahner says that it is. The heart of the parallel between the church and marriage is this: the unity of the love itself in one flesh. Creation is incorporated into the order of grace. Creation has significance for grace. All human moral activity has "a hidden relation to Christ" (p. 420), in which this activity has its fulfillment.

In summary, then, Rahner states that marriage is a sign of God's love. "Whenever there is a unity in love between two persons . . . in their final and definitive validity, this is the effect and the manifestation of the grace which . . . becomes manifest in the unity between Christ and the church" (p. 420). There the church is present as "the smallest community of the redeemed and sanctified" (p. 421). The married couple is the church in miniature.

F. Penance and the Anointing of the Sick

(VIII.2.F, p. 421). Penance and Anointing reflect the reality that our new life in Christ is always the threatened life of a sinner. "If we have experienced how hopeless real guilt before God is just from our human perspective, then we long to hear the word of forgiveness from God" (p. 421). In forgiveness, God communicates the divine self. In Penance, a person who has said "no" to God receives that forgiveness.

"God's word of forgiveness is not only the consequence, but is also and ultimately the presupposition of the conversion in which a guilty person turns to God and surrenders himself" (p. 421). The word has been extended throughout history. It found its irrevocable expression in Jesus Christ. "He entered into solidarity with sinners in love, and he accepted God's word of forgiveness for us in the final act of his faith, hope, and love in the midst of the darkness of his death, the death in which he experienced the darkness of our guilt" (p. 422). His death was as dark as the guilt of human beings.

The church offers forgiveness in many ways. The church promises the forgiveness of sins in Baptism, in prayer, and in confession (whether privately or when the individual confesses "before God and his Christ in the common confession of a community," p. 422). By sin, we place ourselves "in contradiction to the essence of the holy community" (pp. 422–23). So when, in God's word of forgiveness, the church extends forgiveness, it extends it by forgiving the injustice that the sinner has done to the church.

The Anointing of the Sick must be seen in its fundamental context, the situation of final illness. Alone the faithful individual must decide how he or she will understand the meaning of life. In this loneliness, the individual is never wholly alone. With God "there also surrounds him the holy community of believers, of those who love and pray, of those who in life try to exercise the obedience of death, and who in life try to gaze upon the dying one in faith" (p. 423). We live, says Rahner, "from out of the death" of the Lord. Jesus accepted God's word of forgiveness for us in his own death, accepted in complete obedience. So we want the church, Christ's body, present at the sickbed.

The church, through its minister, speaks a holy word to the person who is ill. He allows not only the interior acceptance of grace for the sick person, but he allows the grace of the Spirit-filled church to be present as an event. Grace takes place by becoming corporeal. The very sickness becomes a situation of grace and salvation. The person receives grace because he or she believes and is longing for forgiveness.

G. The Eucharist

(VIII.2.G, p. 424). The Eucharist is the sacrament of the church in a very radical sense. The Lord's Supper was essential to the founding of the church.

It is essential to Jesus' own understanding of himself as a mediator of salvation. Although we speak of the sacrament of the Eucharist as one of the seven sacraments, nevertheless it stands alone.

Understanding Jesus' role as mediator of salvation helps us understand the institution of the sacrament. On the night before he died, Jesus ate a meal, within which he gave to his followers his own body and blood under the appearance of receiving bread and wine. Jesus had accepted his death and connected it with the content of his preaching. He regarded the celebration as an anticipation of the final banquet. It was the foundation of the community of his friends and followers.

The eucharistic food is the body of the one who gave his life in free obedience. The Eucharist is a real meal. By eating it, one is incorporated into the body of Jesus' spiritual community. It assures us of Christ's presence wherever the Lord's Supper is celebrated.

It is not just the presence of Christ in general, but the presence of the suffering and dying servant of God. In that sense, the Eucharist is a sacrifice as well as a meal. It is a sacrifice in that within the Eucharist, the one sacrifice of Jesus continues to be effective, to live on in the liturgical act of representation.

Fundamentally, the Eucharist is connected to thanksgiving. It is the church's way of making real God's offer of the divine self and of giving thanks for it. It is God's "most intense" self-communication, says Rahner, because Jesus gave it the form of his own life, the life that God loved and definitively accepted.

Finally, Rahner describes the individual and the ecclesial effects of the Eucharist. It is individual in that it gives one a participation in the life of Jesus, the life of love, obedience to the Father, gratitude, forgiveness, and patience. It is ecclesial as well. In the Eucharist, God's saving will—God's will to give the divine self to humanity—becomes visible and tangible. The Eucharist is the very tangibility and permanence of God's gift of self. The Eucharist is "the fullest actualization of the essence of the church," Rahner concludes, because it is "the presence of Christ in time and space" (p. 427).

H. Common Aspects of the Sacraments

(VIII.2.H, p. 427). What are the common aspects of the seven sacraments? Every sacrament is the presence of God's efficacious Word. When any of the sacraments are received fruitfully (as well as validly), human beings respond. They respond not just in inner freedom but also in a public, historical, and social way. That is why the sacraments involve words and things: water, bread, oil, touch. But of words and things, words are primary. In some sacraments (i.e. Matrimony and Penance), God's Word is present in human words alone. That is why Rahner defines every sacrament as an "efficacious word of God."

All sacraments, moreover, relate a person to the church. They are not just administered by the church, but they are the self-actualization of the church. In the sacraments, the church is actual (and not just potential) for both the minister and the receiver. That is why Rahner calls the sacraments a dialogue. In the dialogue, God addresses humanity and "establishes creatures in their own reality and freedom" (p. 428). God speaks to humanity from creation onward. In every moment God addresses us. And God has created us to be able to hear God and respond in a way that is worthy.

Sacraments address the individual more specifically than the kind of general address to be found in a sermon. In the sacraments, the church makes a specific demand on the human being. Every sacrament is not only the self-actualization of the church, but "an event in the relationship between the individual and the church" (p. 428). In the sacraments the faithful person recognizes his or her place and function: as a member, as a eucharistic concelebrant, as a reconciled sinner, etc.

Finally, the sacraments are mysteries that unite the past, present, and future in a way that corresponds to the essence of humanity and of God. Rahner speaks of this in the language of Thomas Aquinas. Sacraments are a memory of God's offer in Christ (*signa rememorativa*); they effect what they express (*signa demonstrativa*); and they anticipate the fulfillment of eternal life (*signa prognostica*).

I. OFFICIAL-ECCLESIAL SALVIFIC ACT AND EXISTENTIELL SALVIFIC ACT

(VIII.2.I, p. 429). In this brief section, Rahner shows the unity of the sacraments as both official acts of the church and as moments in the salvation of an individual. The sacraments, as an "operative work" of the church (an *opus operatum*), are not to be distinguished from the sacraments as the "operating work" of Christ on an individual's life (the *opus operantis*). It is wrong to say that the sacraments as the work of the church are alone the act of God upon the person in grace and that the individual's acceptance of the grace of the sacraments is merely a free human act. Both are aspects of a single dialogical relationship with God in grace. The *opus operatus* manifests human salvation in an ecclesial way, and the *opus operantis* manifests salvation in a merely existentiell (but nonetheless grace-filled) act.

Rahner draws a parallel between the sacraments and the official and explicit history of human salvation. There is a history of salvation that (while coexisting with the history of the human spirit) finds an unsurpassable expression in the Bible and the tradition of the church. In the same way, there is a gift of God's grace that (while being given in myriad ways to humanity) finds official, explicit, and juridical presence in the sacraments. "Everything in human life is indeed the history of salvation," says Rahner, "but not everything is for this reason sacramental in this narrower and stricter sense" (p. 430).

J. REDUCTIO IN MYSTERIUM

(VIII.2.J, p. 430). In this final section, Rahner returns to the opening remarks of chapter VIII. Christians accept life as it really is. "The ultimately Christian thing about this life is identical with the mystery of human existence" (p. 430). The Christian is the one who "allows himself to fall into the mystery which we call God." The Christian believes that, by falling into God, he or she is "really falling into a blessed and forgiving mystery which divinizes us." The Christian knows that he or she is committed to God in an explicit and conscious way and not just living unreflectively. To be sure, other human beings may be living an anonymously Christian existence, to the degree that they strive to hear God's invitation and respond to it, and they may find salvation as well. But the Christian seeks life as it is—the life to which God's explicit, tangible, and historical revelation belongs.

·IX·

Eschatology

Chapter IX has three parts. In part 1, Rahner lays out the presuppositions for understanding eschatology, the doctrine of the last things. He states that we must understand eschatological statements as a projection by the Christian community about its own future. That future is not to be understood merely as the future of individuals but also as the collective destiny of all persons. It cannot be reduced to a single scenario. In part 2 of the chapter, Rahner examines the individual aspect of eschatology. Rahner distinguishes individual eschatology (the destiny of the individual at death) from collective eschatology (the destiny of creation as a whole). He rejects, however, the idea of two eschatologies, for together they make up a single reality. The eternal life that is God's will for human beings is their participation in the good, the good which God invites them to choose. Once they have chosen it, their participation in God has communal consequences. Part 3 looks at the collective dimension of eschatology. The death of an individual is not simply a moment of his or her escape from history. It is rather the moment in which the individual's contribution to history—that is, to history as the fulfillment of human destiny—begins to achieve its final form. The individual's concrete acts of love are a participation in the salvation and love of God and contribute to it.

1. Presuppositions for Understanding Eschatology

(IX.1, p. 431). Eschatology is traditionally the doctrine of the "last things"—death, judgment, heaven, and hell. But fundamentally, says Rahner, it is about the human being, "a being who ex-ists from out of his present 'now' towards his future" (p. 431). The human being lives by anticipating and choosing. As creatures, we human beings cannot dispose of our future as if it were wholly in our control. But we can say what possibilities we hope will be freely given to us and freely accepted by us.

A. ON THE HERMENEUTICS OF ESCHATOLOGICAL STATEMENTS

(IX.1.A, p. 431). When Christians read eschatological statements in the Bible, they are tempted to interpret them "as anticipatory, eyewitness accounts of a future which is still outstanding" (p. 431)—in other words, as predictions. But although the Bible and the church say a lot about the future, Rahner asserts that their statements should not be read as if they denied the human ability to make choices. Eschatological statements do not destroy human freedom.

To be sure, every human being is a member of a community. That means that every human being belongs to a collective history. One corollary of this "belonging" is the existence of a collective eschatology. It makes sense to say that every human being will face the last things. But a collective eschatology does not mean that every person will share the same fate. Eschatology is the realm of freedom. Christian statements about the future, says Rahner, speak of this eschatology as "the milieu and environment of transcendental spirit" (p. 432). We are not merely actors reading our lines, but manifest the human spirit in our choices. Hence eschatological statements are not the plot of a drama whose final act we know in advance. They are rather "conclusions from the experience of the Christian present" (p. 432). They are the Christian community's collective projections about the future. In imagination we project our own future and understand the present as the coming-to-be of that imagined world.

Rahner distinguishes between eschatology and apocalyptic. Eschatology is a view of how the future "has to be" if the Christian's view of the present is correct. Apocalyptic is a mode of expression that takes seriously the concreteness of the eschatological future. Biblical apocalyptic speaks of the future as if the writers were eyewitnesses. Eschatology is what the apocalyptic writers mean. They are projecting their interpretation of the present into the future. We have to distinguish between the form of thought and expressions they use (on the one hand) and the true content of their assertions (on the other).

Apocalyptic images speak of what is real, namely, our hope for the future. It is real because it is based on a real experience of the present. But often the images suggest a future that we, with our present Christian anthropology, may not be able to affirm. As an example (not proposed by Rahner), consider the statement by the author of Revelation (7:4) that the number of those "sealed" (under God's protection) is 144,000. It is hard to believe that the number of the saved is so small. A deeper analysis suggests that this apocalyptic number does not predict the number of the saved but connotes an eschatological truth, namely, that God's salvation will be complete. We have to use caution when interpreting apocalyptic statements.

Undoubtedly there are implications in biblical apocalyptic from which we can learn. That is the task of hermeneutics, to discern the truth that the biblical authors intend. But Rahner warns against extravagant claims. "We know no more about the last things," he writes, "than we know about people who have been redeemed, who have been taken up into Christ, and who exist in God's grace" (p. 434). We know about them from their life in our midst, prior to their death, but not from their present experience.

B. THE PRESUPPOSITION FOR A UNIFIED ESCHATOLOGY

(IX.1.B, p. 434). A unified eschatology includes both the body and the soul. Rahner contrasts it with the partial eschatology that looks only to the salvation of the soul. Rationalists in the style of the Enlightenment understood eschatology in this partial way. The problem with this partial understanding is that it ascribes immortality to the soul as an abstraction from the body. It is an individualistic and private salvation. But the destiny of the soul, Rahner asserts, is not "independent of the transformation of the world" and not independent of the resurrection of the flesh. To be sure, it is correct to speak of the immortality of the soul. It is a part of the salvation of the single person. But there is more to eschatology than the fate of the individual. The last things have to do, not just with the individual soul, but with the body in general, with the collective destiny of all persons.

C. THE HIDDENNESS OF THE LAST THINGS

(IX.1.C, p. 434). An eschatology that "is not apocalyptic" (one that does not mistake the language of allegory for the realities it expresses) remains focused on the incomprehensible mystery of God. It is hidden. Such an eschatology does not speak as if it could predict the future. When Christians speak about eschatology, they move "beyond all images into the ineffable" (p. 434).

2. The One Eschatology as Individual Eschatology

(IX.2, p. 435). The second part of this chapter is about the last things understood from the viewpoint of the individual. Rahner distinguishes individual eschatology (the destiny of the individual at death) from collective eschatology (the destiny of creation as a whole). He rejects, however, the idea of two eschatologies. Although one can speak of them as individual and collective, they mutually influence one another and make up a single reality. Rahner begins by noting that, although it is customary to distinguish between the body and the soul, this is the language of apocalyptic, and the two form an eschatological unity (A). The eternal life that is God's will for human beings is their participation in the good, the good which God invites them to choose and which, once chosen, has eternal consequences (B). Purgatory is the doctrine that expresses the interval between an individual's fundamental decision for God and the integration of that decision in the whole of one's reality (C). The many statements in tradition about the last things represent a plurality of viewpoints, and we should not expect to synthesize them into a neat concept (D). Hell represents the possibility of eternal loss, a possibility that exists throughout all of one's life, but which is not equal in weight to God's will that all will be saved (E).

A. The Definitive Validity of Free Human Actions

(IX.2.A, p. 435). Rahner begins this section by recalling chapter III. There he argued that statements about heaven and hell are not parallel. "Heaven" is a much more potent symbol. Why? Because Christian faith teaches that "the history of salvation as a whole will reach a positive conclusion" (p. 435). Hell, by contrast, is a negative symbol. It symbolizes what God does not want, namely, the rejection by human beings of God's vision for the world. To be sure, we cannot simply hold a theory of "apocatastasis" (i.e., the restoration, reestablishment, or renovation of the world by an act of God that makes all things right). But we are not obliged either to say that the history of salvation will result for some people in absolute loss. God wills that all will be saved but allows creatures to reject salvation.

When Christians speak of the last things, they normally distinguish between the fate of the body (which undergoes corruption) and that of the soul (which is immortal). But Rahner questions the value of the distinction for a unified eschatology. What does it mean, he asks, to speak about a person whose body is buried and whose soul or transcendental being enjoys God's presence? The human being is a unity. We only meet the human spirit as corporeal and historical. It is "superfluous," says Rahner, "to ask what a person does while his body is in the grave and his soul is already with God" (p. 436). The dichotomy is more apocalyptic than eschatological. In other words, we distinguish between body and soul to express a profound truth, namely, that the spiritual reality of the person does not die. We express this reality in terms of the traditional concepts of beatific vision and resurrection of the flesh. They mean that the entire person, body and soul, is fulfilled in God.

What, then, does the church mean by speaking of a "time" between the death of the individual and his or her ultimate destiny? Rahner answers this question by speaking of two "finalities." One finality is that of the individual's personal history. That personal history ends at the moment of death. The other finality is that of the human collective reality. It refers to the ultimate destiny of humanity, including the effect that every individual has on that ultimate destiny. Thus the two finalities are not separate. The finality of each individual's death is linked to the finality of human destiny, a destiny to which each individual contributes.

B. DEATH AND ETERNITY

(IX.2.B, p. 436). What does it mean to say that the dead are "still alive"? It certainly does not mean that life continues unaltered after death. "Death marks an end for the whole person," says Rahner (p. 437). But it is equally wrong to reject the concept of eternity and to say that human life is over at death. The individual has a proper end, an end that begins in life and continues after his or her death. The new does not simply annul the old that has died.

Rahner expresses the doctrine in this way: "Eternity subsumes time by being liberated from the time which came to be temporarily so that freedom and something of final and definitive validity can be achieved" (p. 437). What does this mean? Eternity subsumes time because what was achieved in time becomes eternal. It is no longer time-bound. Yes, our actions are temporary, but their value is not. Their value expresses our freedom.

When we act freely—that is, in true spiritual freedom, unhindered by what would prevent us from obeying God—then we are joined with God's eternal life. Our deeds in time flower in eternity. They flower in that they are the mature expression of God's Spirit in us. Death, the end of the whole person, allows that person to reach or express his or her God-given freedom in a final way. Our final validity comes to be in time, not to continue on in time, but to "form" time. In other words, we are co-creators with God, and we put God's stamp on time.

Personal existence survives despite biological death. It does so because the person is more than time. He or she is part of an "inexhaustible and indestructible mystery" (p. 438). The person's real self does not simply fall into nothingness after death but rather shares in an absolute good. The self has produced something in time that cannot be erased by time. Our good, that is, the good we have chosen and to which we have committed ourselves, has "ripened into an experience of immortality" (p. 438). Death is not the end because we have already experienced immortality before death. It is the immortality of a commitment to the good. It is the immortality of a hope that God's grace and promise are real.

The good we do, and the hope we have, are experienced in moral decisions. These decisions are "incommensurable" with transitory time. Our present assessment of them is not a final assessment. There is more to them than we can say. In a decision for absolute goodness, we transcend time. When we choose the good, we participate in the eternal life of God, the source of good.

It is not uncommon to hear today that by rejecting Christianity's moral law, one is ultimately expressing one's freedom. The rejection of Christian morality, some say, frees people from superstition and the inhibitions of outmoded belief. Liberated individuals, it is said, make responsible choices without a slavish belief in religion's "ultimate good." But Rahner questions this assertion. He states that the very concept of free choice, even the supposedly free choice to reject the moral laws that society (including Christian society) defines as good, implicitly affirms the basis for the moral law. It does so by affirming the existence of freedom, which is a spiritual good. When a person proclaims himself or herself as "liberated" from morality, he or she implicitly affirms the spiritual freedom that is the foundation of morality.

The materialist states that all evolution is owing to chance. He or she believes that what Christians call the "good" is merely a radical and empty arbitrariness or a set of conventional moral expectations. Christians affirm, however, that one choice is truly better than another. They mean that there is a spiritual reality, unseen by the materialist, namely, the good itself. This has consequences for the understanding of eternity. When people commit themselves to the good, they are setting this commitment over against time. The very act of making a commitment to the good is an experience of eternity. Eternity lives in our choices, which are our participation in the good.

Christian revelation suggests that God allows every person to experience eternity in this life. We experience what St. John called eternal life in our moral choices. Rahner puts the matter this way: "Scripture does not know of any human life which is so commonplace that it is not valuable enough to become eternal" (p. 441). When we experience this eternity in time, that is, the eternal life of our good choices, we experience our final and definitive validity. God validates our contribution by adding it to the final destiny of human beings. This final and definitive validity is what the church calls the resurrection of the flesh.

C. On the Doctrine about a "Place of Purification"

(IX.2.C, p. 441). The doctrine of purgatory expresses two main ideas. One is that the basic disposition of the human being, a disposition that has come about in the exercise of free actions, acquires a final validity at death. The other is that the person continues to mature after death. Even at the moment of death the basic disposition of the human being has not permeated his or her concrete, corporeal existence. The person has made an ultimate and basic decision, but this decision has not yet been fully integrated.

Rahner explains this, first of all, by distinguishing between language and what it intends to convey. We commonly say that there is a "time" that arrives "after" death during which the person still can become his or her true self. The meaning of such temporal categories (e.g., "after" death) is far from clear. Moreover, symbols such as purgatory's "purifying fire" are apocalyptic images whose eschatological import must be rightly interpreted. We cannot simply accept the traditional language without asking what truth it means to convey.

Next, Rahner focuses on the temporal categories themselves. His main point is that there must be an interval between an individual's death and the person's corporeal fulfillment. One such interval exists between the act of making a fundamental decision for God and the full integration of that decision. Another interval exists between the fulfillment of the individual in death and the fulfillment of the world. A third interval exists between the final validity of a person in death and the manifestation of that fulfillment in the glorification of the body. This notion of interval is problematic, he says, and it is not clear in what senses such a temporal category can be applied. Ultimately, the dogma of purgatory needs to be retained, says Rahner, but not necessarily its mode of expression.

D. On the Necessary Pluralism of Statements about Fulfillment

(IX.2.D, p. 443). In this section, Rahner distinguishes between the fulfillment of the human being and the various statements used to speak about this one reality. The church has transmitted a number of ways to express this fulfillment. Immortality of the soul, resurrection of the flesh, interval after death, and collective eschatology are all ways to speak of the destiny of the person. The plurality of statements cannot be synthesized into a neat conceptual model. The Bible speaks of the last things in a straightforward way, but not all of its statements can be easily reconciled with one another.

E. The Possibility of Eternal Loss

(IX.2.E, p. 443). The most important thing to know about hell, says Rahner, is that it always remains a possibility for the human being. Up to the very end of life, a person must reckon with "absolute loss as the conclusion and outcome of his free guilt" (p. 443). This is fundamental to human freedom.

But the individual "does not need to know anything more than this about hell." For example, people do not have to resolve the question of the relation between the content of biblical statements about hell and their mode of expression, even the content of the words about hell ascribed to Jesus.

Finally, Rahner repeats his remark from chapter III that statements about heaven and hell are not parallel. Christian faith affirms that the history of the world as an entirety will in fact enter into eternal life with God. By contrast, the possibility of eternal loss is merely a possibility, not God's will.

3. The One Eschatology as Collective Eschatology

(IX.3, p. 444). The collective dimension of eschatology is the theme of part 3. Eschatology is one, embracing both the human individual and the collective human race. The death of an individual is not simply a moment of his or her escape from history. It is rather the moment in which the individual's contribution to history—that is, the fulfillment of human destiny—begins to achieve its final form (A). Christians believe that history is tending toward a goal, God's sharing of the divine life with humanity, uniting all creation with God's own self (B). Ultimately, one cannot divide salvation in God (the salvation we anticipate after death) from the salvation of the temporal order (expressed in acts of love in this world), because concrete acts of love show forth our participation in the salvation and love of God (C).

A. THE ANTHROPOLOGICAL NECESSITY OF COLLECTIVE STATEMENTS

(IX.3.A, p. 444). Eschatology necessarily speaks about the human being in two ways: first as an individual, and second as an element in the collective human reality. To be sure, the person is a transcendental, personal spirit; in short, an individual. Rahner discussed that in part 2 of this chapter. But the person is also a part of history, a member of the human race, a component within a milieu and an environment. That is part 3.

To ignore collective eschatology is to separate the human being from the world. It is to suggest that the fate of the individual is separate from the fate of the whole. Undoubtedly death and final destiny liberate individuals from history and grant them fulfillment. But every individual contributes and belongs to a collective. Christians believe that history itself is moving toward such a collective fulfillment. The history of the world, the history of spirit, and the history of salvation are all part of a "one-directional" history that is "moving towards its final and definitive validity" (p. 445).

B. THE CULMINATION OF THE HISTORY OF MANKIND
IN GOD'S FULL SELF-COMMUNICATION

(IX.3.B, p. 445). Rahner here expresses the belief that the history of the cosmos will culminate in the full self-communication of God. The inner momentum of all history is God's self-gift to creatures and their acceptance of this gift.

Rahner then raises the question of whether history would continue if all humanity (or rather, if all "spiritual, corporeal and free beings who work out their destiny before God") were destroyed. His answer is no, it would not continue. To be sure, the human race might fail, but that would not necessarily be the end of history. Even if human beings were destroyed, says Rahner, we can assume that there would be other spiritual and corporeal creatures capable of receiving God's gift of self. Only if all such creatures were to die would history end.

Why? Because "we know matter only as the seedbed of spirit and of subjectivity and of freedom" (p. 445). Christians believe that there is no creation independent of God's desire to share with us the divine life. Even inanimate matter, the basic building blocks of atoms and molecules, has an ultimate purpose. The preparation of matter to receive God's spirit—the eons of evolution—lasted a very long time, but that is the sense in which the Christian interprets evolution. The eons of evolution prepared matter to receive God's gift of self.

Rahner goes so far as to speculate that all matter will eventually be "subsumed into the fullness of God's self-communication" (p. 446). It is not just the human race, he says, that will be fulfilled in God. All matter will be fulfilled as well. It is in a process of transcending itself. This includes more than just human beings. It includes all sentient life and even inanimate matter. The very meaning of the world is to be "the realm of spiritual and personal history" (p. 446), the realm in which God is working to divinize all things.

For that reason, we cannot reduce eschatology to the destiny of individuals. That would be a "purely existential" and inadequate interpretation. Each individual contributes to the fulfillment of creation. "After individuals have played their role here, they do not depart from a drama which as a whole continues on endlessly" (p. 446). The drama itself has an ending. This drama is the dialogue between spiritual creatures and God. It had its climax in Christ. We are now, Rahner suggests, in the denouement.

C. INNER-WORLDLY UTOPIA AND CHRISTIAN ESCHATOLOGY

(IX.3.C, p. 446). What is the relation between our desire for salvation in God and our desire for a better life on earth? Rahner begins with the premise that God is the future of human beings. The future is not just a human construct. It is not just created and finite possibilities that we accomplish out of our own emptiness, possibilities with no end other than to return to the nothingness from which they arose. No, the future is the culmination of God's gift of self. God is both the future of the individual person and the future of collective humanity. The future is the creative and infinite being of God.

Every inner-worldly act of love for our neighbor, says Rahner, is an expression of love for God. Love for neighbor is the concrete way in which we love God. Every one of our acts of love, acts in which we commit ourselves responsibly to neighbor and to God, has "eternal significance and validity" (p. 447). When we perform an act of love for our neighbor, the miracle arises of God's love for us. It is "the miracle of the love and of the self-communication in which God gives himself to man" (p. 447). That is the unity and difference between love for God and for human beings. They are different but never separate.

• EPILOGUE •

Brief Creedal Statements

In this section, Rahner concludes *Foundations of Christian Faith* with three brief creedal statements. He prefaces them, first of all, with an explanation of the need for them. Brief creeds concentrate the faith into a formula that highlights its most important dimensions and their significance for contemporary readers. Next, Rahner explains the relation of his brief formulas to official symbols of the faith, like the Apostles' Creed. It cannot be superseded, to be sure, but new formulas, reflecting different situations in the world, are permissible and legitimate. After that, Rahner enumerates the requirements for writing a brief creedal statement. It ought to express the fundamentals of Christian faith as grounded in the history of Jesus Christ.

Finally, Rahner presents three brief formulas of faith. The first, a "theological" statement, emphasizes that the human experience of transcendence has its term or goal in the Father-God who invites and sustains the possibility of transcendence. The second and "anthropological" creed connects the love of human beings for one another with love for God, whose relationship with humanity reached its climax in Jesus Christ. The third, "future-oriented" creed portrays Christian faith as open to an absolute future. God draws humanity toward this future by sharing with it the Holy Spirit. After presenting these brief creeds, Rahner reflects on the Christian belief in the Trinity, the three divine "persons" in whom the one God is accomplishing the salvation of all.

Introduction

(P. 448). Could it be, asks Rahner, that the foregoing nine chapters have obscured the "idea" of Christianity toward which he has striven? He intends this epilogue, he says, for those readers who have found the scope of the earlier material daunting, the length of the presentations challenging, the development of the thought difficult—yes, and even for those readers who wish that he had clarified his insights more. The epilogue, he says, aims

166

"to try again and in another way to bring the whole of Christianity into view" (p. 448).

A. THE NEED FOR BRIEF CREEDAL STATEMENTS OF CHRISTIAN FAITH.

(Epilogue.A, p. 448). Two basic motives spur the effort to express Christian faith in brief creeds. One motive is to sharpen the focus of faith. Brief creeds enable believers to distinguish between the heart of faith and secondary aspects of it. They help a believer to take responsibility for faith.

The second basic motive for brief creedal statements is to make the faith intelligible to non-Christians. In a situation where many people disbelieve in Christ, short creeds can indicate the essence of Christianity, an essence that will differ considerably from mistaken but popular notions of it.

B. THE MULTIPLICITY OF POSSIBLE CREEDAL STATEMENTS.

(Epilogue.B, p. 449). Although Rahner concedes that the Apostles' Creed cannot be superseded by a new, universal creed, nevertheless different basic creeds are necessary. The differences among the various situations in the world where the gospel is preached requires various creeds. There can be, within the Christian church, no single theology.

The pluralism of theologies can no longer be integrated completely into a single theology, as they perhaps were in the homogeneous world of Hellenistic, Roman, and Western culture. Pluralism within theology is legitimate and necessary. Since no profession of faith exists without an implicit theology, theological pluralism requires a pluralism of creeds.

To be sure, the church has power to make definitive doctrinal decisions, and it will continue to do so, especially in the form of negative anathemas. But this does not mean that only the official representatives of the church can fashion creedal statements. Such statements can and should arise, adapted to the differences among nations, cultures, and histories.

C. REQUIREMENTS FOR A BASIC CREEDAL STATEMENT.

(Epilogue.C, p. 452). Every creedal statement should "contain what is of fundamental importance and what provides a basic starting point for reaching the whole of the faith" (p. 452). Short creedal statements will express— as indeed every really Christian creed must express—faith in the historical Jesus as Lord and savior. To be sure, Rahner's second, "anthropological" creed does not mention Jesus Christ. Nevertheless Rahner insists that even this creed has a "Christological implication."

i. A Brief Theological Creed

(Epilogue[i], p. 454). This sixty-seven-word creed (fifty-six words long in the German), emphasizes that human transcendence has its "term" or goal in God. God communicates the divine self to humanity in "forgiving love." Such love shows itself in God's ever-renewed invitation to transcend what we were—by making free and responsible choices—in accord with our conscience and innate abilities. God's forgiving love reached its climax in Jesus Christ. In him the divine self-communication became manifest as irreversible and victorious.

A. EXPLANATORY REMARKS

(Epilogue[i].A, p. 454). The brief theological creed has three main statements. The first is about the identity of God. Thomas Aquinas confidently affirmed that God exists. Rahner's creed, by contrast, indicates how we understand what the word "God" really means. We understand God as the goal of our everyday acts of knowledge and freedom.

God gives the divine self, second, to human beings as their fulfillment. In traditional terms, this means two things. First, God offers the divine self historically in the Logos or Son, that is, in Jesus Christ. Second, God sends the divine self "existentielly" in the Holy Spirit as the grace of justification. The self-communication of God in the two missions of Son and Spirit expresses the Trinity.

The third statement of the theological creed is that God's self-communication reaches its climax in Jesus of Nazareth. In Jesus, God not only offers the divine self. God also shows that, in Jesus' life, death, and resurrection, this divine gift of self has been accepted in the human race. Jesus Christ is the "firstborn among many" (Rom. 8:29), the first human being to have been completely united with God. He enjoyed a hypostatic union with the Father. This is the starting point for a theology of the church as the sacrament of God's work in Christ.

ii. A Brief Anthropological Creed

(Epilogue[ii], p. 456). This creed expresses the faith that, when human beings risk themselves in love for one another, they discover themselves and grasp the meaning of God. In terms of this creed, God is "the horizon, the guarantor, and the depth" of human love. Such love is possible only where God gives the divine self to human beings. Human love, made possible interpersonally and socially by God, is the church's ground and essence.

A. EXPLANATORY REMARKS

(Epilogue[ii].A, p. 456). The second, anthropological creed connotes the theology of the first creed. First of all, it states that love for one's neighbor contains an experience of God, at least implicitly. Human beings transcend themselves in interpersonal relationships, wherein one's neighbor becomes the concrete occasion for a free and responsible response. As we transcend what we were by responding to our neighbors, we encounter God—explicitly or implicitly—as the mysterious source of transcendence.

The second statement of the creed is that God creates the possibility of interpersonal love. By offering the divine self, first in existentiell terms as the justifying grace of the Holy Spirit, and second in historical terms through the incarnation of the Logos, God has established a relationship with humanity. God makes human love possible.

The church is the unity of God's self-gift as existentiell communication and historical achievement. God offers the divine self in Spirit, truth and love. Humanity accepts the offer and manifests it as community, history, and law. The two are not identical but united.

iii. A Brief Future-Oriented Creed

(Epilogue[iii], p. 457). This creed begins with a statement about Christianity as the religion that is open to the future. It awaits the "absolute future"—the future that "wills to give itself in its own reality by self-communication" (p. 457). God is the future of humanity. By raising Jesus from the dead, God showed that the unity of divinity and humanity is irreversible.

A. EXPLANATORY REMARKS

(Epilogue[iii].A, p. 457). Just as the first creed spoke of God as the goal of human transcendence, so this creed speaks of human transcendence by speaking of the future. This is the future of God's self-communication. Divinely led, humanity orients itself toward what God intends for it, namely, unity with God. This is its absolute future, as distinct from finite and partial futures. The life, death, and resurrection of Jesus Christ reveal this unity as eschatological. It is the final destiny of human beings.

The absolute future implies a Christology and a doctrine of the Trinity. It also implies a theology of grace, understood primarily as God's gift of self. Christianity holds open the future of God's self-communication. Insofar as the future remains to be achieved in human freedom and responsibility, it remains a question and a mystery.

B. REFLECTION ON THE TRINITARIAN FAITH

(Epilogue[iii].B, p. 458). The three brief creedal statements are "reflections and consequences of Christian belief in the Trinity" (p. 458). The first creed, which speaks of God as the term or goal of transcendence, refers to the "Father" of Christian doctrine. The second creed, which speaks of the radical union of human and divine love, signifies the incarnate Logos. In the "Son," humanity and divinity reached a fundamental, "hypostatic" union. The third creed, which refers to humanity's absolute future, corresponds to the "Holy Spirit." God, the absolute future of humanity, invites us to accept the divine gift of self in love and freedom.

Human experience is the most intelligible approach to understanding God, concludes Rahner. God's turning to the world as Trinity expresses the basic substance of Christian faith.

Detailed Table of Contents

This detailed table of contents is identical to the table found at the end of *Foundations* with two exceptions. First, the page numbers given below correspond to the paraphrase, not to William V. Dych's translation of Rahner's work. Second, this table indicates not only the part numbers for each chapter but also the sections (indicated by a lower-case letter), and the subsections (indicated by an upper-case letter).

II. Man in the Presence of Absolute Mystery

V. The History of Salvation and Revelation

VI. Jesus Christ

VII. Christianity as Church

VIII. Remarks on Christian Life

IX. Eschatology

Epilogue: Brief Creedal Statements

Topic Index to the Translation by William V. Dych of Karl Rahner's *Foundations of Christian Faith*

The following index supplies the English word and principal page number of the English edition of the *Foundations* in which the word appears. The index also provides a fuller treatment to words used in the headings of individual sections of *Foundations*. In these cases, the index supplies the German original and identifies the section in which the English word appears in a heading. For example, a reference to section VI.5(b).E means that the word appears in the heading to chapter VI, part 5, section b, subsection E. The Introduction is abbreviated "Intr." The Epilogue is abbreviated "Ep."

Midrash, 376
Miracle, as call, 261 (*das Wunder als Anruf*, VI.5[f].F)
Miracles, or signs in the life of Jesus, 255 (*Wunder im Leben Jesu*, VI.5[f]); cf. 160, 255-60; and laws of nature, 25 (*Wunder und Naturgesetze*, VI.5[f].D); and the relationship between God and World, 260 (*das Wunder vom Gott-Welt-Verhältnis aus gesehen*, VI.5[f].E); in comparison to the unique resurrection [*see* Resurrection, in comparison . . .]; the general concept of, 257 (*zum allgemeinen Begriff des Wunders*, VI.5[f].C)
Modality of human subjectivity, 129
Modern Period (*Neuzeit*), 169
Modernism, 15
Monads, 189
Monophysitism, 226, 249, 287, 290-93, 300, 303
Monothelitism, 226, 287, 292
Moral situation or experience, 408
Mystagogy, 59
Mystery, experience of, 57 (*Erfahrung des Geheimnisses*, II.2.C); cf. 57; Holy, 65 (*heiliges Geheimnis*, II.2.E); cf. 65, 125; presence of in the human being, 42 (*Getragensein durch das Geheimnis*, I.6.A); cf. 12, 21, 54, 60-61, 67, 73, 85, 205, 217; the absolute (the person in the presence of the absolute), 44 (*der Mensch vor dem absoluten Geheimnis*, II); cf. 12, 44, 60, 69, 73, 77, 106, 129, 194, 204, 232
Mysticism, 274
Mythology, mythological, 39

Nature, and history, 180; human, 217, 219, 224; laws of, and miracles, 258 (*Wunder und Naturgesetze*, VI.5[f].D); proceeding from first level of reflection, 246 (*Eigenart*, VI.5[c].A); pure, 207
Necessary, 322 (*notwendig*, VII.1.A), 153

Nestorian, 287, 302
Norma non normata. See Scripture as *norma non normata*.

Object of Faith (in dogmatic theology), 245
Objectifications, categorical (of transcendental freedom), 96 (*transzendentale Freiheit und ihre kategorialen Objektivationen*, III.2.C)
Office, Teaching, 377 (*Lehramt*, VII.6.G); cf. 381
Old Testament as normative for Christian faith, 371
Ontic (i.e., categorical), 126, 149
Ontological, in contrast to ontic, 126 (*ontologischer Satz*, IV.3.A); cf. 149
Ontologism, 52, 64, 67
Openness of the human spirit, essential and a priori, 19 (*grundsätzliche Offenheit*, Intr.3.C); cf. 83, 332
Opus Operantis, work operating (on the individual), 413 (VIII.2.C); cf. 429
Opus Operatum, work that causes (by itself), 413 (VIII.2.C); cf. 412, 427, 429
Orders, Holy, 417
Origin of Christianity. See Criterion of continuity.
Original, knowledge of God, 68; possession of self, 14; word of God, 50
Original Sin, 106 (*Erbsünde*, III.4); cf. 116, 118, 120-21, 315, 387; Christian teaching about, 110 (*die christliche Rede von der Erbsünde*, III.4.D); cf. 79, 261; the consequences of, 115 (*die "Folgen der Erbsünde,"* III.4.H)

Pagan, 449
Pantheism, 62-63, 219
Paraclete, 340
Paradosis, 338
Participation in the divine nature, 213
Pastoral Epistles, 338, 341
Paul, 337 (*zur paulinischen Theologie der Kirche*, VII.3.C); cf. 265, 285, 302, 348, 372, 433

Biblical Index

Index of Proper Names

D.S. stands for Denziger-Schönmetzer, the editors of the *Enchiridion Symbolorum*

Abraham, 145, 166
Action française, 324
Adam, 110-13, 162, 314, 388
Apocalypse (Book of Revelation), 441
Augsburg Confession, 353, 355, 358.
Augustine, Augustinianism, 2, 91, 135, 147, 214, 222, 319, 411

Blondel, Maurice, 52
Bultmann, Rudolf, 13

Calvin, Jean, 147, 366
Carthage, Council of (D.S. 229), 411
Catechism, Tridentine, 450
Cephas, 334-35
Chalcedon, 211, 285, 290

Darlap, Adolf, 139
Denziger-Schönmetzer, 285-86
Deutero-Isaiah, 283
Drey, Sebastian, 4

Enchiridion Symbolorum. *See* Denziger-Schönmetzer.
Ephesians, Letter to the, 390
Ephesus, 285

Feuerbach, Ludwig, 436
Florence, Council of (D.S. 1310), 413

Gasparri, Cardinal Pietro, 450

Hebrews, Letter to the, 265
Hegel, G. W. F., 1, 259, 297

Johannine Letters, 340
Johannine theology, 441
Judas, 443

Käsemann, Ernst, 339

Leo XIII, Pope, 374
Lexikon für Theologie und Kirche, 332
Lieth, von der, Elisabeth, xv
Luke, 336, 341, 387
Luther, Martin, 91, 366, 386-87

Maccabees, 278
Marx, Karl, 47
Matthew, 336, 387
Moses, 145, 167, 314

Neufeld, Karl H., xv
Newman, John Henry, 10
Nicaea, 285

Origen, 94

Pascal, Blaise, 91
Paul the Apostle, 265, 285, 302, 337, 348, 372, 433
Paul VI, Pope, 2
Pilate, Pontius, 232
Pius XI, Pope, 450
Pius XII, Pope, 374, 376, 388

Raffelt, Albert, xv

Schelling, von, F. W. J., 4
Schnackenburg, Rudolf, 332, 337
Schöndorf, Harald, xv
Seneca, 404
Staudenmaier, Franz Anton, 4

OF RELATED INTEREST

KARL RAHNER
FOUNDATIONS OF CHRISTIAN FAITH
An Introduction to the Idea of Christianity

"There is no finer introduction to this Jesuit genius."
—*Journal of the American Academy of Religion*

"A master work. [It] recapitulates all that Rahner has been about in the construction of his systematic theology." —*Thought*

"With systematic talent unequaled in contemporary theology. [Karl Rahner] lays out the basic concepts and development of his own remarkable forty-year intellectual journey." —*Commonweal*

"The theologically and intellectually alert will find this a volume of incomparable pleasure." —*The Christian Ministry*

"A brilliant synthesis flowing from an incomparable mastery of Scripture, the Church Fathers, the great medieval theologians, the theology of the Schools, and contemporary thought." —*Theological Studies*

"As a fresh and stimulating account of the Christian faith this volume is likely to become a classic. . . . High praise must be given to the translator; it is even possible to forget that the original is German." —*Choice*

"This challenging, original, helpful, and rich volume . . . is a work of rare intellectual power and profound religious sensitivity."
—*Religious Studies Review*

ISBN: 0-8245-0523-9 Paperback

*Support your local bookstore or order directly
From the publisher at www.CrossroadPublishing.com*

*To request a catalog or inquire about
Quantity orders, please e-mail
sales@CrossroadPublishing.com*

crossroad

About the Author

Herder & Herder is honored to welcome Mark F. Fischer to our house. Dr. Fischer is Professor of Theology at St. John's Seminary in the Roman Catholic Archdiocese of Los Angeles (since 1990). He is the past chairman of the Ecclesiology Seminar of the Catholic Theological Society of America. His website devoted to *The Foundations of Christian Faith* is one of the most visited websites in the world for people looking for information on Karl Rahner, and he is webmaster of the Karl Rahner Society. Mark is married and has three sons.